EXPLORATIONS

STUDIES IN CULTURE AND COMMUNICATION

VOLUME 2

*Edited by Edmund Carpenter and
Marshall McLuhan*

WIPF & STOCK · Eugene, Oregon

Wipf and Stock Publishers
199 W 8th Ave, Suite 3
Eugene, OR 97401

Explorations 2
Studies in Culture and Communication
By Carpenter, E S and Easterbrook, W T
Copyright©1954, Edmund S. Carpenter & Marshall McLuhan Estates
ISBN 13: 978-1-62032-428-8
Publication date 9/22/2016
Previously published by University of Toronto, 1954

This is an anniversary new edition of the eight co–edited issues of Explorations, with annotations by Michael Darroch and Janine Marchessault, in conjunction with students and researchers at the University of Windsor and York University, Canada. Research for the annotated editions was made possible by a grant from the Social Sciences and Humanities Research Council of Canada. Additional research was provided by Lorraine Spiess in conjunction with the Estate of Edmund Carpenter. Permissions research was provided by Jonathan McKenzie. This republication project was a joint initiative undertaken by the estates of Marshall McLuhan and Edmund Carpenter.

Funding for Issues 1–6 (1953–1956) was originally provided by a grant from the Ford Foundation's Behavioral Sciences Program. Issues 7–8 (1957) were sponsored by the Telegram of Toronto.

Typography for Issue 1 was designed and printed by Rous & Mann Press Limited, Toronto. The cover of Issue 7 and the cover and typography of Issue 8 were designed by Harley Parker and printed courtesy of the University of Toronto Press. Please see individual issues for further notes on contributors and acknowledgements.

Every effort has been made to contact copyright holders and to ensure that all the information presented is correct. Some of the facts in this volume may be subject to debate or dispute. If proper copyright acknowledgment has not been made, or for clarifications and corrections, please contact the publishers and we will correct the information in future reprintings, if any.

EXPLORATIONS . . .

is designed, not as a permanent reference journal that embalms truth for posterity, but as a publication that explores and searches and questions.

We envisage a series that will cut across the humanities and social sciences by treating them as a continuum. We believe anthropology and communication are approaches, not bodies of data, and that within each the four winds of the humanities, the physical, the biological and the social sciences intermingle to form a science of man.

Volumes 1 through 6:

Editor:
    E. S. Carpenter
Associate Editors:
    W. T. Easterbrook
    H. M. McLuhan
    J. Tyrwhitt
    D. C. Williams

Address all correspondence to EXPLORATIONS
University of Toronto
Toronto, Canada

Volumes 7 & 8:

Editors:
    Edmund Carpenter
    Marshall McLuhan

Sponsor Telegram of Toronto
Publisher University of Toronto

April 1954

Explorations, 1953–57

Foreword to the Eight-Volume Series of the 2016 Edition, Volumes 2–8

(The main Introduction to this series is in Volume One)

Michael Darroch (University of Windsor) and
Janine Marchessault (York University)

Explorations was an experimental interdisciplinary publication led by faculty and graduate students at the University of Toronto in which the media theorist Marshall McLuhan and the radical anthropologist Edmund Carpenter formulated their most striking insights about new media in the electric age. The journal served to disseminate some of the insights and experiments of the Culture and Communications graduate seminar (1953–55), an innovative media think tank of the 1950s. The eight coedited issues of *Explorations* are republished here for the first time since their original printing in the 1950s.

The Explorations research group aimed to develop a "field approach" to the study of new media and communication. While inspired by a postwar, modernist discourse of universality, no single mode of research was dominant. By their own account, the team sought "an area of mutually supporting insights in a critique of the methods of study in Economics, Psychology, English, Anthropology, and Town Planning."[1] *Explorations* published writings by group

---

1. Herbert Marshall McLuhan Fonds, held in Library and Archives Canada (LAC) in Ottawa. Further references to the McLuhan Fonds will be identified as LAC followed by the call number MG 31, D 156, the volume number, and the folder number (here: LAC MG 31, D 156, 145, 35).

members along with contributions on topics ranging from ethnolinguistics to economic theory, from art and design to developmental psychology, from psychoanalysis to nursery rhymes and bawdy ballads, from urban theory to electronic media. The journal treated culture, and cultural studies, as a landscape of experiences and knowledge. An experimental space in its own right, *Explorations* counted among its more than eighty contributors both established and emerging scholars, scientists, and artists.

The think tank and the journal were supported by a grant from the Ford Foundation's newly established interdisciplinary research and study program in behavioral sciences (most likely cowritten by McLuhan and Carpenter and assisted by the then doctoral student Donald Theall). The group obtained $44,250 for a two-year research project devoted to studying the "changing patterns of language and behavior and the new media of communication."[2] Within North America, the Toronto group's proposal can be counted among the very first attempts to combine explicitly the study of culture *and* communication. The timing of this grant is significant given the scope of contemporaneous studies of media underway in the United States and Europe: functionalist and critical cultural studies of mass communications, theories of cybernetics, studies of social interaction, as well as psychological studies of the effects of media on human perception. Carpenter, initially the driving force behind *Explorations*, acted as editor of the first six issues before becoming coeditor with McLuhan for issues 7 and 8, which were sponsored by the *Toronto Telegram*. A ninth and final issue, entitled *Eskimo* (1959), combined Carpenter's writings on indigenous art and culture of the Aivilik juxtaposed with images from filmmaker Robert Flaherty and drawings by Frederick Varley. After Beacon Press published a selection of *Explorations* contributions in 1960, coedited by Carpenter and McLuhan as *Explorations in Communication*, McLuhan later resuscitated the spirit of *Explorations* as a "magazine within a magazine," a publication inside the University of Toronto's alumni magazine, the *Varsity Graduate* (1964–72).

2. *Ford Foundation, 1953, Ford Foundation Annual Report 1953*, New York: Ford Foundation: 67. The Ford Foundation's Behavioral Sciences Program had the stated goal of "improving the content of the behavioral sciences" by specifically supporting "interdisciplinary research and study." Launched in 1952, the program aimed to help the "intellectual development of the behavioral sciences" by "improving their relationship with such disciplines as history, social and political philosophy, humanistic studies and certain phases of economics" (67).

The group's proposal to Ford's Behavioral Sciences Program is revealing of the central assumptions that would underpin the graduate seminar and *Explorations*. The proposal's point of departure is not yet an assumption about the power of media forms to shape content, but rather the understanding that methods for studying new media required recognition of new patterns emerging across technological, cultural, and urban life. Underpinning the proposal is a conversation that McLuhan in particular had started with advocates of cybernetic theories. Carpenter was also of course conversant with the writings of anthropologists who were deeply involved with developing cybernetic models and metaphors within the social sciences, among others Gregory Bateson and Margaret Mead. Cybernetic theories also came to the group through Donald Theall, who would complete his PhD dissertation in 1954 on "Communication Theories in Modern Poetry: Yeats, Pound, Joyce and Eliot" under the supervision of both McLuhan and Carpenter.

"Well aware of the brilliant new developments in communication study at Massachusetts Institute of Technology," the Ford grant explains, gesturing both to Norbert Wiener's cybernetic conferences and to Claude Shannon and Warren Weaver's mathematical theory of communication, "the undersigned propose to utilize these insights but to employ also the technique of studying the forms of communication, old and new, as art forms," an approach already "implicit in the very title of Harold Innis' *Bias of Communication*."[3] The Toronto group proposed to study the effects of new media forms on patterns of language, economic values, social organization, individual and collective behaviour, always keeping in mind accompanying changes to the classroom and the networks of city life. In their eyes the central problem consisted of two aspects. First, "the creation of a new language of vision" that "arises from all our new visual media and which is part of the total language of modern culture." Second, the Toronto group proposed to study "the impact of this total social language on the traditional spoken and written forms of expression." These two core objectives they would pursue in the pages of *Explorations* through numerous contributions. As clearly indicated in an early draft of their Ford proposal, the core research group

3. Edmund S. Carpenter, Jaqueline Tyrwhitt, H. M. McLuhan, W. T. Easterbrook, and D. C. Williams, 1953, "University of Toronto: Changing Patterns of Language and Behavior and the New Media of Communication." Ford Foundation Archives. Grant File PA 53–70, Section 1, 1–11. Rockefeller Archive Center, New York: 4.

represented the five key disciplines that would supplement each other: anthropology, psychology, economics, town planning, and English.[4]

While no one discipline was privileged above the others, anthropology played a special role in creating a strong comparative framework from the start. In addition to anthropological discussions of cybernetics, the Sapir-Whorf theory was an important intellectual foundation. As with Innis, Edward Sapir (a German-born American who spent fifteen years in Ottawa working for the Geographical Survey of Canada) offered a multifocal habit of vision, working between linguistics, anthropology, and psychology. For the grant applicants, Sapir "brought together European attitudes towards psychoanalysis (emphasis on socially-situated personality) and North American attitudes towards social structure (culture)." Moreover, Sapir "fused the European concern with philology with [the] North American concern with dynamic patterns in language."[5] The anthropologist and ethnolinguist Dorothy Lee was arguably one of the group's "most influential force[s],"[6] contributing six articles on language, value, and perception. Her insight that peoples such as the Trobrianders perceived lineal order differently from Western cultures had already been cited by Bateson and Ruesch (1951), and was central to the delineation of acoustic and visual cultures undertaken by the Explorations group, and in later studies by both McLuhan and Carpenter.

In developing their methodologies, seminar faculty and graduate students undertook a number of critical media experiments on changing patterns of perception resulting from new media. The CBC and the then Ryerson Institute placed studio space and media equipment at their disposal. The experiment tested their central hypothesis that different media (speech, print, radio, television) lend themselves to different kinds of pedagogical experiences.[7] It is surprising that such findings have never been fully taken up by educational media researchers. Hopefully, the republication of these early studies will

4. "Changing Patterns of Man and Society Associated with the New Media of Communication." Draft of Ford Foundation Proposal, likely 1953. LAC MG 31, D 156, 204, 26.

5. Carpenter et al, 1953: 2.

6. Edmund Carpenter, 2001, "That Not-So-Silent Sea," in Donald F. Theall (Ed.), *The Virtual Marshall McLuhan* (p. 240), Montreal: McGill-Queen's University Press.

7. Edmund Carpenter, 1954, "Certain Media Biases," *Explorations* 3:65–74; Edmund Carpenter and Marshall McLuhan, 1956, "The New Languages," *Chicago Review* 10(1): 46–52; Edmund Carpenter, 1957, "The New Languages," *Explorations* 7:4–21.

renew interest in the cognitive studies of media which have focussed too narrowly, according to Carpenter and McLuhan, on attention and inputs and not enough on the creative and critical aspects of perception.

What is clear in reading through the *Explorations* issues is that Carpenter and McLuhan were most interested in the new kinds of learning made possible through the media. McLuhan, in particular, was influenced by research into human perception as part of his approach to media studies since he believed that these media were altering our senses, our forms of attention and knowledge production. Carpenter and McLuhan would assert that the media are transforming the human sensorium, an idea captured perhaps most playfully in the final coedited issue, *Explorations* 8, an ode to James Joyce devoted to the oral, to the new "acoustic space" of the electric age: "Verbi-Voco-Visual." The issue features seven essays, including one by McLuhan, that explore different aspects of oral culture—mostly concerned with a transition to a new orality. Twenty-four non-authored "Items," which include some previously published essays by McLuhan and Carpenter, appear as humorous intellectual sketches exploring topics like "Electronics as ESP," car commercials, bathroom acoustics, dictaphones, and of course wine. The final "Item," number 24, entitled "No Upside Down in Eskimo Art," reiterated McLuhan and Carpenter's core assertion that "after thousands of years of written processing of human experience, the instantaneous omnipresence of electronically processed information has hoicked us out of these age-old patterns into an auditory world." In the history of media studies in Canada and internationally, the *Explorations* journal is an important starting point for defining the rich new insights around new media cultures that the Toronto School helped inaugurate.

References

Carpenter, Edmund S., Jaqueline Tyrwhitt, H. M. McLuhan, W. T. Easterbrook, and D. C. Williams. 1953. "University of Toronto: Changing Patterns of Language and Behavior and the New Media of Communication." Ford Foundation Archives. Grant File PA 53–70, Section 1, 1–11. Rockefeller Archive Center, New York.

Carpenter, Edmund. 1954. "Certain Media Biases." *Explorations* 3:65–74.

Carpenter, Edmund. 1957. "The New Languages." *Explorations* 7:4–21.

Carpenter, Edmund. 2001. "That Not-So-Silent Sea." In Donald F. Theall (Ed.), *The Virtual Marshall McLuhan* (pp. 236–61). Montreal: McGill-Queen's University Press.

Carpenter, Edmund, and Marshall McLuhan. 1956. "The New Languages." *Chicago Review* 10(1): 46–52.

Ford Foundation. 1953. *Ford Foundation Annual Report 1953*. New York: Ford Foundation.

Ruesch, Jurgen, and Gregory Bateson. 1951. *Communication, the Social Matrix of Psychiatry*. New York: Norton.

Theall, Donald. 1954. *Communication Theories in Modern Poetry: Yeats, Pound, Eliot and Joyce*. Doctoral dissertation. Toronto: University of Toronto.

Summaries of All Eight
Explorations Volumes

Explorations 1

Explorations 1 took an audaciously new approach to communications and cultural research "cutting across" studies in anthropology, literature, social sciences, economics, folklore, and popular culture. From Copernican revolutions (Bidney) to a seventeenth-century translation of Sweden's Mohra witchcraft trials (Horneck); from senses of time (Leach) to the meaning of gongs (Carrington); from Majorcan customs (Graves) to a typography of functional analysis (Spiro); from Veblen's economic history (Riesman) to contemporary stress levels (Selye), the issue also included one of György Kepes's earliest drafts on fusing "art and science," an essay on Freud and vices (Goodman), and a return to childhood in Legman's work on comic books, before concluding with now classic essays by McLuhan and Frye. The cover of *Explorations* 1 depicts a series of masks from the award-winning film *The Loon's Necklace* (Crawley Films, 1948).

Explorations 2

Explorations 2's mischievous spoof covers, both front and back, inside and outside, were labelled "Feenicht's Playhouse," a reference to the Phoenix playhouse of Joyce's *Wake*. The key playful headline, "New Media Changing Temporal and Spatial Orientation to Self," was accompanied by multiple hoax articles, including "Time-Space Duality Goes" and "TV Wollops MS," a reference to television's apparent power over manuscript culture as evidenced by the group's media experiment at CBC studios. Exemplifying the playfulness of the core faculty's discussions about new media and behaviour, it is not surprising the McLuhan would publish in this issue his now famous article "Notes on the Media as Art Forms" alongside essays by other seminar participants: Tyrwhitt resuscitated an unpublished article, "Ideal Cities and the City Ideal," a historical survey of proposals for ideal urban designs (originally drafted for the defunct journal *trans/formation: art, communication, environment*). Carpenter's "Eternal Life" is a first analysis of Aivilik Inuit concepts of time; then student Donald Theall's "Here Comes Everybody" offered a snapshot of his research on Joyce and communication theories in modern poetry; anthropologist Dorothy Lee, who would visit the seminar in March 1955, offered a review of David Bidney's challenge to scholarly traditions in his 1953 book *Theoretical Anthropology*. In addition, Carpenter fleshed out the contents with contributions from political economy, anthropology, psychology, and English: the second part of Riesman's Veblen study; Lord Raglan on social classes; Derek Savage on "Jung, Alchemy and Self"; the *New Yorker*'s Stanley Hyman on Malraux's thesis of the "museum without walls"; and A. Irving Hallowell's extended essay on "Self and its Behavioral Environment"—the inspiration for the spoof cover.

Explorations 3

Explorations 3 was initially planned as a volume dedicated to Harold Innis. In the end, the issue would only include Innis's essay "Monopoly and Civilization," introduced by Easterbrook, and a series of reflections in "Innis and Communication" by seminar participants. In November 1954, the *Explorations* researchers attended the "Institute on Culture and Communication" organised by Ray Birdwhistell at the University of Louisville's Interdisciplinary Committee on Culture and Communication. A number of the contributions to *Explorations* 3 are essays or early drafts of contributions related to this conference (Birdwhistell, Lee, Trager & Hall). The issue also includes the initial, and substantially divergent, assessments of the group's first "media experiment" at CBC studios (April 1954) in the contributions by Carpenter and Williams. The issue is rounded out with an excerpt on reading and writing (Chaytor), a new translation of Kamo Chomei's *Hojoki* (Rowe & Kerrigan), a study of utopias (Wolfenstein), a reading of *Tristram Shandy* (MacLean), reflections on Soviet ethnography (Potekin & Levin), a reading of Shelley's hallucinations as narcissism and doublegoing (McCullough), a critical reassessment of the science of human behaviour (Wallace), and "Meat Packing and Processing," an anonymous entry, likely by McLuhan, alluding to Giedion's *Mechanization Takes Command* (1948). Like *Explorations* 1, the cover depicted an indigenous mask from the Northwest Coast also represented in the Crawley film *The Loon's Necklace* (1948).

Explorations 4

According to McLuhan, *Explorations* 4 was planned as an issue devoted to Sigfried Giedion. Published in February 1955, with a cover adapted from Kandinsky's *Comets* (1938), *Explorations* 4 was devoted to issues of space and placed a strong emphasis on modes of linguistic and poetic thought across multiple media. Poems by e. e. cummings and Jorge Luis Borges mingle with essays by seminar leaders McLuhan on "Space, Time, and Poetry," Carpenter on "Eskimo Poetry: Word Magic," Tyrwhitt on "The Moving Eye" (regarding comparative perceptual experiences of Western cities and the ancient Indian city of Fatehpur Sikri), and Williams on "auditory space"—a notion that "electrified" the group, as Carpenter later recounted. Northrop Frye and Stephen Gilman's essays on poetic traditions were juxtaposed with Millar MacLure and Marjorie Adix's odes to Dylan Thomas, who had died in 1953. Case studies by then graduate students Walter J. Ong on "Space in Renaissance Symbolism" and Joan Rayfield on "Implications of English Grammar" were aligned with Dorothy Lee's contribution on "Freedom, Spontaneity and Limit in American Linguistic Usage" and Lawrence Frank's early draft of "Tactile Communication." Both Lee and Frank had presented their contributions at Ray Birdwhistell's "Institute on Culture and Communication" in Louisville, in 1954. A "Media Log" and the now famous entry "Five Sovereign Fingers Taxed the Breath," both largely replicated from McLuhan's 1954 *Counterblast* pamphlet, were published anonymously. In addition to "Our Enchanted Lives," a memorandum of instructions for television programming adapted from a Procter & Gamble memo, "The Party Line" offered a second alleged memorandum "To All TIME INC. Bureaus and Stringers." An "Idea File" containing insights on oral, written, and technological cultural forms was culled from writings by Robert Graves, Edmund Leach, Walter Gropius, and E. T. Hall, among many others. With *Explorations* 4, the group revealed its commitment to the belief that communication studies was deeply rooted in anthropological and literary-poetic traditions, but equally informed by studies of mechanisation, technology, and culture.

Explorations 5

The cover of *Explorations* 5 returned to the playfulness of issue 2: the image of the famous Minoan "Our Lady of the Sports" figurine, held at the Royal Ontario Museum (the authenticity of which has long been disputed) was set in front of the *Toronto Daily Star*'s 8 April 1954 Home Edition front page, featuring the headline "H-Bomb in Mass Production, U.S." This juxtaposition between ancient artefact, contemporary media, and techno-logical production set the stage for the issue: starting with Daisetz Suzuki's description of "Buddhist Symbolism", the issue follows with McLuhan's fa-mous analysis of TV and radio in Joyce's *Finnegans Wake*. Such contrasts of new media forms continue with a "Portrait of James Joyce," an excerpt of a 1950 "Third Programme" BBC documentary edited by W. R. Rodgers, and the two-page "Anna Livia Plurabelle" section of Joyce's *Finnegans Wake*, set in experimental typography designed by Harley Parker and Toronto's Cooper and Beatty Ltd. The issue further juxtaposes essays by E. R. Leach on cultural conceptions of time and Jean Piaget on time-space conceptions of the child; anthropologists Claire Holt and Joan Rayfield on interpen-etrations of language and culture and Carpenter's study of Eskimo space concepts; Rhodra Métraux on differences between the novel, play, and film versions of *The Caine Mutiny*; Roy Campbell on the fusion of oral and writ-ten traditions in the writings of Nigerian author Amos Tutuola, including an excerpt of his 1954 novel *My Life in the Bush of Ghosts*, and Harcourt Brown on Pascal; economist Kenneth Boulding on information theory and Easterbrook on economic approaches to communication; and an excerpt from Daniel Lerner and David Riesman's work on the modernisation of Turkey and the Middle East. Tyrwhitt and Williams contributed reflec-tions on the seminar's second media experiment in "The City Unseen," an analysis of students' perceptions of the environment of the then Ryerson Institute. Anonymous entries included "Colour and Communication" and a transcription of satirist Jean Shepherd's radio broadcast "Channel Cat in the Middle Distance," likely courtesy of Carpenter. The issue is rounded out with a Letters File and an Ideas File, with contributions from E. R. Leach, Patrick Geddes, and Lawrence Frank.

Explorations 6

Writing to the Explorations Group in 1954, Carpenter worried about the funds from the Ford grant that were available for publishing this issue. *Explorations* 6 was funded through the sales of issue 5 and possibly Carpenter's own funds. The cover image for this issue was a section of *The Great Wave*, by Katsushika Hokusai. According to Carpenter's letter, this issue summarizes the group's "ideas and findings," which though "not fully articulated" were "new and exciting." He saw the issue as "a full seminar statement." Indeed, the issue brings together the interdisciplinary reflections and comparative media studies that characterized the group's methodology: a brilliant essay by radical anthropologist Dorothy Lee on "Wintu thought" (Lee would ultimately publish six essays in *Explorations* and had a significant influence on the seminar) and two essays on television that were solicited to reflect upon different geographical differences that shaped the experiences of the new medium—one in the US (Chayefsky) and the other the Soviet Union (Sharoyeva, the "top man" in the USSR television system). Also included were Giedion's classic essay on cave painting; a reflection on the phonograph alongside a consideration of "print's monopoly" by C. S. Lewis; as well as essays by McLuhan on media and events; language and magic (Maritain); writing and orality (Riesman); color (Parker); the evolution of the human mind (Montagu); and the anonymous entries "Print's Monopoly" and "Feet of Clay," likely drafted by McLuhan and Carpenter, which take up conflicts between old and new media environments. This issue contains the full spectrum of the weekly seminar's research undertakings over a two-year period.

Explorations 7

Explorations 7 (1957), the only issue without a table of contents, was edited by Carpenter and McLuhan solely and, with issue 8, sponsored by the *Toronto Telegram*. Easterbrook and Tyrwhitt were away, and Williams wanted his name taken off the masthead, allegedly because of the publication of American writer Gershon Legman's infamous "Bawdy Song . . . in Fact and in Print," a history of erotic writing. McLuhan had contributed to Legman's short-lived but hugely influential magazine *Neurotica* (1948–52), so the two had a previous connection. But the tension between Williams

xv

and the editors might have also been due to their different interpretations of the CBC/Ryerson media experiments which explored media sensory biases with a group of students discussed in issue 3 by Williams in scientific terms, and here again by Carpenter in his essay "The New Languages" in cultural terms. Carpenter argues that each medium (radio, TV, print) "codifies reality differently." To accompany this opening essay, they each included anonymous entries: the essay "Classroom Without Walls," later attributed to McLuhan, explores the ubiquitous mediasphere outside educational institutions, which teachers must begin to consider as an inherent and unavoidable pedagogical experience, followed by "Songs of the Pogo," a reference to the popular comic and LP of the period, which pervaded the McLuhan home. McLuhan saw relationships between "Jazz and Modern Letters," juxtaposed with Carpenter's reflections on the acoustic character of ancient and preliterate symbols, masks, and traditions in "Eternal Life of the Dream." Dorothy Lee contributed two essays to the issue on lineal and non-lineal codifications examined in the Trobriand language with responses by Robert Graves. The focus on educational matters also included a review of Riesman's *Variety and Constraint in American Education* as well as examinations of the cultural specificity of the Soviet press, Soviet novels, and Soviet responses to Elvis Presley. The particularity of an oral and noncapitalistic culture had been an important point of comparison for the Explorations Group, especially Carpenter and McLuhan. Harley Parker designed the issue's cover.

Explorations 8

Explorations 8 (1957) is perhaps the most famous of all the issues. It was devoted to the oral—"Verbi-Voco-Visual"—and was edited primarily by McLuhan and again published by the *Toronto Telegram* and the University of Toronto. The issue was filled with visual experimentation; framed by extensive play with typography in the spirit of the Vorticists and for the first time the extensive use of "flexitype" by Harley Parker, then display designer at the ROM. Seen throughout are Parker's experiments with typography as well as color printing, the first time in the history of the journal. A photomontage from László Moholy-Nagy's *Vision in Motion* (1947) depicting a man's face with an ear juxtaposed over an eye is the frontispiece to the issue. The issue features seven essays, including one by McLuhan, that explore different aspects of oral culture—mostly concerned with a transition to a new orality. Twenty-four non-authored "Items," which include some previously published essays by McLuhan and Carpenter, appear as humorous intellectual sketches exploring topics like "Electronics as ESP," car commercials, bathroom acoustics, dictaphones, and of course wine. The final "Item," number 24, entitled "No Upside Down in Eskimo Art," reiterated McLuhan and Carpenter's core assertion that "after thousands of years of written processing of human experience, the instantaneous omnipresence of electronically processed information has hoicked us out of these age-old patterns into an auditory world."

Michael Darroch (University of Windsor)
Janine Marchessault (York University)
2016

VOLUME 2

The use of the term 'mass media' has been unfortunate. All media, especially languages, are mass media so far at least as their range in space and time is concerned. If by 'mass media' is meant a mechanized mode of a previous communication channel, then printing is the first of the mass media. Press, telegraph, wireless, telephone, gramophone, movie, radio, TV, are mutations of the mechanization of writing, speech, gesture. Insofar as mechanization introduces the 'mass' dimension, it may refer to a collective effort in the use of the medium, to larger audiences or to instantaneity of reception. Again, all of these factors may create a difficulty of 'feedback' or lack of rapport between 'speaker' and audience. There has been very little discussion of any of these questions, thanks to the gratuitous assumption that communication is a matter of transmission of information, message or idea. This assumption blinds people to the aspect of communication as participation in a common situation. And it leads to ignoring the *form* of communication as the basic art situation which is more significant than the information or idea 'transmitted'.

At many levels, printing established a divorce between 'literature and life' which was scarcely heard of before printing and which is meaning-

1

less today when print is recessive, on one hand, or mainly pictorial in impact, on the other. The well-established view of culture which assumes that it filters down from *élites* to popular levels will not stand up for a moment to the facts of linguistic history and formation. Yet language is the great collective work of art transcending all individual works. Today this naive content-view of culture prevents us from directing serious critical attention to the media, old and new, as art forms. It is a charley horse inhibiting all education in a technological society.

Today the advance of TV as a communication channel helps us by contrast to focus some of the basic features of cinema. The very word 'Hollywood' suggests the sacred grove from which has issued in our century a new pantheon. The power of the movie projector to evoke gods and goddesses is not accidental. On one hand, there is the movie camera with its analytical power to arrest, dissect, and record motion. The camera rolls up the carpet of existence. On the other hand, the projector reconstructs the dissected scene and unrolls the daylight world as a magic carpet, a dream-world. The camera records the day-world; the projector evokes the night-world. The daylight world intensified by the 45 degree vision of the camera reveals on the dark screen its obverse. The movie patrons assemble in the 'cave' to observe the shadows of the phenomenal world as projected by the dreaming eye of the movie god. Plato and Hollywood join hands in a metaphoric dance on the sands of California.

The spatial image offered by camera eye and projector has a peculiar limitation. It tends to by-pass everything in existence characterized by routine, repetition and continuous effort. Like the short story or the lyric poem, cinema works best with the single mood, state of mind, or metaphor. These it can elaborate or sustain for minutes or hours. The transforming magic of the short poem and short story appear as unexpected associates of camera-eye as an art form. And cinema would seem to be closely related to the romantic art of the esthetic moment, the moment of arrested attention. As Christopher Caudwell put it in *Illusion and Reality*: 'There is a poetic instant and as time vanishes, space enters; the horizon expands and becomes boundless. The art reveals itself as double.'

It is the technological equivalent of the process by which we recreate within ourselves the exterior world. The artist arrests his cognitions by recognition. He then reverses the process and embodies in an exterior work the drama of apprehension. The stages of apprehension, reversed and embedded in new matter, enable us to contemplate, purge and dominate the drama of cognition, the dance of existence. This reversal leading to contemplation is a catharsis. But this is precisely the action of camera and projector *vis-à-vis* the visible world. So that anything whatever taken up into this seemingly banal mechanical process is nevertheless metamorphosed. Here it is possible to suggest an answer to the mysterious question raised by Seigfried Giedion in *Mechanization Takes Command*. In his masterly account of the mechanization of the bread industry he expressed bewilderment at the fact that European immigrants accustomed to excellent bread were in America eager for the ersatz loaf. The answer lies in the fact that we are also eager for ersatz dreams, blondes, houses and entertainment. Is it not the sheer magical power of the technological environment which leads us to prefer the artificial to the natural? Bread in the first place is a product of art. But when the entire economy is on an artistic or magical basis, sparked by the magical appeals and promises of the ads (visual ads are in themselves magical in their habit of transforming ordinary objects and situations) is it not repugnant to the total pattern and promise of the new life to accept 'natural' effects even at the level of physical taste? The power of the machine to transform the character of work and living strongly invites us to transform every level of existence by art. In a collective way we seem to have followed the esoteric counsels of Baudelaire 'sur le maquillage' in seeking by art to re-discover an Edenic world.

Gilbert Seldes mentions how in the early days of TV crowds would stand by the hour watching a TV screen in a shop window when the only picture on the screen was of the traffic in the street in which they stood. Such is likewise the magical power of the press. Reportage takes up the ordinary events, the weather and the municipal events in which we all participate, and changes them simply by virtue of the medium of print and photography. Any communication link or channel necessarily possesses this mythic dimension. Much more are the ineluctable modalities of sight and sound charged with powers of metamorphosis which have been magnified by technology into the size and posture of mighty djinns.

The TV camera is not the movie camera. It does not arrest the flow of action in a series of still shots. Its continuous pick-up is like the radio mike with respect to the voice. Again the TV screen is not the movie screen. In some sense the spectator is himself the screen. The cathode tube carries 'the charge of the light brigade'. The tube carries both the charge and the answering barrage. The result is the painting of images by the ballet of electrons. Again, the small screen and the small audience of TV completely alter the relation of image to external world and to audience.

3

As Erasmus was the first to grasp the character of the revolution of the printing-press, James Joyce was the first to exploit the multiple revolution of telegraph, press, radio, cinema, and TV. *Finnegans Wake* has already begun to appear as an orchestration of all the media of communication, ancient and modern. And it was his mastery of the art process in terms of the stages of apprehension that enabled Joyce to install himself in the centre of the creative process. Whether it appears as mere individual sensation, as collective hope or phobia, as national myth-making or cultural norm-functioning, there is Joyce with cocked ear, eye and nose at the centre of the action. He saw that the change of our time ('wait till Finnegan wakes!') was occurring as a result of the shift from superimposed myth to awareness of the character of the creative process itself. Here was the only hope for a world culture which would incorporate all previous achievements. The very process of human communication, Joyce saw, would afford the natural base for all the future operations and strategies of culture. Towards this vivisectional spectacle of the human community in action we have been led ever more swiftly in recent decades by increasing self-consciousness of the processes and effects of the various media of communication. Our knowledge of the modes of consciousness in pre-literate societies together with our sense of the processes of culture formation in many literate societies past and present, have sharpened our perceptions and led to wide agreement that communication itself is the common ground for the study of individual and society. To this study Joyce contributed not just awareness but demonstration of individual cognition as the analogue and matrix of all communal actions, political, linguistic and sacramental.

What Erasmus saw was that the printed book was to revolutionize education. He saw that the book gave new scope and power to the classroom. What we have to see is that the new media have created classrooms without walls. Just as power technology has abolished 'nature' in the old sense and brought the globe within the scope of art, so the new media have transformed the entire environment into an educational affair.

Concentrating briefly on one aspect of photography as it revolutionized painting technique as well as the conditions for contemplation of art, André Malraux came up with his news of 'museums-without-walls'. The main force making in that direction he saw was the clarification of the painter's medium itself. The canvas gradually freed from anecdote and narrative became in our time not a vehicle but sheer expression. This was the heritage of Cézanne, whose concentration on one formal problem ('the realization of space by the juxtaposition of areas of pure color') led to a break-through as spectacular as that of Planck and Einstein. But this discovery occurred simultaneously in poetry and music. And it enables us to see that each channel of expression (even press, radio, cinema) awaits a similar day of emancipation. Every medium is in some sense a universal, pressing towards maximal realization. But its expressive pressures disturb existing balances and patterns in other media of culture. The increasing inclusiveness of our sense of such repercussions leads us today hopefully to investigate the possibilities of orchestral harmony in the multi-levelled drive towards pure human expressiveness.

Eramus, the text-book, and the Renaissance classroom constitute a subject for meditation related to the interaction of the printed page as new art form and the older cultural equilibrium between manuscript and oral communication. The Renaissance classroom was transferred to America minus the manuscript tradition and conversation minus the plastic milieu of European art and architecture. The intensely abstract character of the printed page was to be the matrix of the technology of America. But paradoxically, the new technology was to produce a new set of arts and a new architecture which was anything but abstract. Yet the original trauma of cultural translation from old to new world has remained.

In this century, however, we have seen James, Pound and Eliot revolutionizing the verbal culture of Europe by their technological impact on the old world. And contrariwise, we have had LeCorbusier and Giedion verbalizing our technological culture. Here it would seem is the formulated means of healing the wounds caused in our Western culture at the Renaissance.

North American children respond asthetically to the powered objects in their world. Streetcars, locomotives, airplanes and motorcars are the first objects of delighted contemplation. But in the classroom the student is confronted with verbal culture in book form. For the European, on the other hand, verbal culture is as much an object and area of spontaneous delight and play as machinery for us. The conclusion is obvious. We can master verbal culture and European art only by approaching it *at first* as a technical problem, just as some Europeans have mastered our sports, jazz, machinery, and architecture by translating it into their verbal cultures. Once the bridge has been crossed in either direction the bridge is no longer necessary. It functions only as a grammar and crib in early stages of reading a new language.

But such temporary bridges are necessary today not only between cultures but within our own culture as a means of mastering the different languages of sight and sound spoken by the new media of communication. It is not only at the political level that we have to know several languages. Locked up for four centuries in the dominant language of the printed page, we unconsciously attempt to handle all communication problems in its rectilinear, form-content language. So unconscious are we of this problem that we have even lost the ability to read the printed page through the sheer distraction created by the other media. Many people have noted how ours is an 'eye-minded' culture. But we do not have educated eyes. Similarly our ears are assailed by messages as no ears have ever been assailed, but we do not have educated ears. The printed page has blinkered us until we have lost the clues to the nature of communication and its relation to the art process.

Such a view would seem to provide a solution to 'the case of the missing anecdote'. In *Encounter 4*, a student at the University of Utah recorded the conversation between Dylan Thomas and some members and students in the Department of English. That record is worth all the critical essays that have been written on Thomas. Thomas poured out stories, comments and observations during his tours. So have many other poets and artists. But nobody has seen fit to record them. The spoken word we seem to regard, along with our own popular culture, as illegitimate, not really culture. Europeans, on the other hand, unparalyzed by the art-form of the book, have always allowed great cultural and literary value to the anecdote, the chance remark and the 'first acquaintance' with a poet or painter. Here they expect to see the mind of the artist in spontaneous action, just as they seek in conversation to awaken and rally creative resources.

In this regard the pocketbook can be seen as a form which exorcises the cultural bogey of the book. Cheapness and convenience are scarcely the clues to the success of the pocketbook today. Rather, as Delmore Schwartz suggested in the *New York Times Book Review* (Jan. 17, 1954): 'The pocket book reader's only desire is pleasure and he is not likely to be suspected of being an intellectual and a highbrow, as he might be if he frequented the public library. He feels no solemn duty toward the pocketbook and he does not feel that his intelligence is at fault if it bores him, since it has not been presented as a monument of human culture which confers superiority upon the reader.'

The pocketbook takes the hex off culture. In our particular milieu, it is a new *form* of communication. Earlier Mr. Schwartz had pointed to the fact that at college people read books because such a habit promoted communication. Later they gave up books because it interfered with normal social life. But the pocketbook permits one to return to solitary vice without interfering with one's social acceptability.

Some years back the *Partisan Review* did a study of its readers and found that they were mostly in the 18–25 group. The success of the pocketbook suggests that a saddle-shoe format for the little mag might corral a much larger group of readers.

From a somewhat different angle, it has been suggested that the current large audience for L. P. polyphony offerings is due to the technical interest in music developed by jive and bebop groups a few years back. A technical analysis and history of music in terms of written and, later, of printed scores is needed to clarify some of the relations between sight and sound. Presumably printed scores had something to do with divorcing words and music after the 16th century. But printed scores would seem to have made possible the maximal freedom of expression of 'pure music'. The visual, printed form permitted the release of the formal aspects of sound from the oral and verbal ground of music. In the same way *vers libre* was an effort to get away from the domination of printed poetry over the free oral patterns of verbal music. *Vers librists* consciously cut back to Gregorian chant, to communal litanies and popular speech rhythms as structural base.

The habitual contemplation of the media of communication as art forms necessarily invokes the principle that the instruments of research are also art forms, magically distorting and controlling the objects of investigation. Critical awareness of this fact has saved the modern scientist from many blunders, but such awareness has arrived tardily in the popular sphere. Naturally the great communication and entertainment trusts of North America are not eager to promote such critical awareness. The existing cultural paralysis engendered by orthodox élite-theories of culture are greatly to their advantage. But we might consider how far we have evaded the direct political control of the media by the expedient of indifference to the impact of the media so long as they can be exploited for public fun and private profit. This may prove to have been a piece of unconscious political wisdom. But so far it has been based on the dubious assumption that 'control the message and you control all'. The actual history of any of the media suggests the reverse. What is at stake is whether the new magical forms of communication are to be kept for laughs and the old forms of communication reserved for politics. Roosevelt's radio talks would have been less effective if the newspaper and editorial world had been on his side. By pretending that the new magic can be contained in the entertainment sphere we assume the old form-content split which is based on the doctrine that the form of communication is neutral. Even Hitler and Goebbels, fortunately, shared this illusion with the Western world. At present we appear to be living *by* an illusion but *with* magical media. Of course this may prove to be an enduring formula.

Marshall McLuhan

In some respects it was an unfortunate decision of the publishers to open the new collected edition of the works of C. G. Jung with volume 12, *Psychology and Alchemy*, a work first published in German in 1944 and now for the first time available to the English reader; for it is not one of Jung's best books, and will sadly disappoint those whose interest was aroused by the essay on alchemy included in *The Integration of the Personality* (1940). The latter was a brilliantly suggestive though curiously incomplete book, and the same impression of incompleteness, of fragmentariness, is conveyed by the present work, in which no essential advance is made on the earlier alchemical essay, the same ideas being repeated at greater length, with ampler illustrative matter, and a full apparatus of notes. *Psychology and Alchemy* consists of an Introduction; an essay, 'Individual Dream Symbolism in Relation to Alchemy', embodying a series of remarkable dreams by a patient illustrating the so-called individuation-process in the psyche, with a commentary in which Jung draws a parallel between the dream-symbols and the symbols found in alchemical writings; and a further essay on 'Religious Ideas in Alchemy', in which the underlying concerns of the alchemists are interpreted in terms of analytical psychology. A quotation will show the character of Jung's approach:

This [the mediaeval period] was a time when the mind of the al-chemist was really grappling with the problems of matter, when the exploring consciousness was confronted by the dark void of the unknown, in which figures and laws were dimly perceived and attributed to matter although they really belonged to the psyche. Everything unknown and empty is filled with psychological projection; it is as if the investigator's own psychic background were mirrored in the darkness. What he sees in matter, or thinks he can see, is chiefly the data of his own uncon-scious which he is projecting into it. In other words, he encounters in matter, as apparently belonging to it, certain qualities and potential meanings of whose psychic nature he is entirely unconscious.

It is with this supposition that Jung elucidates the alchemical writings; and he does in fact succeed in throwing a partial and fitful light, and at time something more than that, upon their obscurities. In particular, he finds in them indications of that same progress towards psychological wholeness which he has watched at work within his own patients, and of which he writes:

The symbols of the process of individuation that appear in dreams are images of an archetypal nature which depict the centralizing process of the production of a new centre of personality . . . I call this centre the 'self', which should be understood as the totality of the psyche. The self is not only the centre but also the whole circumference which em-braces both conscious and unconscious; it is the centre of this totality, just as the ego is the centre of the conscious mind.

One can accept this, and many other of Jung's perceptive and illumi-nating observations, for instance, his remarks on the meaning of the squaring of the circle and of the androgynous nature of the integrated self, without being overwhelmingly impressed by the general endeavour to circumscribe alchemy within the boundaries of his system of psy-chology. One can't, indeed, avoid thinking that, were Jung in a position fully to interpret the alchemists to us, he would approach their writings in a more orderly and systematic way; he would attempt to arrange the known literature in some order of intelligibility, and thereafter select some few examples for sustained examination. But he does not do this; nor does he take into account the conscious philosophy of the alchemists, their world-view, as found, for example, in the writings of Paracelsus and, later, Jacob Boehme; instead he takes, in the most carefree way in the world, and from whatever text comes to hand, whatever elements seem susceptible of incorporation into his own system. The pictorial illustra-tions are similarly heterogeneous and do little to help the text.

To go into the reasons for the unsatisfactory character of *Psychology and Alchemy* would take us into the obscure backgrounds of Jung's thought, in which there seems to be a perplexity or an equivocation which I would like to see tracked down and laid open. It has to do, I am sure, with Jung's ambiguous position in the matter of religious faith. There are those who, like the *Listener* reviewer (20.8.53) acclaim Jung as 'a religious thinker, the most important of his time' who has 'given us a key by which to unlock the old wisdom, whether Hindu, Buddhist, Christian, or that of our own dreams'; and indeed, it might be supposed, from certain passages in the present book, that Jung's viewpoint was that of mystical Christianity. For instance—

With the methods employed hitherto we have not succeeded in Christianizing the soul to the point where even the most elementary demands of Christian ethics can exert any decisive influence on the main concerns of the Christian European. The Christian missionary may preach the gospel to the poor naked heathen, but the spiritual heathen who populate Europe have as yet heard nothing of Christianity. Christianity must indeed begin again from the very beginning if it is to meet its high educative task. So long as religion is only faith and outward form, and the religious function is not experienced in our own souls, nothing of any importance has happened. It has yet to be understood that the *mysterium magnum* is not only an actuality but is first and foremost rooted in the human psyche. The man who does not know this from his own experience may be a most learned theologian, but he has no idea of religion and still less of education.

Sharp as these words are, it nevertheless becomes clear at the crucial point that Jung will not commit himself to the *truth* of Christianity, but confines himself to stressing its psychological relevance and utility; to do more, he claims, would be to stray beyond the proper bounds of an empirical psychology. Such an attitude would be reasonable, were not Jung continually straying beyond them. How 'scientific' is he? The 'scientific' Freudians regard him as a deplorable example of what happens when a man wilfully strays from the path of scientific rectitude into obscurantism and black magic; yet he has hit on things which the Freudians have quite missed, and will go on missing. The candid reader will probably conclude that for all his disclaimers Jung is a bold thinker striving towards a personal *weltanschauung* through an arrangement of the materials coming into his hands not only through his clinical work but through his experience of life and his wide reading in the fields of anthropology and comparative religion. Of course, his findings can support themselves by an appeal to empirical observation, but they come

11

to us not as mere naked facts, but clothed in the very fabric of Jung's mentality. The truth appears to be that Jung, taking his point of departure from Freudian psychology with its wholly materialistic assumptions, its endeavour to ground itself in the natural sciences, has been impelled both by innate disposition and by his clinical experience towards the territory of religion, of mysticism and the occult, without, however, radically questioning and revising the naturalistic presuppositions with which he began. The quandary in which he then finds himself he seeks to escape by appealing to the merely empirical character of his work. The appeal fails, because after all he is out for a *weltanschauung*, as the reviewer sees who hails him enthusiastically as 'a religious thinker, the most important of his time'.

The difficulty here is that you cannot arrive at a world-view in one field of thought alone; if you try to do so with psychology, you are open to charges of 'psychologism'. This is the weak spot in Jung which makes him vulnerable to the assaults of theologians and others who see clearly enough that psychology, a branch of philosophy, cannot stand square on its own feet but must continually be making postulates and assumptions which carry it beyond itself into the field of philosophy proper— where it may not, perhaps, put up a very good showing. This observation has been most cogently made by a sympathetic critic, Victor White, O.P., in his recent book, *God and the Unconscious*. While a purely empirical science can proceed for some time on the basis of rough and ready working hypotheses, Fr. White points out, even unconsciously assumed ones, sooner or later it will be compelled to the endeavour to their precise examination and definition; that in fact it is impossible to interpret the simplest psychological phenomena without at least tacit trans-empirical assumptions.

Let me suggest one example [writes Fr. White]. I may, for instance, call a particular psychological phenomenon a *projection*, and I may accurately describe a projection as an unconscious 'process of dissimilation wherein a subjective content is estranged from the subject and, in a sense, incorporated in the object'. Provided I understand by 'subject' and 'object' no more than descriptions of conscious phenomena, *i.e.*, what is *perceived* as 'I' or 'not-I' respectively, I do not seriously transgress the strict limits of purely empirical observation. But then my definition precisely does *not* describe the phenomena as the projector perceives them; the content which, on other grounds, the psychologist calls subjective, he, in virtue of the projection itself, experiences as objective. Once he has assimilated the content to his empirical ego-consciousness, it is no longer a projection. I am driven therefore, wittingly or unwittingly, to assertions which overstep my empirical datum: to affirmations not merely of what 'appears' but of what 'really is'—even in spite of appearances. Thus, with Professor Jung, I shall go on to describe a projection in much more absolute terms: 'In the obscurity of something outside of me I discover, without recognizing it to be such, something which belongs inside me and to my own psyche.' But in so speaking I at once raise a hornet's nest of questions and assumptions which take us very far beyond the bare phenomena, or the scientist's cautious 'provisional view of the psyche as a relatively closed energic system'.

If I am to be entitled to dismiss the old alchemists' *Lehre der Entsprechung* (correspondence theory) as a rationalization, and to establish my own projection-theory of the same phenomenon as genuinely rational and scientific, I must be able to give a rational and critical account of my own terms. A purely pragmatic 'suitability' for attaining practical results, to preserve the phenomena, will no longer suffice; for by that criterion the alchemists' theory was at least as successful as my own. If I am to claim validity and even meaningfulness for my statement that the phenomenon is a projection, I must claim also the reality of a subject other than that of the phenomenal empirical ego, an objectivity other than that of the phenomenal objectivity experienced by the empirical ego (for this the alchemist or the patient also experiences and affirms). I claim, albeit tacitly, that I can define the psyche at least sufficiently to enable me to attribute to it an 'outside' and an 'inside'—again other than the purely phenomenal (for it is 'without recognizing it to be such')— and this in its turn implies that I have found justification for applying these or any other spatial concepts to the psyche. In further asserting that the projected content is really not 'outside' but 'belongs to my own psyche', I am claiming in effect that I can discriminate what belongs essentially to the psyche from what merely *happens in* it and *to* it, perhaps from 'external' agency or energy: that in this particular phenomenal event, at any rate, the psyche functions, not as a merely relatively, but as an absolutely, closed system. I am furthermore assuming that I can talk of it as 'it' at all, and that I have some intelligent meaning when I refer to 'it' by nouns and pronouns indicative of 'things' rather than by adjectives indicative of (for instance) the organism, or verbs indicative of operations.

Fr. White adduces the projection-theory, he says, as 'only one example (but perhaps a particularly acute one) of the fashion in which the practical necessities of analysis, and indeed of any interpretation of psychological phenomena which goes beyond the merely descriptive or quantitative, drive us willy-nilly into a maze of philosophical, you may call them "metaphysical", problems.' That is so; but it might equally well be adduced as an especially pointed example of the tacit and uncritical dualism of the 'within' and the 'without', the psyche and the world of nature, which, a heritage from Freudian naturalism, runs through Jung's thinking and is accountable for its incoherent and unfinished character.

Freud's definition of the mind as '. . . a psychical apparatus, extended in space, appropriately constructed, developed by the exigencies of life, which gives rise to the phenomena of consciousness only at one particular point and under certain conditions',—a hypothesis which, he claims, puts us in a position 'to establish psychology upon foundations similar to those of any other science, such as physics'—was thoroughly undermined by Jung's hypothesis of the collective unconscious with its archetypes: a hypothesis, or a discovery, to which he was led by his rejection of the exclusively sexual-instinctual character of the Freudian *libido*, tied as that was to the restricted theory of the Oedipus-complex. Where Freud saw the 'psychical apparatus', however, as a phenomenon of external nature—a device for the precarious reconciliation of instinctual drives with the inhibiting demands of civilization—in Jung the psyche has become something mysterious, autonomous, purposive and vast, whose affiliations with nature are, to say the least, obscure. So far as one can see, if Jung intends anything in this matter, he intends us to presume the collateral existence of a collective, subjective psyche on the one side, and an objective world of nature on the other: collateral but presumably independent. If so, it is an assumption which leads to some insuperable difficulties, for it makes man the simultaneous inhabitant of two heterogenerous realms of mind and matter. In practice, Jung deals with the problem by ignoring it and concentrating on mind; but that, too, has its dangers in that it leads him covertly towards a form of subjectivistic Gnosticism. It is a little risky, is it not, to speak as Jung does in the passage I have already quoted, of the *mysterium magnum* as an actuality first and foremost rooted in the human psyche, instead of *vice versa*, and to disparage mere 'faith and outward form'. 'Too few people', he says again, 'have experienced the divine image as the innermost possession of their own souls. Christ only meets them from without, never from within the soul.' One knows well enough what he means to convey, but the expression is unfortunate. We don't, in reality, find Christ by searching into our own depths, but, if at all, through real meeting with an other, in a realm where 'within' and 'without' cease to be contradictory; and of meeting, in this sense, Jung throughout his writings has nothing whatever to tell us. Everything for him, we might say, comes from 'within' the soul, never from 'without'.

The contradiction becomes acute when, having rejected the notion of a specious 'normality' as a sufficient criterion of psychological wholeness, one is faced with the religious and metaphysical question of man's final end. In the present book Jung speaks somewhat slightingly of 'the early days of analysis . . . with their pseudo-biological interpretations and their depreciation of the whole process of psychic development'; he now confesses that there is in the analytical process, the dialectical discussion between the conscious mind and the unconscious, 'a development or an advance towards some goal or end'—a goal or end the perplexing nature of which, he says, has engaged his attention for many years; and he now believes that 'there is in the psyche a process that seeks its own goal independently of external factors', *viz.*, the realization of a new centre of personality, the 'self', embracing both conscious and unconscious elements in a marriage of opposites. Just as his 'archetypes' bear some resemblance to Plato's 'ideas', so here he appears to approach the mystical teaching as to the Self, the Logos. Yet the question of man's final end, which must surely be bound up in that of the goal of any psychic process, is after all not merely a psychological but a metaphysical one. In other words, since man is a part of nature standing in vital relation to everything in the visible cosmos, the question of his final end is involved with that of the cosmos itself. The psyche and nature must equally have their origin and end in a God who is transcendent to and immanent in both, and not by any means merely a *mysterium* 'rooted in the human psyche'. This God Jung does not know, and faith in him he does not require; he is content simply to point to the actuality of God as an archetype within the psyche; as to which he confesses:

. . . We simply do not know the ultimate derivation of the archetype any more than we know the origin of the psyche. The competence of psychology as an empirical science only goes so far as to establish, on the basis of comparative research, whether for instance the imprint found in the psyche can or cannot reasonably be termed a 'God-image'. Nothing positive or negative has thus been asserted about the possible existence of God, any more than the archetype of the 'hero' proves the actual existence of a hero.

We can, I think, come to a clearer understanding both of the 'perplexing' goal of the autonomous psychic process now believed in by Jung, and of Jung's attitude to faith, if we turn to the early *Psychology of the Unconscious*, in which he first drew extensive parallels between an individual case-history with its wealth of dream and phantasy material, and the content of universal religious myths and cults. In this work he was able to point, *pace* the Freudians, to the utility of the religious symbol

15

in effecting that transformation of the incestuous libido which alone can liberate psychic energy for man's cultural tasks. Without fully realizing its significance, Jung had in fact, through psychological investigation, stumbled upon the age-old and world-wide mystery doctrines concerning *regeneration*; and it is enlightening to see how, with his naturalistic presuppositions, he misunderstood and mishandled this great theme.

Christianity was originally accepted, says Jung in that book, in order that humanity might escape from the brutal licentiousness of antiquity; and as soon as Christianity is discarded, the licentiousness and brutality return. We imagine, he says, that our incest wish has long been got rid of, and do not realize that all the while we unconsciously commit incest, symbolically, in religion. Here, the unconscious incest wish has been transformed into symbolic acts and concepts which cheat men, 'so that heaven appears to them as a father and earth as a mother and the people upon it children and brothers and sisters. Thus man can remain a child for all time and satisfy his incest wish all unawares.'

The religious myth, consequently, is one of the most important human institutions which, however misleadingly, nevertheless strengthens the psyche in the face of the threatening universe. 'The symbol, considered from the standpoint of actual truth, is misleading, indeed, but it is *psychologically true*, because it was and is the bridge to all the greatest achievements of humanity.' The following passage is of the greatest interest for the light it throws on Jung's earlier attitude to religious faith, which he has since modified, but which would still seem to condition his way of thinking:

But this does not mean to say that this unconscious way of trans-formation of the incest wish into religious exercises is the only one or the only possible one. There is also a conscious recognition and under-standing with which we can take possession of this libido which is bound up in incest and transformed into religious exercises so that we no longer need the stage of religious symbolism for this end. It is thinkable that instead of doing good to our fellowmen for 'the love of Christ', we do it from the knowledge that humanity, even as ourselves, could not exist, if among the herd, the one could not sacrifice himself for the other. *This would be the course of moral autonomy, of perfect freedom, when man could without compulsion wish that which he must do, and this from knowledge, without delusion through the religious symbol.*

It is a positive creed which keeps us infantile and, therefore, ethically inferior. Although of the greatest significance from the cultural

16

point of view and of imperishable beauty from the aesthetic standpoint, this delusion can no longer ethically suffice humanity striving after moral autonomy.

The infantile and moral danger lies in belief in the symbol because through that we guide the libido to an imaginary reality. The simple negation of the symbol changes nothing, for the entire mental disposition remains the same; we merely remove the dangerous object. But the object is not dangerous; the danger is our own infantile mental state, for love of which we have lost something very beautiful and ingenious through the simple abandonment of the religious symbol. I think *belief should be replaced by understanding*; then we would keep the beauty of the symbol, but still remain free from the depressing results of submission to belief. This would be the psychoanalytic cure for belief and disbelief.

The ominous introduction of such a breach between 'psychological' truth and truth as such should put us at once on our guard; and we might then look with reasonable suspicion both upon the naive assumption that 'moral autonomy' can be a sufficient human goal and upon the curiously unreal supposition that understanding can ever become a *substitute* for belief, as if reason and will were not both indispensable and complementary human faculties. Jung's muddle over the significance of the connection between *incest* and *rebirth*, so reminiscent of Nietzsche's confusion in *The Birth of Tragedy*, arises precisely from his lack of faith in the transcendant reality of the spiritual life; failing to discriminate the spiritual from the natural, and still more from the unnatural, he becomes confounded between the related movements of *regeneration* on the one hand and *degeneration* on the other. The confusion is perfectly understandable, and is quite plainly revealed in the brash treatment of Christ's reply to Nicodemus, and in the comments on Christ's self-comparison to the brazen serpent lifted up by the Israelites in the wilderness.

To be born of water means simply to be born from the mother's womb. To be born of the spirit means to be born from the fructifying breath of the wind. . . . One recognizes very clearly the ethical demand as the foundation of these mythologia assertions: *thou must say of the mother that she was not impregnated by a mortal in the ordinary way, but by a spiritual being in an unusual manner*. This demand stands in strict opposition to the real truth; therefore, the myth is a fitting solution. One can say it was a hero who died and was born again in a remarkable manner, and in this way attained immortality. The need which this demand asserts is evidently a prohibition against a definite phantasy concerning the mother. A son may naturally think that a father has generated

17

him in a carnal way, but not that he himself impregnated the mother and so caused himself to be born again into renewed youth. This incestuous phantasy which for some reason possesses an extraordinary strength, and, therefore, appears as a compulsory wish, is repressed and, conforming to the above demand, under certain conditions, expresses itself again, symbolically, concerning the problem of birth, or rather concerning individual rebirth from the mother. In Jesus' challenge to Nicodemus we clearly recognize this tendency: 'Think not carnally or thou art carnal, but think symbolically, then art thou spirit.'

Jung's grave error is his literal, naturalistic interpretation of the incest wish, which applies only to its regressive aspect. As a 'righteous philistine of culture'—his words for Nicodemus—he is unable to grasp the inner meaning of the exhortation and is forced to interpret it as a useful but strictly untruthful device serving the therapeutic aim of somehow raising the nature above the repressed incestuous desire. This appears when, later, he writes of the mythological hero's battle with the dragon:

The hero battling with the dragon has much in common with the dragon, and also he takes over his qualities; for example, invulnerability. As the footnotes show, the similarity is carried still further (sparkling eyes, sword in the mouth). Translated psychologically, the dragon is merely the son's repressed longing, striving towards the mother; therefore, the son is the dragon, as even Christ is identified with the serpent, which, once upon a time, *similia similibus*, had controlled the snake plague in the Wilderness. John III.14. *As a serpent he is to be crucified: that is to say, as one striving backwards towards the mother, he must die hanging or suspended on the mother tree.*

This is, of course, both blasphemous and wildly wrong. But the passage serves to reveal both Jung's ineptness, at times, when faced with the spiritual teaching, and the intrepidity with which he approaches his self-appointed task of assimilating it to his psychoanalytical *weltanschauung*.

Yet to endeavour to measure the mystical teachings by the uncertain standards of analytical psychology is to attempt the assimilation of the greater to the lesser. For the plain fact is that that psychology is not comprehensive enough, and not firmly grounded enough, to be a criterion for the evaluation of another system—it is itself in need of fundamental evaluation and verification. It is well enough when the great psychologist contents himself with pointing out the similarities between the symbols manifested in the course of the individuation-process and those of religious mysticism or the occult teachings; but it is far from well when he

18

takes the further step of utilizing his psychological theories to explain, i.e., to explain away, spiritual truths.

To return, then, to alchemy. In pointing out that beneath their apparent concern with the transmutation of metals the alchemists were in fact brooding over the problems of psychical transformation, Jung is on the face of it uncovering a novel truth, when, in fact, not only was this perfectly well known to the alchemists themselves, as he of course admits, but it has long been a commonplace to those who have given the matter any serious attention. In a work, *The Doctrine of the Subtle Body in Western Tradition*, published in 1919, the author, G. R. S. Mead, speaks of '. . . a supra-physical, vital and psychical side to alchemy—a scale of ascent leading finally to man's perfection in spiritual reality.' The gross alembic, says Mead, in which the inner work of transmutation was wrought, was the physical body of man. The fervour of his attentive brooding was the fire which had to be so watchfully maintained and warily graded for the 'hatching out of the spiritual man-chick from the mysterious philosophic egg of his subtle nature'. Thus,—'the wild riot of symbol, myth and allegory in which they delighted, was intended by the best of them to set forth the sequence of a natural inner process of the life of the soul.'

All such puzzling devices, when rightly interpreted, they held, would be found to fit into an ordered whole, which told the story of the development of man's inner nature as it could be intensified and quickened by the deliberate application to it of the knowledge of the greatest of all arts—namely, the purification and reorganizing of man's psychical apparatus and the perfecting of the life of his spiritual selfhood. . . . For their grand secret was the soul-freeing doctrine of regeneration, which as a demonstrable fact of history was undisguisedly the chief end not only of the higher mystery-institutions but of many an open philosophic school and saving cult of later antiquity.

Despite the interest and value, in detail, of his commentaries, Jung not only adds nothing *essential* to this, he positively detracts from it by his ignorance of the theoretic background of occultism in general, and of alchemy in particular, in which, as a matter of course, psychology does not stand apart by itself but is integrated with cosmology through the well-known insistence that in man, the microcosm, there occur processes analogous to and connected with those taking place in the macrocosm, the universe. Having no cosmology, however, Jung wrenches the two apart; and when he encounters the cosmological side of the occult teachings he either ignores it completely or 'interprets' it psychologically, *via* the projection-formula.

19

Take for example his treatment of the alchemists' theory of psycho-physical transformation, the creation of an immortal body. With the remark that the term *imaginatio*, like *meditatio*, is of particular importance in the alchemical opus, he turns to Martin Ruland's *Lexicon Alchemiae* of 1612, and finds the statement: 'Imagination is the star in man, the celestial or supercelestial body.' This astounds him; but instead of going more closely into the Paracelsian doctrines which lie beyond this statement in order to discover, if possible, what it meant to the alchemists, and indeed, what it might conceivably still mean to contemporary expounders of occult systems, he rationalizes it as follows:

. . . This astounding definition throws a quite special light on the fantasy processes connected with the *opus*. We have to conceive of these processes not as the immaterial phantoms we readily take fantasy-pictures to be, but as something corporeal, a 'subtle body', semi-spiritual in nature. In an age when there was as yet no empirical psychology such a concretization was bound to be made, because everything unconscious, once it was activated, was projected into matter—that is to say, it approached people from outside. It was a hybrid phenomenon, as it were, half spiritual, half physical; a concretization such as we frequently encounter in the psychology of primitives. The *imaginatio*, or the act of imagining, is thus a physical activity that can be fitted into the cycle of material changes, that brings these about and is brought about by them in its turn. In this way the alchemist related himself not only to the unconscious but directly to the very substance which he hoped to transform through the power of imagination.

In a later section dealing with 'The Lapis-Christus Parallel', Jung writes, again: 'It is clear enough from this material what the ultimate aim of alchemy really was: it was trying to produce a *corpus subtile*, a transfigured and resurrected body, *i.e.*, a body that was at the same time spirit. In this it finds common ground with Chinese alchemy, as we have learned from the text of *The Secret of the Golden Flower*. There the main concern is the "diamond body", in other words, the attainment of immortality through physical transformation. The diamond is an excellent symbol because it is hard, fiery, and translucent.' If, then, we turn to Jung's *Commentary* on the above work, we find that he takes the attainment of the 'diamond body', or of 'any other sort of indestructible body', to be expressions which are merely 'psychologically symbolical of an attitude which is invulnerable to emotional entanglements and violent upheavals; in a word, they symbolize a consciousness freed from the world'. Do they only serve to 'symbolize'? Is it not at least conceivable that, given the bi-unity of mind and matter, they may be subtle-physical realities as well? Given the postulates of a philosophy of mysticism, there seems to be no inherent absurdity in the idea, whereas in Jung's implied dualism of mind and matter, if the position be pushed to its conclusion, there *is* such an absurdity. Jung's psychology, indeed, *qua* psychology, would seem only to be capable of reaching full intelligibility when it is brought into line with, and corrected in the light of, a philosophy of mysticism.

II

The Jungian account of the unconscious is somewhat fluid and elusive. Below the psyche's conscious, waking surface, Jung tells us, there is a more or less superficial layer of the unconscious which is undoubtedly personal; below this again is a deeper layer that does not derive from personal experience but is inborn. This collective unconscious is not individual but universal, constituting a psychic foundation, superpersonal in its nature, that is 'identical in', although not, explicitly, common to, all Western men. Although Jung speaks of the contents of the collective unconscious, by which it is made 'sufficiently conscious for recognition as the archetypes', deriving this term from St. Augustine's explanatory paraphrase of the Platonic *ideas*, he by no means attributes to them a transcendent reality, but thinks of them as immanent in the psyche. The Jungian psyche has been pictured as a house built above ground (the individual, personal consciousness), beneath which is a cellar, the personal unconscious, each cellar having a trapdoor leading down into a subterranean labyrinth of great antiquity, where lie the traces left by our human and pre-human ancestors which have moulded the configuration of the psyche.

In some of his more recent pronouncements, nevertheless, Jung seems to trench upon the 'subliminal self' outlined by the theorists of psychical research. Thus, in *Psychology and Alchemy*, he writes: 'In my experience the conscious mind can only claim a relatively central position and must put up with the fact that the unconscious psyche transcends and as it were surrounds it on all sides. Unconscious contents connect it *backwards* with physiological states on the one hand and archetypal data on the other. But it is extended *forward* by intuitions which are conditioned partly by archetypes and partly by subliminal perceptions depending on the relativity of time and space in the unconscious.' Compare this with an observation in G. N. M. Tyrrel's *The Personality of Man*—'In telepathy and precognition we catch a glimpse of something at work in the personality which bears no ordinary relation to space and time; something, also, which is no mere unintelligent "unconscious", but is full of planning

21

and directed effort.' Now what the psychical researchers claim to reveal is precisely the tenuousness of the borderline between psyche and nature, between thoughts and events, the subjective and the objective aspects of reality which in the Jungian conception are kept separate. 'If', writes Tyrrel, 'the evidence of psychical research shows anything, it shows that the phenomena it studies are not "supernatural". They are "natural" in the sense of belonging to an ordered whole. They are evidently governed by different laws from those which govern the physical world; but there is no reason to suppose that they are separated from the latter by any intrinsic boundary. There is probably continuity, the apparent sharp division being the result of the limited character of our sense-perception. We should regard paranormal phenomena as constituting an extension of the sphere of nature; but "nature" with an extended meaning.'

The basic dualism in Jung's thinking about the relations of psyche and nature is evidenced in many places; take for instance the account of mythological origins given in *The Integration of the Personality*. There Jung asserts that myths are not to be interpreted as solar, lunar, vegetal or other comparisons, but are to be seen as first and foremost psychic manifestations representing the nature of the psyche; the mind of the primitive is 'little concerned with an objective explanation of obvious things', but has an irresistible unconscious urge to assimilate all experience through the outer senses into inner, psychic happening. 'All the mythologized occurrences of nature, such as summer and winter, the phases of the moon, the rainy seasons, and so forth, are anything but allegories of these same objective experiences, nor are they to be understood as "explanations" of sunrise, sunset, and the rest of the natural phenomena. They are, rather, symbolic expressions for the inner and unconscious psychic drama that becomes accessible to human consciousness by way of projection—that is, mirrored in the events of nature. This projection is so thoroughgoing that it has taken several thousand years of culture to separate it in some measure from the outer object.' I do not know what this last sentence implies, if not that the end of human efforts is an entire detachment of the subject from the object; for Jung does not, apparently, grasp that subject and object are correlatives and that their *end* can only be through reconciliation in a third term which transcends while embracing both. In leaving us suspended between an inner subject and an outer object in no way connected except that the one may serve as a passive frame for the 'projection' of the other, he solves a mystery by submerging it in a mystery yet greater and more perplexing. At least it might have occurred to him that the human psyche which 'projects' its drama upon the events of nature must have been itself formed and developed through the ages by a corresponding 'intro-

22

jection' of those very events, and that the relation between them must therefore at bottom be somehow intrinsic and indissoluble.

We find the same dualism already present in the opening chapter of *Psychology of the Unconscious*, where it issues in a sharp dichotomy between the two types of thinking, 'directed' and 'dream or phantasy' thinking; the first, of which the perfected expression is science and its resultant techniques, being 'incessantly occupied in stripping off all subjectivity from experience', and the second, found prëeminently in the mentality of children and primitives, founded upon an inextricable confusion of subject and object. This is a surprising oversimplification in that it leaves out of account that active region of the mind in which thought is imaginative, concrete and symbolic; for directed thinking is not in fact synonymous with scientific objectivity, but must include that poetic or religio-philosophical way of thought which demonstrably and knowingly rests upon a mythic or symbolic foundation. Still, having made the dichotomy, how does Jung overcome it?—as he needs must in order to proceed at all. Finding himself without a *tertium quid* to bring the two distinct and opposed types of thinking into unity, he is forced to the bare assertion that they are connected, when by definition they are not connected and having nothing in common. He asserts, bluntly: 'By means of phantastic thinking, directed thinking is connected with the oldest foundations of the human mind, which have been for a long time beneath the threshold of consciousness.' The lacuna here would seem to match that between his view of 'psychological truth' and truth as such, which enables him to acknowledge the indispensability of the religious symbol in the work of healing, while recommending the 'replacement' of belief by understanding.

Thus, throughout, the dualistic presupposition obstructs Jung's intuitive grasp of psychological realities which demand a triune structure for their substantiation, that structure itself requiring a root of *faith*. This is especially so in the later works where he arrives at the concept of the 'self', defined as 'a virtual point between the conscious and the unconscious' which provides the psyche with a new centre of gravity, as the mysterious goal of the psychic process. It happens that the Self is a central concept of mysticism. Mysticism holds that realization of the Self presumes a transcension of the dualities which condition mortal existence—life/death, pleasure/pain, I/not-I—and the union of the individual will with the universal Logos. Jung's 'self' is, therefore, a psychologized version of the Self of mysticism, shorn of its transcendental character and restricted to a position of immanence in the psyche. Accordingly, when Jung comes to comment upon the text of a mystical work like the *Golden*

23

Flower, he explains the attainment of the psychological condition symbolized (for him) by the 'diamond body', as a dualistic disinvolvement of subject from object, when what the text really means is something quite different: the detachment alike from ego and non-ego through the slaying of desire and the consequent realization of the Self which transcends and unites subject and object.

I return to the point that what is needed in order to make intelligible the findings of analytical psychology is an account of the unconscious which does not dualistically involve the suppression of nature for the sake of an introverted, capsulated psyche, but which is capable of making room for psyche and nature, mind and matter alike within a single system. There would be no great novelty in this: philosophical monism has a long and honourable tradition. And in fact, such an account is to be found in an admirable work already extant when Jung was still at school, *The Philosophy of Mysticism* by Baron Carl du Prel, of which an English translation appeared in 1889.

The unconscious for du Prel is not confined to the human psyche as distinct from the world of nature, but the term comprises all that ultimate reality or being which lies behind the phenomena of consciousness, both objective and subjective, and thus behind consciousness itself. To the question whether this 'unconscious' lies immediately behind our physically conditioned consciousness, or may be pushed back indefinitely, so that there is room (to quote the translator's preface) for a root of conscious individuality, only *relatively* unconscious for the organism of sense, du Prel finds an answer in the recognition of the psycho-physical 'threshold of sensibility', and in its occasional mobility or displacement. Du Prel links his conception with the organic world by pointing to the fact that in the scale of biological evolution, from the oyster to the man, organization and consciousness rise parallel to each other. In other words, from the standpoint of every animal organism, external nature can be divided into two parts, which are the more unequal as the organic grade is lower. The one includes that part of nature with which the sense-apparatus establishes relations; the other is for the organism in question transcendental, in that it lives in no relation to it. In the biological process the boundary-line between these two world-halves has been pushed continually forward in the same direction. The biological rise and the rise of consciousness thus signify a constant removal of the boundary between representation and reality at the cost of the transcendental part of the world, and in favour of the perceived part. With the increase in the number of senses and the rise in their functional ability, the psycho-physical threshold was continually pushed forward: influences behind it do not come into consciousness. There is thus a transcendental world, unknown to us, but which may be known in part through the shifting of the psycho-physical threshold, as it occurs in certain hypernormal psychical conditions—which have latterly been the subject of psychical research. There is also the possibility of further evolution, further encroachment upon the transcendental world through a rise in the biological scale.

Correlative to this is the question of our self-consciousness. If self-consciousness does not exhaust its object, then corresponding to the transcendental world must be a transcendental Ego; and our sense of personality, by which we know ourselves as mere willing beings, does not coincide with our whole Ego. 'The sphere of our earthly personality would be only the smaller circle included in the larger concentric circle of our metaphysical subject, and the earthly self-consciousness would not cast its beams to the periphery of our being.' This metaphysical subject is not in itself unconscious, but only relatively so, as lying beyond the illuminated sphere of the earthly self-consciousness. 'The thought that individuality extends its roots down into the thing-in-itself is thus at least logically admissible', and: 'If there is a transcendental Ego, we stand with only one foot of our being in the phenomenal world.'

Du Prel accounts for the dramatic processes of dream-construction, and for forgetting and remembering, etc., in terms of a duality of persons within the single subject. The individual lies this side and that side of the threshold of sensibility, and the two halves are related as two scales of a balance, the one rises above the threshold as the other sinks below it. How far the soul, the unconscious, projects beyond the consciousness we do not know, except that the projection is very extensive. We have to distinguish between our sense-consciousness, our soul-consciousness, and the still problematical Subject-consciousness:

. . . Representing these as three unequal circles one within the other, the sense-consciousness filling the smallest, the soul-consciousness the middle one, and the Subject-consciousness the largest, the periphery of the innermost circle would stand for the psycho-physical threshold. By its displacement in the rising series to the ecstatic conditions, sleep, somnambulism, trance, apparent death, etc., the centre of the inner circle is more and more obscured; that is, the sense-consciousness tends more and more to disappear, but the circle itself is widened; that is, the consciousness extends itself more over the region of the so-called Unconscious. Already in common sleep the Ego of sense sinks; in the magnetic sleep the line of the inner circle is so far thrown back towards the periphery of the outer one that the somnambulists speak of their sense-Ego—the inner circle—only in the third person. . . . The *content* of consciousness in these conditions naturally retains its full reality, even when it is dramatically transferred to another person. Now there is no condition of ecstasy in which the outermost circle can be completely reached. The proof of this is easily adduced. There is no condition of sleep with ecstasy *without* visions. Visions depend on the dramatic severance, but the latter is only possible on the condition that a conscious and an unconscious, with a threshold dividing them, are both present. Whence it follows that the foundation of visions must be our own unconscious spirit, with which we are in communication, and with dramatic severance, just because the consciousness does not illuminate the whole outer circle, but an Unconscious always remains.

There is nothing here which conflicts essentially with the empirical findings of analytical psychology, or for that matter of psychical research, and much that could go far to substantiate them; the conclusion that 'the foundation of visions must be our own unconscious spirit' is already an anticipation of Freud and Jung, while the following plainly points toward Jung's 'subliminal' account of the psyche:

. . . we must recognize that the Ego below the psycho-physical threshhold, the so-called unconscious, is only relatively unconscious, from the standpoint of the Ego above the threshold of sensibility, not unconscious in itself. This transcendental half of our being, lying beyond the sphere of our normal consciousness, stands in other relations to things than does the man of five senses, and has other modes of perception than his, and in these also the scale by which we measure time and space in the day-consciousness undergoes a change. When, however, this transcendental Ego comes forth in dream and somnambulism, its perception often takes on allegorical and symbolical forms, or even the form of the dramatic sundering of the Ego, and then, indeed, we should decline to superstition should we take this mere form of knowledge for real.

We have noted that Jung, while allowing to the alchemists some knowledge of the processes of psychical transformation, tacitly denies the possibility of a coincident physical transmutation. The reflections given below follow those already quoted concerning the alchemical *imaginato*:

The singular expression 'astrum' (star) is a Paracelsian term, which in this context means something like 'quintessence'. Imagination is therefore a concentrated extract of the life forces, both physical and psychic. So the demand that the artist must have a sound physical constitution is quite intelligible, since he works with and through his own quintessence and is himself the indispensable condition of his own experiment. But, just because of this intermingling of the physical and the psychic, it always remains an obscure point whether the ultimate transformations in the alchemical process are to be sought more in the material or more in the spiritual realm. Actually, however, the question is wrongly put: there was no 'either-or' for that age, but there did exist an intermediate realm between mind and matter, i.e., a psychic realm of subtle bodies whose characteristic it is to manifest themselves in a mental as well as a material form. This is the only view that makes sense of alchemistic ways of thought, which must otherwise appear nonsensical. Obviously, the existence of this intermediate realm comes to a sudden stop the moment we try to investigate matter in and for itself, apart from all projection; and it remains non-existent so long as we believe we know anything conclusive about matter or the psyche. But the moment when physics touches on the 'untrodden, untreadable regions', and when psychology has at the same time to admit that there are other forms of psychic life besides the acquisitions of personal consciousness—in other words, when psychology too touches on an impenetrable darkness—then the intermediate realm of subtle bodies comes to life again, and the physical and the psychic are once more blended in an indissoluble unity.

'We have', Jung enigmatically adds, 'come very near to this turning-point today.'

Yet if we accept the hypothesis of a moveable threshold of sensibility which marks off our conscious ego with its limited area of perceived reality, from our Subject with its field of transcendental knowledge, then the dichotomy of 'psyche' and 'nature' had already been resolved. Matter and force, du Prel points out, as distinct and separate entities, are mere mental abstractions which are never in experience found apart; their apparent dualism is referable to a dualism in our powers of perception, since it pertains to the position of the psycho-physical threshold whether the force side or the material side of the nature of things is perceived, they being always present together, and only distinguishable in thought. Every force acting upon us must thus have its material side, even if it is not sensible to us: what is for us insensible is not therefore immaterial. If the dualism of matter and force is suppressed, all metaphysics must from the standpoint of another faculty of perception be only physics. If all matter is visible force, and all force invisible matter, it depends simply on the position of the threshold, whether I can read the thought of another, or whether I not even feel its impact. Our senses, then, are a quite arbitrary and relative scale by which to assign the boundary between matter and force, body and mind. Each threshold of sensibility draws the boundary at a different place. 'Below all senses there must be the insensible, and the aggregate conditions of solid, fluid and gaseous are only condensed products of a fourth aggregate condition, which Faraday and Crookes term radiant matter, and in which matter—from the standpoint of our sensibility—appears volatilized into bare force.' The more the material side of a thing presents itself to us, as in a block of granite, the more its force side disappears; the more the force side emerges, as in thought, the more its material side vanishes. But it is inadmissible to regard this ideal distinction of force and matter, mind and body, as a real separation, and to hypostasize these two sides of a thing as independent. —Which provokes the reflection that perhaps the alchemists were sounder in their views on the materiality of the 'diamond body' than Jung is disposed to allow.

Now Jung finds the mysterious goal of the individuation-process, which he assimilates psychologically to the alchemical *opus*, to be the production of a new centre of personality, the 'self', which is 'not only the centre but also the whole circumference which embraces both conscious and unconscious; it is the centre of this totality, just as the ego is the centre of the conscious mind'. How does this fit into the above schema?

In our self-consciousness, according to du Prel, is revealed, not our whole Subject, but only our Ego posited in the phenomenal world. We have therefore to distinguish our transcendental Subject from the Ego, the self-consciousness of sense. Now in this Subject, *a priori* to our whole sense-phenomenon, the dualism between our organism (subject) and organically mediated consciousness (object) is certainly annulled; but in its place there arises another and deeper dualism, namely that between the transcendental being on the one side, and our organic phenomenal form with its sense-consciousness on the other side. There is thus simultaneous duplication of persons in the single Subject, and we are simultaneously members of two worlds, the phenomenal world to which we are tied by our senses and the transcendental world in which our Subject already lives, and of which we become conscious only through a shifting of the psycho-physical threshold. Because its transcendental faculties are not mediated by the sense-organism, but are evinced in spite of it, it is apparent that our transcendental Subject is the life-principle in us: as organizing principle in us, it is for the organism, *a priori*, prior to it, our earthly phenomenal form being only its transitory tracing.

Since the biological process is a raising of the unconscious into the conscious, making the possession of the Subject the possession of the person, and its ideal consummation coincides with the transcendental existence of our Subject, the transcendental faculties of the latter, glimpsed by us in hypernormal states, provide us with the sole opportunity of anticipating in thought the biological process also. This progress presses into a world which is, in its kind, material and subject to law, and to which as Subjects we already belong. More, the biological aim of our existence coincides for the race with the transcendental aim for the individual. We attain the aim of earthly existence, says du Prel, when we subordinate the interests of our person to those of the Subject. Herein is the explanation of conscience: the moral imperative comes ultimately from the transcendental Subject; and the conflict in us between two wills, the one rational, the other egoistical and unjust, is explained by the thorough difference of the situation of the pre-existing Subject, a member of the transcendental order of things, and its transient phenomenal form in the world of sense.

But to return to the mystical conception of the realization of the Self through a transcending of the dualities of mortal life, and to Jung's 'integration and birth of [the] superior personality . . . invulnerable to emotional entanglements and violent upheavals', which he identifies with the alchemical 'diamond body'. It would appear, would it not, that the approximation of our Ego (in du Prel's language) to our transcendental Subject must result precisely in 'the production of a new centre of personality' which would in very fact be located at 'a virtual point between the conscious and the unconscious', seeing that our Subject and its field is unconscious to the personality of sense; and in this respect at least analytical psychology is accommodated within the wider scope of a philosophy of mysticism. 'If such a transposition succeeds', Jung says in the *Golden Flower*, 'it results in doing away with *participation mystique* [*i.e.*, non-differentiation between subject and object], and there develops a personality who, so to speak, suffers only in the inferior parts of himself, but in the superior region is singularly detached from painful as well as pleasing events.' This detachment appertains, not to the ego, but to the Self; and it is therefore remarkable that du Prel should adduce instances which prove that the transcendental being considers the personality of senso in a purely objective relation—'in an attitude of as much indifference to its fate as to that of a stranger—as it must be, since the two halves of the being lie this side and that side of a threshold of sensibility'. Moreover, there is nothing to exclude the inference that this indifference of the transcendental consciousness, which regards objectively the pleasure and pain of the ordinary man, and estimates it according to a standard of its own, extends to the whole sum of our fate in life. Insofar as we shift the centre of our existence from our ego to our Self, therefore, we shall ourselves share in this indifference to our personal fate; shall, in other words, be 'singularly detached from painful as well as pleasing events'. We may, further, come into possession of subliminal faculties; and there is nothing to contradict the alchemical supposition that there will be a transmutation of our physical organism. Du Prel says:

If there takes place biological adaptation to the same transcendental world to which we as Subjects already belong, the identity of both worlds being apparent from the fact that this Subject is the true quintessence and supporter of our phenomenal earth-form, then must this quintessence, as the monistic cause at once of our bodily phenomenon and of our earth-consciousness, determine, both organically and mentally, the future man, and conduct him further and further into the transcendental mode of existence. The difficulty that we are so disposed to think of every super-sensuous existence as immaterial, and of every material existence as one of gross substance, disappears when we recognize the dualism of force and substance as existing only for the mode of perception. If force and substance are only two inseparable sides of one thing, we cannot disclaim materiality altogether for our transcendental Subject, even if only in the sense of a fourth aggregate condition; we can but conceive in the bosom of the biological future an organism of a mode of existence like that of our Subject. If thus considering the question we proceed from nature, we can already recognize in the succession of her kingdoms, from the stone, through the vegetable and animal up to man, a continual material attenuation; proceeding from the transcendental Subject, we cannot logically represent its existence, as we attain to it in death, as diametrically different from the earthly.

The employment here of the alchemical term "quintessence" to denote the Subject, the Self, as supporter and informer of our phenomenal earth-form and the cause equally of our physical frame and our sense-consciousness, is perhaps accidental: it is nevertheless suggestive. The 'fourth aggregate condition' of matter in which the physical aspect of our Subject may perhaps be found, and in which, from the standpoint of our sensibility, matter must appear volatilized into bare force, du Prel refers to as 'radiant matter'—a quintessential substance of which the aggregate conditions of gaseous, fluid and solid known to us are but condensed products. We touch here on the *four elements* of alchemy, and of the tradition behind alchemy. Brewer (*Dictionary of Phrase and Fable*) has: 'The ancient Greeks said there are four elements or forms in which matter can exist:—Fire, or the imponderable form; air, or the gaseous form; water, or the liquid form; and earth, or the solid form. The Pythagoreans added a fifth, which they called ether, more subtile and pure than fire, and possessed of an orbicular motion. This element, which flew upwards at creation, and out of which the stars were made, was called the fifth essence; *quintessence*, therefore, means the most subtile extract of a body that can be procured.'

There is some interesting information about the symbolism of the four elements, in which psychology is integrated with cosmology, in Colin Still's, *The Timeless Theme.* If we bear in mind that what Jung has stumbled upon in his researches into the soul is the process of *regeneration*, we shall find it of interest to compare what Still has to say on the same theme; for Still, who appeals throughout to mystical tradition, is principally concerned with the elemental symbolism in the initiation rites of the Greek mysteries, those rites being concerned precisely with regeneration, and thus having much in common with the symbolism of alchemy. Behind the experiences of the pagan initiation, then, says Still, lay a complete philosophy, of which each of the incidents in the ritual proceeding allegorized a salient feature. It was a philosophy of Redemption, and its ceremonies were designed as a reversal of the process of *descent through the elements* implied by the Fall.

Granted what we learn from writers on occultism, that the real *elements* are not physical, but are the informing, energizing principle of the physical phenomena, Still tells us that from the earliest times the physical body of man has been described as earthly, the emotional part of him as watery, the rational part as airy, and the intuitional part as fiery or aethereal. He relates this to the ancient belief that the human constitution comprises, besides the physical body, a series of super-physical bodies or vehicles:

Earth . . . physical body.

Water . . . the sensuous or passional or impressional element in man—the 'natural' or 'psychic' body. The Egyptian *Ka*, the Zoharic *Nephesh*, and the Greek *Psyche*.

Air . . . . rational, intellectual or spiritual element in man. *Ba, Ruach* and *Pneuma*.

Fire . . . . supergaseous state of matter ('water above the firmament' in Genesis.) Aethor. The divine or intuitional element in man—the 'heavenly' body. *Khou, Neshamah*, and *Nous*.

These four main bodies in the human constitution are the four main planes through which the consciousness rises and falls in the cycle of subjective moods—a passage from *earth* to *water* 'may be employed as

31

a piece of natural symbolism to represent a rising of the consciousness from the physical plane to the plane of sensuous emotion'. Turning from microcosm to macrocosm, he continues, we find that ancient mystical philosophies regarded the external universe as itself consisting of four main spheres, likewise designated by the four elements, and conceived as regions of habitation during this life and the 'next'.

Stated in terms of natural symbolism, death consists in the Soul's shedding of the successive elements as bodies and in its concurrent ascent through the successive elements as regions of habitation. Thus at death the Soul sheds the EARTHLY body and quits the region of EARTH. Clothed now in the WATERY body, it passes to the region of WATER. It then sheds the WATERY body; and, clothed in the AIRY body, it rises to the region of AIR. Finally, when perfectly purified, it sheds the AIRY body; and, clothed now in the FIERY body as in a 'fiery garment', it rises to the region of FIRE (AETHER).

As to the former aspect of this dual process [incarnation and 'death'], note that the shedding of the successive bodies, when it is expressed in terms of the elements, corresponds to the changes whereby objective matter turns from the solid state into the liquid and from the liquid state into the gaseous. In short, death is a process in the microcosm which is analogous to the process of rarefaction in the macrocosm. Similarly, of course, incarnation is analogous to condensation.

Still, of course, has much more to say on this theme; but so much is sufficient to indicate how closely these traditional beliefs correspond with du Prel's hypothesis; how they accord with the alchemical writings; and how little they need conflict with the purely psychological findings of Jung.

'The spiritual regeneration of man', writes Franz Hartmann in his *Paracelsus* (c. 1890), 'requires the opening of his inner senses, and this, again, involves the development of the internal organs of the spiritual body, while the latter is intimately connected with the physical form. Thus this regeneration is not an entirely spiritual process, but productive also of great changes in the physical body. He who rejects, neglects, or despises his physical body, as long as he has not outgrown the necessity of having such a corporeal form, may be compared to the yolk in an egg wanting to be free from the white of the egg and the shell, without having grown into a bird.'

D. S. Savage

To write a Utopia, to live in an imaginary world, implies a dissatisfaction with one's immediate environment, and the periods that have produced the greatest number of Utopias—of visions of an ideal environment—have all been periods of upheaval.

There was the Renaissance, the period of the revolution of learning. Following this, the Age of Reason saw few Utopias but the Industrial Revolution gave rise to a number of new idealists—the Idealists of Material Progress—who had an entirely different outlook from their successors, the Idealists of Decentralization (or Escape) whose first wave broke at the end of the 19th century, and whose third wave is still with us, covering over the new Idealists of Humanism whose voices are barely audible as yet.

THE 'NATURAL' TOWN

The rise and growth of towns themselves—the 'real' towns and not the Utopias—can be divided into three groups. There are the 'natural' towns that have developed slowly through the ages, proceeding at the pace of their inhabitants from barbarism to civilization. The form of these towns has been determined by their geographical position and their history.

The cow-path—that early route of least resistance between pasture and homestead that skirted round steep places, boulders and bogs—may still underlie the route of the main road that leads from the suburbs to the city hall. Bends and sudden turns in side streets may have been caused by the projections of half-remembered fortifications or quite forgotten quarrels over rights of way between neighbouring owners. The effects may be delightful, quaintly charming or wildly inconvenient, but everything has a certain inevitability because it was determined by the gradual parallel evolution of place and people.

THE 'COLONIAL' TOWN

This type of 'natural' town is unknown west of the Atlantic where the first town-builders were people already far advanced in civilization. Most towns in America belong to a second type which includes almost all 'colonial' towns created in undeveloped parts of the world during periods of rapid trade expansion. Under these conditions, the prime considerations are speed, ease and economy of construction and immediate efficiency of operation. In all parts of the world and at all periods of history, these considerations have led directly to towns based on a simple rectangular pattern of streets and buildings, derived from the basic shape of the buildings which, in turn, has been derived from the basic shape of the prime unit of construction—a rectangular brick or a longer but still rectangular plank of wood.

This 'colonial' type of town includes the Greek settlements of the Hellenistic period around the shores of the Mediterranean; the camps and settlements of the Roman Empire throughout Western Europe and North Africa; the new trading settlements founded during the Middle Ages, particularly in devastated or less closely settled parts of Europe; the early Spanish and English settlements of America during the 16th and 17th centuries; and indeed most of the later colonial towns all over the world.

THE GOVERNMENT CENTRE

The third main type of towns covers those that were designed from the start, or radically re-designed, to become centres of government. The focus of these towns might be the palace of the King, as at Versailles (1624), or of the ruling prince as at Karlsruhe (1715); the home of the President and the memory of a national hero as at Washington (1791) or the centre of administration and the memory of national victories as at Paris (1858). Other schemes that come into this group are the new plans made for Hitler's Berlin and Stalin's Leningrad during the last

34

world war. No matter what the political credo of the regime in power, each such town inevitably displays the radiating avenues of the parade of pomp.

In contrast to these actual towns of gradual maturity, of immediate efficiency and of the display of power, Ideal Cities or Utopias have more often never been built at all, but have remained mere story-tales or diagrams. Even when one has been built, it has seldom taken the form patterned in the dream of its inventor. Utopian pioneers have usually had to try out their ideas within an environment already established by others. And yet, abortive and frustrated as is the history of the visionary Utopias, they are the sources from which flow all current idealism in town planning and urban redevelopment.

Imagining or creating an Ideal City—a perfect environment for human life—is a God-like act. It is about as near as man can get to the Divine Act of creating a world for Man formed 'in His own image'. This last concept is important, for man cannot consciously envisage an environment (or a God) higher than the ideal of his own period. So, a study of contemporary Utopias enables us to see both what was the ideal picture of life at each particular era, and also to realize what evils and difficulties were most apparent to the minds of idealists of that time.

It is partly due to this contemporary flavour that Ideal Cities, whether described or built, seldom retain their validity as 'ideals' for succeeding generations. They rapidly become 'period pieces' with the nostalgia or interest that attaches to the particular period in which they were conceived or created. They represent in fact the crystallization of an ideal environment for a particular moment of time and, by reason of their very perfection and completeness, they are not susceptible to the flux and change of the living environment around them. Although often considered well 'in advance of their time', most Utopias or Ideal Cities crystallize the 'might-have-beens' of the generation that is on the decline. To take a simple example, the Garden City crystallized the ideal of escape from the crowded dirt of the industrial revolution within the limitations of movement of the latter end of the nineteenth century. By the time the ideal was formulated (the turn of the century) it was already behind advanced technology; by the time the first prototype was built our time-scale had changed, the motor car was upon us; and by the time the Garden City idea really became a popular panacea, the original pattern—the first crystallization of the idea—had become obsolete.

Conditions that have favoured the creation of Utopias have followed periods of crisis, of mental, spiritual and physical revolution: periods when the results of pouring new wine into old bottles were becoming evident. The Renaissance—the revolution of learning—produced the prototype of all Utopias by Thomas More in 1516, which had been preceded by the Italian cult of the star-shaped city. Thomas More's work bears little relation to these schemes but a close affinity with three other Utopias written almost one hundred years later in quick succession by Tomasso Campanella, Valentin Andreae and Francis Bacon.

A second outburst of Utopias was an effect of the *revolution of religion*. In the 17th and 18th centuries the Mennonites, Shakers, Rappites and others founded a number of 'perfect' communities in Europe and North America. The latter phases of this period overlapped the next crop of Utopias which followed upon the *revolution of industry*. These included Robert Owen's New Harmony, settlements inspired by the writings of Charles Fourier and Etienne Cabet and the careful plan of J. S. Buckingham's New Victoria. After this we enter upon the first stages of our own period, that of the *revolution of movement*, with a series of Ideal Cities that include the Lineal City of Soria y Mata (1882) and the Garden City of Ebenezer Howard (1898). We can also catch a glimpse of the dawning period the *revolution of humanism* in the Radiant City of Le Corbusier (1935) and Broadacre City of Frank Lloyd Wright (1937).

IDEAL CITIES OF THE REVOLUTION OF LEARNING

The Ideal Cities of each of these periods have portrayed, in a disciplined and crystalline form, the ideals of their own time. In the period following the *revolution of learning* the main emphasis was laid upon the promotion of culture, represented by alertness of mind, beauty of body and harmony between man and his surroundings. A general standard of education was required for all, acquired by a close relationship between life and study, or a form of practical guidance in taking part in the ordered life of a consciously beautiful environment. All Renaissance Utopias lay value upon the careful selection of gifted scholars, artists and poets who received great freedom and the best the environment could offer.

They dividing the day into 24 hours appoint 6 of these for work; 3 of which are before dinner and 3 after. They then sup and at 8 o'clock, counting from noon, go to bed and sleep 8 hours. The rest of their time, besides that taken in work, eating and sleeping, is left to every man's discretion; yet they are not to abuse that interval to luxury and idleness,

36

but must employ it in some proper exercise according to their various inclinations, which is for the most part reading. It is ordinary to have public lectures every morning before daybreak, at which none are obliged to appear except those marked out for literature; yet a great many, both men and women, of all ranks, go to hear lectures of one sort or other according to their inclinations . . . After supper they spend an hour in some diversion in summer in their gardens, and in winter in the halls where they eat, where they entertain each other with music or discourse.   THOMAS MORE
Utopia, 1516

Everyone is taught all the arts . . . After their seventh year all the children follow courses in natural sciences . . . and when they are older they study mathematics, medicine and other sciences . . . they continually debate among themselves and emulate one another and eventually become magistrates of that science or mechanical art in which they are the most proficient . . . They also go into the country to learn the work in the fields and pastures, and he that has studied most arts and knows how to practise them is considered most noble. They laugh at us who consider our workmen ignoble and hold to be noble those who have learned no trade and live in idleness and also keep in idleness and lasciviousness so many servants that it is the ruin of the republic.
TOMMASO CAMPANELLA
The City of the Sun, 1602

The whole city is divided into three parts, one to supply food, one for drill and exercise, and one for books. The remainder of the island serves purposes of agriculture and for workshops . . . All is open, sunny and happy, so that with the sight of pictures they attract the children, fashion the minds of the boys and girls, and advise the youths. They are not baked in summer nor frozen in winter; they are not disturbed by noise nor frightened because of loneliness. Whatever is elsewhere given over to luxury and leisure of palaces is here devoted to honourable recreation and pursuits.

VALENTIN ANDREAE
Christianopolis, 1619

IDEAL COMMUNITIES OF THE REVOLUTION OF RELIGION

Several of the aspects emphasized in these Ideal Cities of the Renaissance were reactions from mediaeval obscurantist doctrine and the unimportance of individual personality. The Ideal Communities of the *revolution of religion* also reacted against the manners of their period—the pomps and ceremonies of civil and religious custom—and demanded the utmost

simplicity. These Utopias place their emphasis upon the spiritual brotherhood of man at an elementary level of equality. All displays of virtuosity
were suspect or condemned, except perhaps in the field of manual craftsmanship to which the superb furniture of the Shaker communities bears
eloquent witness.

The major difference between these Ideal Communities and those of
the Renaissance is that these were practised as a way of life with an
emphasis on the individual conscience, while the former were described
as a formal pattern for living. The impact of the writings and diagrams
of the Renaissance Utopias on the design of many places and buildings
is considerable and many institutions were created as a direct result of
their ideas: e.g., the Royal Society in Britain which was a direct result
of Bacon's 'New Atlantis'.

The direct influence upon physical design of the communities of the
revolution of religion is not easy to discern but their indirect effect upon
the moral outlook of North America has been decisive.

The streets are quiet; for here you have no grog shop, no beer house,
no lock-up, no pound . . . and every building, whatever may be its use,
has something of the air of a chapel. The paint is all fresh; the planks
are clean bright; the windows are all clean. A sheen is on everything;
a happy quiet reigns.   W. H. Dixon
                                                    New America, 1867

The greater part of the day was spent in labour, but the evenings
were given up to study and meditation, to religious meetings and other
spiritual occupations. On most days everyone was in bed with lights out
by 9.00 or 9.30, having previously spent an hour in silent meditation,
seated upright upon a chair in the retiring-room.
                              Charles Nordhoff
                              Communistic Societies of the United States, 1875

IDEAL CITIES OF THE REVOLUTION OF INDUSTRY

The Utopias of the *revolution of industry* had another emphasis. The
early part of the nineteenth century was a maelstrom of events. Clouds
from the cataclysmic eruption of the French Revolution still hung in the
air; the long Napoleonic Wars had left behind them a legacy of great
increases in mechanical invention and factory production, coupled with
widespread unemployment. On the far side of the Atlantic were the wide
open spaces of North America. Every idealist of this period felt confident
it was possible to combine equality of opportunity with mechanical

efficiency. Like all Utopians, they laid considerable emphasis upon discipline, though now this was directed to a system of elected councils or committees. Their Ideal Cities contain labour-saving mechanisms of all sorts, simple living standards are enforced, and there are many opportunities for communal social life. Although these Utopias were based upon reaction to the 'soul-less' industrial slums of Europe, their authors were all imbued with the nineteenth century faith that mechanization and progress were synonymous. The age of disillusion had not yet dawned. Like the Ideal Communities of the religious sects, these industrial Utopias had no place for the eccentric, whether he be a gifted artist or a tiresome rogue. The Renaissance emphasis upon the cultivation of beauty belonged to a totally different outlook upon life.

I early noticed the great attention given to dead machinery and the neglect and disregard of the living machinery . . . Mechanism may be made the greatest of blessings to humanity instead of its greatest curse... Mechanism and science will be extensively introduced to execute all the work that is over-laborious, disagreeable or in any way injurious to human nature . . . to render mechanism and science the only slaves or servants of man.   ROBERT OWEN
Life of Robert Owen, 1857

The progress of industry renders the establishment of the community of goods easier than ever before; the present limitless development of the power of production, thanks to the use of steam and machinery, can bring equality of abundance, and no other system is more favourable to the perfecting of arts and the reasonable pleasure of civilization.   ETIENNE CABET
Voyage to Icaria, 1839

[In Icaria] there is always a committee of experts which after careful study sets forth a model plan for the best town house, dining table, farm, programme of study or monument. This is unanimously adopted by the whole nation and becomes law.
M. L. BERNERI
Journey Through Utopia, 1950

[In a Fourierist Phalanx] work will be rewarded according to its usefulness and the most disagreeable work will receive the highest pay. The beneficent passions so operate in children as to grant them pleasure in playing with dirt and refuse; they will therefore combine in scavenging groups known as 'The Little Hordes' to do that work which is most repellant to adults—for which reason they will be honoured more highly

39

than any other group, taking their place at the head of all parades and receiving the Salute of Esteem.

CHARLES FOURIER
Universal Harmony, 1803

The objects chiefly kept in view have been to unite the greatest degree of order, symmetry, space and healthfulness in the largest supply of air and light, and in the most perfect system of drainage, with the comfort and convenience of all classes; the due proportion of accommodation to the probable numbers and circumstances of different ranks; ready accessibility to all parts of the town under continuous shelter from sun and rain . . . and in addition to these a large admixture of grass lawn, garden ground and flowers . . . the whole to be united with as much elegance and economy as may be found practicable.

JAMES SILK BUCKINGHAM
National Evils and Practical Remedies, 1859

THE REVOLUTION OF MOVEMENT

As the 19th century grew older the belief that the millenium could be materialized by mechanization faded. The ideas of the new dreamers were stimulated by the *revolution of movement* which has now borne two crops of Utopias: those around the turn of the century—the age of the electric railway and street car; and those since the first world war— the age of the internal combustion engine.

THE GARDEN CITY

All Utopians are romantic, but the Anglo-Saxon Utopians of the turn of the century were the first to be nostalgic. Edward Bellamy (*Looking Backward*, 1887), William Morris (*News from Nowhere*, 1890) and Ebenezer Howard (*Tomorrow*, 1898) dreamt that we could recover the idyllic qualities of bygone periods renowned for their balance between spiritual life and physical exertion. They believed this could be re-discovered if we would but turn our back on large-scale industry and revert to living in small communities with only small units of production.

The new London bears little resemblance to the old [in the year 2100]; it has become an agglomeration of villages separated by woods, prairies and gardens, and the ugly houses, dirty with soot, have been replaced by beautiful cottages and buildings . . . England was once a country of clearings amongst the woods and wastes, with a few towns interspersed, which were fortresses for the feudal army, markets for the folk, gathering places for the craftsmen. It then became a country full of huge and foul workshops and fouler gambling dens, surrounded by ill-

40

kept, poverty stricken farms, pillaged by the masters of the workshops. It is now a garden, where nothing is wasted, nothing is spoilt, with the necessary dwellings, sheds and workshops scattered up and down the country, all neat and pretty.   WILLIAM MORRIS
News from Nowhere, 1890

['Town-Country' has] Beauty of Nature; Fields and Parks of easy access; Low Rents; Low Rates; Low Prices; Field for Enterprise; Pure Air and Water; Social Opportunity; High Wages; Plenty to do; No Sweating; Flow of Capital; Good Drainage; Bright Homes and Gardens; No Smoke; No Slums; Freedom; Co-operation.
EBENEZER HOWARD
Tomorrow, 1898

THE LINEAR CITY

The Latins, Soria y Mata (*The Linear City*, 1882) and Tony Garnier (*The Industrial City*, 1901) were less affected by nostalgic sentiment. Both accepted large-scale industrialization and concentrated their efforts upon the clear classification and separation of incompatible factors. Soria y Mata was the first to lay down the policy of the distinction between traffic arteries and residential streets, and Tony Garnier produced the first complete design for a modern industrial town with careful separation of industrial and residential traffic and a system of super-blocks intersected by footpaths—an early recognition of the threatened rights of the pedestrian by the revolution of movement.

The means of locomotion determine the design of a city. The plan of a city should precede its construction. The form of a city should be that of its main road or street axis, or what we might call the spine of the urban system, by making this as wide as practicable (a minimum of 130′) in the central part of which two or more street car tracks should be constructed. Furthermore, as the regular geometrical forms (squares, rectangles, trapeziums) are the most perfect and have less perimeter than other irregular ones in the same area, it follows that the detached portions of the city—which are the vertebrae of this vertebrate system—should be determined by drawing rectangular lines to the street car tracks in the main street.
DON ARTURO SORIA Y MATA
The Linear City, 1882

The reasons for establishing such a town could be either proximity to primary industrial materials, or the existence of a source of natural power, or again favourable transport facilities . . . The principal industries are upon a level plain at the junction of a mountain torrent and the river. A main railway line separates the factory area from the town, which lies higher up the slopes on a plateau. Higher still lie the hospital buildings . . . Each of the principal elements—factories, dwellings and hospital—is isolated and situated so that extensions are possible should the need arise.

TONY GARNIER
The Industrial City, 1901

The influence of both of these schemes lay dormant for twenty years, but the Garden City idea of Ebenezer Howard and the work of his follower Raymond Unwin in building the first Garden Cities at Letchworth (1904) and Welwyn (1920) set a standard that electrified suburban planning throughout the world.

THE INTER-WAR PERIOD

During the period between the world wars the dormant ideas of Soria y Mata and Tony Garnier were developed in the plans for the revolutionary towns of Soviet Russia (before the period of imperialist reaction had set in) and part of the Garden City idea of Ebenezer Howard (cum Raymond Unwin) was carried on in Radburn and the Greenbelt Towns of the U.S.A. The Garden City definition was 'A town planned for industry and healthy living, of a size that makes possible a full measure of social life, but no larger, surrounded by a permanent rural belt, the whole of the land being in public ownership or held in trust for the community', but the U.S. towns were simply planned dormitories for commuters with living areas for their wives and small children.

In the same period London saw the birth of a descendant from the Lineal City idea: The MARS Plan for London (1937), which concentrated industry and commerce into a central belt across the London area, and concentrated residential areas into narrow, parallel strips running out into the countryside, each household being between a rapid transit system (leading directly to work and entertainment) and wide acres of open park land and playing fields untraversed by traffic. A similar approach underlies a new plan for greater Copenhagen (1947).

At the same time a caricature of the Garden City was being produced in Germany. The main lines of Ebenezer Howard's Utopia were adopted as official policy by the Nazi Party for their new single-industry settlements in Pomerania and other less populous parts of Germany. Decentralization of industry was associated with concentration and isolation of the industrial workers, and with the close supervision of their social life made possible by a system of widely dispersed small towns. It was held that the provision of secure employment, a cottage home and a good-sized garden plot—in other words the removal of conditions of instability—showed results in the form of early marriages and a high birth-rate; and the organization of each town into community units, each under the observation of a reliable member of the Party, ensured the maintenance of a high standard of good behaviour.

IDEAL CITIES OF THE REVOLUTION OF HUMANISM

Apart from these hang-overs from the earlier period, the inter-war years produced the first Utopias of the revolution of humanism—the Radiant City of Le Corbusier (1935) and Frank Lloyd Wright's Broadacre City (1937). Both these Ideal Cities, perhaps for the first time since the Renaissance, pay tribute to the cultivation of the senses and the intellect. In these Utopias transport—whether by rail, road or air—is no longer a fetish. Rapid forms of transport are accepted as the normal means of getting about, but a factor to be separated from the immediate living environment. Le Corbusier achieves this by grouping the dwellings of cross sections of the community into high blocks raised above open park land and farmhand, and also by raising the main roads upon causeways, (like the New Jersey Turnpike). By these two acts he creates an environment in which all may enjoy the primal needs of man which he lists as air, light, greenery, space, silence, liberty, intimacy, privacy and beauty: rights that have been the prerogative of the peasant and the privileged, but have been lost, both within our large cities and in our suburban developments.

Frank Lloyd Wright achieves the same result by wide spacing of the individual buildings, including the community buildings, over a boundless prairie. The ideals are almost identical. The difference is that Le Corbusier, as a Latin, has a natural affinity for urban life and, as a European, he is aware of the constant pressure of a large population with limited incomes upon a limited area of land. Le Corbusier also approaches the urban-rural relationship of man from the standpoint of the strip farming of continental Europe, where the farmer's fields may be at some distance from his village homestead. Frank Lloyd Wright with his Anglo Saxon tradition believes in the natural virtues of 'homes and gardens' and, against a background of the limitless plains and deserts of North America, he has the viewpoint of the farmer who lives in the midst of his fields. The wide spacing of his community buildings is related both to contemporary ease and speed of movement and also to the technical need for parking places for a population that has almost as many vehicles as people. In Broadacre City the main emphasis is upon

43

the individual family home, though the landscape is punctuated by tall tower apartment blocks for those sections of the population who, by age or temperament, are not suited to the single family house. In the Radiant City the same situation exists, but in reverse. The scene is dominated by the tall, widely spaced slabs of apartment dwellings (each provided with shops and services), but there are also colonies of individual dwellings for those who prefer this form of living.

A written Utopia *The Unknown Land* by Viscount Samuel (1942) also belongs to this new era. Significantly enough it is a lineal descendant of Francis Bacon's Renaissance Utopia *The New Atlantis* (1624) and most of the emphasis is laid upon the cultivation of the 'complete' man. In Bacon's time the people of Bensalem had worked an eight hour day (revolutionary enought at that period), but by the time it has been rediscovered by Samuel, the hours of work (of 'Duties') have been reduced to nine a week. The rest of the time is mainly employed in forms of occupation that give personal satisfaction (called 'Secondaries'). For instance musicians may spend their nine hours, in three hour shifts, in factory work; footballers on the land. Distinctions between amateurs and professional, dilettante and specialist, hobby and job, black coat and cloth cap, are no longer clear-cut; nor is there a premium upon either youth or age.

The duties include all the work that has to be done in order to keep the country going—factory and agricultural work, transport of goods, retail distribution and care of the home; together with education and scientific research. The public authorities arrange for a sufficient supply of labour for these, and workers in them give regular attendance. This is where the nine hour week applies; it is usually worked in shifts of three hours. Everything else is left to the Secondaries. The State does not interfere here in any way. . . . Take for example my wife and myself. Her duty, as with most married women, is looking after the house and household. But she is a very keen gardener and gives a great deal of her time, especially at the busy seasons, to the two acres of land attached to our house. She is also an expert in photography and much interested in music; those are her additional Secondaries. As for me, I do my nine hours' duty as a teacher at what you would call a Higher Grade School. I have four or five Secondaries which I take up and drop at different times; although one of them is fairly continuous. I encourage the boys and girls in my class to come and see me at my house and talk about things, and I always allot regular times for that. Then I am a humble assistant to my wife in her gardening, and look after the woodland round about. I am just finishing a book also . . . I used to work at Eng-

44

lish and one or two other languages, but I gave that up when I knew them fairly well, and became interested in biology. I have a theory of my own about the morphology of insects, which might—or might not—come to something one day. I work at that fairly regularly in one of the laboratories, very well equipped, which are maintained in various parts of the town for the use of amateur scientists like myself.

VISCOUNT SAMUEL
An Unknown Land, 1942

Utopias related to the *revolution of humanism* are still rare. They can be glimpsed between the lines of S. Giedion's *Mechanization Takes Command* (1948) and they run like a gleaming thread through the CIAM discussions on the 'Heart of the City' (1952). They become translated into vision upon the drawing boards of the student architect, the essays of the student political scientists, the sketches of the student artist, but most of the world around us is still inspired by the Utopias of the *revolution of movement* of which we are now in the third phase, the post-war period. For instance, the ideas of Ebenezer Howard are still the main force behind Britain's New Towns Programme, under which fourteen New Towns have already been started. This idea, so revolutionary at the turn of the century that those who accepted it were dubbed the 'reds' of that period, is now the respectable ideal, and the schemes of Le Corbusier or Frank Lloyd Wright are still 'visionary', 'totalitarian' or 'socialist' according to one's personal background of prejudice.

In France, however, the eternal source of civilization and culture, revolution and emotion, the Unité d'Habitation at Marseilles already presents a challenge which at the moment is difficult to estimate, and in South America, which escaped both the Industrial Revolution and the consequent era of Escape from Industrialization, some developments are taking place and some new towns being built that seem, from a distance, to be more in tune with the new time. It is too early to judge, we are too close to see clearly: the new time is in the bud and we do not know the form or colour of the flower. We can but keep the soil moistened, destroy noxious pests that would check its growth or deform its shape, and give some opportunity to the young whose vision is not yet dimmed.

Jacqueline Tyrwhitt

David Bidney's *Theoretical Anthropology* represents ten years of research and reflective thinking, and offers a study of ' . . . assumptions underlying the development of modern cultural anthropology' as well as an exposition of his own theoretical position. Some of the essays are already known to us in their present form, others have been rewritten or written directly for this volume. This is not a book developing a theme, with chapters to be read in the given sequence. Yet there is unity in the book, because Bidney's stand is so firm that everything he says arises inevitably out of a central core, and develops a basic theme. It is significant that twelve out of the sixteen essays are given titles in which terms are paired: for example, *The Problem of Man and the Human World, Evolutionary Ethnology and Natural History.* In this lies the clue to Bidney's theoretical position: that man and nature, freedom and authority, culture and personality, are not isolates mechanistically connected, or in mutual opposition, but are instead to be understood in a relationship of 'polarity'. 'Culture is essentially a polar concept and is unintelligible apart from a reference to nature, human and cosmic.' In fact, he uses the 'and' in the titles only to remove it in the body of the text, to replace it by a dynamic, mutually creative relatedness—his special version of the 'feedback' of Mead and Bateson.

In his 'historical, critical and constructive study' of the theories which form the background of modern anthropology, Bidney gives us what we have never had before in anthropology—a wealth of analytic writing, of precise and careful appraisal, from the pen of a philosopher, trained in incisive analysis and in the search for implication. The theories of Aristotle and Plato, St. Augustine and Maimonides, Kant and Hegel, do not often make their appearance in anthropological works, nor perhaps in the private thinking of anthropologists. Here their theories about man and the universe are presented among those of other philosophers, natural scientists, and social scientists, whose work has been used in developing anthropological theory. And, in every case where Bidney proposes his own theoretical postulates he presents first a selected part of the background of thought against which he has formulated them and from which he differs.

Bidney's view of culture, of man's relation to culture, and of the relation of culture to nature or reality, is a conciliation of two apparently contradictory philosophical views: the Kantian, idealist view of order as inherent in the mind of man and its categories, and of the realist's view of the 'given' as independent of man and his perceptions. Bidney sees man in a creative role, experiencing the given through the formative process of his culture. In these days of defeatist acceptance of passivity, when even schools prepare for a passive, undifferentiated role in life, it is invigorating to read Bidney's rejection of all theories which postulate determinism. Bidney finds such determinism in what he calls the 'culturalistic fallacy'—as well as the 'naturalistic fallacy'. So he takes a position against these, and against sociologists and psychologists and all those who believe that society or man's nature or the 'given' or an ideology or history or in fact anything, determines man's life and fate. In keeping with his polaristic view, he finds all these in interaction, among themselves as well as with man's nature, neither determining the other, but each helping create, move, change, strengthen the other. 'The problem still remains', he writes in his essay on Ethnology and Psychology ' . . . as to the relation of historical, evolutionary culture to human nature. . . . Human nature *may be perfected* [my italics] by proper cultivation of human potentialities.' And it is this 'cultivation' which is the function of culture. So, 'Actual historical human nature varies with the state of human culture and they are not to be conceived as independent of each other. Human nature and human culture are polar entities.' 'The notion that psychology is limited to the study of innate human nature and its processes, while culture is the study of acquired characteristics simply is not tenable.'

47

It is in this relationship of polarity that Bidney finds the dynamic mechanism for change. Man and culture form, in other terms, a feedback circuit: 'Man is the efficient cause of the cultural process', and is in turn affected by culture. Because man has 'self-conscious freedom' it is never possible to predict the course of cultural change, since the directive agency of human intelligence is unpredictable; but the change will be there, since the polar relationship is a dynamic one.

In place of isolates, such as history, culture, human nature, Bidney proposes his 'psychocultural thesis'; he offers a 'psychohistory' and an 'ethnopsychology'.

The essays in this volume were written over a period of ten years, and even when they have been revised for inclusion in this volume, they bear the marks of a developing approach, perhaps of the developing man. Only in his analysis of the work of others, does there seem to be no change; and in fact, here there seems to be insistence and often repetition, since it is usually the same people who are mentioned, the same approach which is analyzed as background. Bidney appears as the social scientist, the anthropologist, only gradually, in what seems to be his later writing. Where, in early papers, he often seems to start with an idea or theoretic approach, and to remain with it without even approaching the concrete, in later papers his thinking often derives from the world of event, or is at any rate tested against it. In a paper written in 1947, he says, 'The theory of the freedom and creativity of thought insists upon the primacy of fact of verified experience over theory.' At that time, this was not yet fully characteristic of his approach, and I think it is not yet so. But this seems to be the direction of his development; and gradually, the thinking which began with the somewhat sterile and narrowly circumscribed examination and criticism of the logical shortcomings of theories, became increasingly free and creative, and is learning to have 'practical respect for the data of experience'. If Bidney does continue to put this principle into practice, he will be enabled to move to new theoretical insights and discoveries.

Bidney's central theory of polarity has itself undergone change through the years. From the beginning, this theory was Bidney's peculiar version of the current holistic approach, with its dynamic mechanism, the feedback. However, perhaps because of the evoked image of the two poles in relation, he shows a tendency to limit his whole to the dualism of a pair, a complementary pair, it is true, and one of which neither member is intelligible apart from the other, but nevertheless a duality, lineally conceived and connected. And so he can speak of 'entities', and of 'elements'—terms which, according to holism, are inapplicable except to artifacts created through man's abstraction. He speaks, for instance, of human nature and human culture as 'polar entities'; and of pattern and process as 'distinguishable but inseparable elements of cultural behavior'. If Bidney had been completely holistic in his approach, I think he could not have spoken of 'elements'; he would have used some such term as 'constituent'—a term I borrow from Lawrence Frank, all mention of whose completely holistic, and greatly influential work, is strangely absent from this volume.

In general, however, the holistic approach is there. So Bidney states: 'A culture is a spatio-temporal process and product, whose essence and existence cannot be understood apart from the ethnohistorical context in which they developed.' And he speaks, not of man and culture, but of the 'cultured man'; not of pattern and process, but of the 'patterned process' and the 'patterned behavior of man in society'. 'If one were to maintain . . . that cultural phenomena and social systems are internally related, then the way would be prepared for a holistic approach which studies human social and cultural phenomena as functional wholes. Social anthropology and cultural anthropology are then understood as two branches of a common discipline.'

Bidney limits his study in the main to the viewpoints of only those writers from whom he differs. He makes scant or no mention of those from whom much of his own thinking derives, or at any rate whose point of view he represents. It is not clear whether the omission is deliberate, or whether Bidney is not acquainted with the works of those anthropologists, for example, whose approach is holistic. It may be that, accustomed as he was to philosophical treatises, he limited his examination only to those anthropological writings where the author declares, in effect, that he will now talk about culture, or freedom, or personality, and so he automatically excluded those works where the authors, without avowed intention, deal with their material holistically. But this cannot explain why there is no mention of the essential holism of those pragmatists, for whom the situation is primary, for whom there is no dualism between knower and known, actor and act, no separation into observation, observer and observed.

The holism which Bidney proposes has been a part of anthropological thinking, for long unrecognized as such, and not named. It is certainly implicit in Sapir's writing, as, for example, in *Sound Patterns in Language*, which was published in 1925. His position is, in general, strongly reminiscent of Sapir's. For example, he presents culture as a part of the personalities of individuals. When he explains how actual historical man appears to vary with the cultural conditions which affect him, the view he proposes is Ruth Benedict's view that culture develops certain potentialities of human nature and neglects others. His view of man as creating experienced reality out of the given through the symbolic function of culture, has of course been held and expressed for years by ethnolinguists whom Bidney—perhaps only slightly acquainted with their writings—regards as deterministic. And when he writes: 'An integrated culture is a moving equilibrium, an ever-changing harmony', he might be quoting from some writing of Laura Thompson's. He is apparently unaware of this debt to other anthropologists, perhaps because their views have been completely incorporated into his own thinking.

When he does present anthropological theory for discussion, his analysis is incisive and penetrating. Yet, at times, his criticism seems to be wasted; he is fighting straw men. When he offers a theory to fill a felt void, the void is often not there; what he offers is a duplicate. He has been trained to examine philosophical writing, and so has looked at the theoretical statements of anthropologists for their views. But anthropologists are usually not interested in the rigorous development of an idea in explicit terms. The views which they hold on value, on the nature of culture, on man's freedom, on process, are implicit in their presentation of concrete data, and especially in their ethnographic work. If they have omitted to state a view in a theoretical writing, this does not mean that they do not have one; they have incorporated it in their ethnographic approach. Bidney shows slight acquaintance with, or at any rate reliance upon, ethnographic literature. Yet it is here that an anthropologist's theory is at work, vital, moving, shaping, changing as the facts themselves force change upon it. It is in the way in which the ethnographer is relating himself to his chosen society, in the selection and perception of his material, in the structuring of the project, in his choice between presentation and representation, in his organization, in the naming of his chapters, that he is expressing his theoretical position.

To my mind, for example, nothing which Malinowski has said about culture or freedom or ethics, equals what is communicated through his minutely detailed ethnographic descriptions in *Coral Gardens and Their Magic*; and, in his statements on methodology, he never did justice to the theoretical assumptions which made possible a perception of culture, a relatedness to society, or a presentation such as this. Yet it is only with the overt, explicit, theoretical statement that Bidney deals here. He takes issue with Malinowski, for example, for completely reversing himself on the subject of human freedom: 'He postulated that human freedom is the condition of cultural development, whereas formerly he had insisted upon the opposite thesis.' Actually, Malinowski's position, as found implicit in his superb ethnographic writing, is consistent. When he describes Trobriand agriculture, the 'taboos' appear as avenues of freedom, not prohibitions; as channels for 'an active participation in the drama of nature', freeing man for an activity which contains the whole meaning of life. Here freedom and culture coexist inseparably, in harmony, and it would be fruitless and pointless to inquire which is a condition of the other.

There is scant mention of Margaret Mead's work, perhaps because she rarely speaks explicitly of the concept of 'culture' or of 'freedom'. True, two of the three references to her work are to one of her best papers: *The Concept of Culture and the Psychosomatic Approach*; but there is no recognition of her insistent holism, which is implicit in her work in recent years, increasingly strong and evident in the last ten. Her work on the Food Habits Committee, her consideration and discussion of induced change in this society and elsewhere, and all her suggested lines of procedure, can be understood only as stemming from holism. Her magnificent first chapter in *Growth and Culture*, is an avowal of holism. When her work and that of other anthropologists was used by others to explain personality development in terms of mechanistic causality, she has written to protest, to explain that child rearing methods could be understood only holistically as channels, not as self-contained entities producing certain results. When she describes the relationship between mother and child, with the mother communicating her culture through the way she relates herself and simultaneously reinforcing her culture through the very act of the communication, she is describing what Bidney would call a polar relationship. All this, along with the works which Bidney discusses at such length, has certainly gone into the 'development of modern cultural anthropology'.

Considerable attention is devoted to Kluckhohn's work; yet here, again, only limited technical points are taken up, only overt, explicit statements. Yet Kluckhohn's profound views about culture are mainly to be found implicit in scattered papers, in essays written with absorption and humility, which do not necessarily deal with the 'concept of culture'. In these we find thinking-in-process, creative and perhaps not yet crystallized into a quotable statement.

If much of what Bidney proposes is not new in anthropological thought, it is certainly new in this type of presentation. Never before has anthropological theory been stated so explicitly, coherently, systematically. Anthropologists are rarely trained in philosophy or in the analysis of implications, premises, logical postulates; or if they have been they have usually put this training behind them. Even when they are clearly aware of these theoretical assumptions, they are often impatient of precise formulation. So when Bidney is pointing out discrepancies in their statements, he is actually pointing to the need for greater precision, awareness and consistency in statement. And inconsistency is always with us. It occurs in Bidney's own work, sometimes between statements in different essays, perhaps written in different years, sometimes within the span of a paragraph. For example, when he discusses nature and culture, he says: 'Supervening upon this given or discovered world there is the cultural world'; yet, further down the page, referring to man, he says, 'the conceptual or symbolic world, by which he interprets and envisages the natural world'. But if we accept the second statement then the 'given' world cannot be used synonymously with the 'discovered' world; and the cultural world does not supervene upon, but helps create the discovered out of the given.

There is inconsistency, also, in his view of man in his universe. He can speak of 'the cultured man', to avoid the dualism of man and culture; and yet he can also refer to culture as external to man, prohibiting activities which man would fain gratify, an 'inescapable burden'. He speaks of man as a part of nature, yet also says, 'Man's dilemma lies in the fact that he is *trying to do* [my italics] the apparently impossible, namely, to be a part of nature and yet to be in a measure independent of it, to be an active participant in the drama of nature and yet a specta-tor at the same time.' This is a dilemma for Bidney, caught in his in-consistency. But it is no dilemma for the Hopi or the Trobrianders, or the Tikopia, who give no evidence of 'trying to' combine these two, since the concept of 'man' or the self, for them, apparently contains all this in its definition. The Wintu actually incorporate the resolution of this dilemma—to continue with this negatively phrased formulation—in their verbal structure, so that the two aspects are presented as complementary within a harmonious whole.

Bidney's inconsistency, however, does not worry me. I find it stimulating, because it is in the nature of process and creativity. There is more con-sistency in the older, the more philosophically closed and self-contained, the more crystallized papers, but there is also less vitality. Where think-ing is coming into being, moving, exposing itself to hard data of concrete experience, shattering itself against the actual and recreating itself, there is process, and its consistency is frequently only one of direction.

There is much of this invigorating, exploring, incisive thinking in *Theoretical Anthropology*, and it makes rewarding, though difficult reading.

Dorothy Lee

Time has been said to be the great problem for philosophers; nor is it otherwise with silent believers. How, and with what, does man fill time? How, and how far, does he pass out of time? Apostates are those who have abandoned the problem; saints are those who have solved it. Their solution, the solution to the problem of eternity, is, in effect, theology.

The Aivilik Eskimos have remained faithful to the problem, refusing to give it up. They have sought the meaning of life in the problem of time, and the answer to both in the nature of man and the definition of life. Their theology does not distinguish between the two systems of metaphysics which in Western thought govern separately illusion and reality. In their daily lives these are bound together by a thousand crossing strands and threads. But they clearly distinguish between 'self' and that which is 'other-than-self'; it is from this distinction that their unique concepts of subjective and objective derive.

The Aivilik's view of self appears to be as clearly demarcated as ours, but is remarkably different, and its precise limits often vary according to different situations. At times it is open at the back, as it were, and over-flows into spheres external to the body both in time and space; it embodies in experience events which, remembered and related in the clear light of day, ought actually to have remained hidden in the imagination.

But then, just what do we mean by 'actually'? The Aivilik assert that man's ego is not a thing imprisoned in itself, sternly shut up in boundaries of flesh and time. They say many of the elements which make it up belong to a world before it and outside it, while the notion that each person knows but one life and can know no other is contrary, they maintain, to everyday experience. It is significant that among these people, what belongs to consciousness generally is thought to constitute the self.

The nature of human life is not clearly defined by Aivilik thinkers, except on two or three points. Beliefs are uncodified, hardly precise enough to be called doctrines, and it is difficult to outline what the individual Aivilik considers the history and destiny of his own soul to be, and what relationship his present life has to that long career through eternity. However, the following appear to be the outstanding features: *Tungnik*, described as representing something close to our notion of the human soul, is the dominant spiritual element in man. Immortal, it is periodically embodied in the flesh at the baptismal. Thus an infant does not become an individual until he is named, for though the body, *teme*, and the mind, *ishuma*, are present, until the *tungnik* appears, life is not thought to be complete. Once *tungnik* has taken possession of the body, it does not become localized in any particular part of the individual, but 'like blood, is everywhere'. *Tungnik* can leave its corporeal home during life, usually at night, and engage in adventures in other estates. All Aivilik agree that at death it permanently separates from the body. Beyond this, opinion differs, for tradition does not specifically state where all ghosts reside during intervals between their earthly lives.

There are those who identify *tungnik* with a person's formal name. Hence, shortly after the birth of a child, an elder may say aloud before all present, 'Spirit of [deceased relative or friend] be with us now. Enter the body of this child.' Individuals are then addressed by the kinship term assigned to them in their earlier lives, and are expected to live up to reputations formerly enjoyed. One sometimes hears individuals reminiscing about pre-natal experiences; others talk of rebirth: 'One cannot get you in this life, but one will be revenged later.'

It sometimes happens that two children born into isolated families about the same time may be named after the same individual. It then becomes a problem to determine which body the known spirit actually entered. To cite an example, both Ooquorluk, born at Povungnetuk, and Evalooaryuk, born a year later at Lyon's Inlet, were named after Kahyukyuk, a deceased hunter whose exploits still figure in the legends of the North. For years now Ooquorluk and Evalooaryuk have engaged in friendly competition—foot races, wrestling—to determine 'who is the real Kahyukyuk'.

Aivilik take new names when they are old, sick or beset by misfortune. When Tomah suffered a series of severe misfortunes, he accepted another name. This was done at a 'gift-scramble' held in his honour. His father placed about two dozen small family possessions in a caribou skin, stepped outside the igloo, and, casting them to the assembled members of the camp, announced Tomah's new name. Tomah tested his new powers the next day by entering, and winning, a specially arranged dog sled race. Thus it is possible for an Aivilik to change, in a sense, his very identity.

Others deny baptismal reincarnation, and hold that the deceased person's spirit merely looks after its namesake, guiding it through life and speaking directly to it should the namesake be an *angakok* or shaman. A man may have several names, each serving as a spirit helper. The principal one is usually acquired along patrilineal lines, but others may come from either side or from friends. There is a certain mystery in these names. Most Aivilik recall the case of the hunter at sea who noticed that he was being followed by a great bird. He paddled as fast as he could, but the bird kept pace. Then the frightened man called upon his sacred name and soon outdistanced the bird. The majority of Aivilik feel, I think, that the *tungnik* somehow resides in these names, but they never clearly state the case.

Christian theology does not seem to have clarified the problem, for some converts now hold that at death a *tungnik* has three choices: to roam this world as either a benevolent or malevolent power as long as acquaintances worthy of aid or vengeance remain; to go beneath the sea and there be tormented eternally by the Goddess *Sumna;* or to remain forever in the company of the good and the saved in the non-terrestrial, eternal and heavenly City of God. But the question is essentially irrelevant, for in spite of a gloss of Christian dogma, the natives remain under the thrall of pagan beliefs. They continue to believe that at death the soul merely vacates its temporary home and then waits to re-enter another. Its fate is of no concern to its owner since continuity of life's journey is guaranteed. Until missionaries came, Aivilik theology contained no theme of soul jeopardy or retributive judgment, and therefore no religious observances for soul salvation. Even

56

today the natives remain uninterested in thoughts of after-life or ultimate destiny. Cessation of the heart beat remains but part of the cycle of life and death where, sooner or later, the body disappears as an entity, and the soul re-enters the cycle. The why of all this does not concern the Aivilik; they claim no transcendent ability to understand it.

They merely assert that death is not an end, but a beginning—a beginning of a new phase in a never-ending cycle. They meet the problem of death by denying the problem itself. I suspect they fear, in the secret depths of their hearts, the finality of death and that their philosophy is more a denial of a reality emotionally felt, than a conviction carrying full relief. Nevertheless, they maintain that they can run all risks, squander their lives, and scatter their possessions, because they are immortal. They know that there is life beyond death, beyond the corruption of the body—beyond every evidence of the disappearance of the body scattered amidst nature and the seasons.

For life, they say, is superior to time. It cannot vanish, because death, like birth, is an event in time, and life is above time. This vivid belief— even if it remains unformulated, a silent assumption—is the very essence of Aivilik philosophy. It is a conviction so strong and so unshakable as to deny and defy the fact of death. Death is never an inevitability, obedient to natural laws. It is the work of a witch or deity and hence dependent upon individual and fortuitous causes. A concept of death, as something that conforms to unalterable natural laws, the Aivilik never recognize. Nor do they recognize it as an ultimate end, as the final stop in the journey of life. The entire concept of man as mortal, by his nature and essence, is alien to them. Just as deities and animals are not imprisoned in time, so human life knows no temporal walls.

The Aivilik feel that death is not a hard, unbearable fact. It is like sleep; in both cases the body reawakens. When confronting death, they clearly reveal this feeling. If they cannot cast derision upon the supersession of breath, they meet it not with anything that can ordinarily be called fear, certainly not with any kind of hope. They are exasperated. They are, in the full sense of both words, desperately angry. For death, the destruction of life, is not so much a thing to be feared as it is first of all a thing incomprehensible, impossible, an offence, a scandal. Not-to-be is nonsense for the Aivilik. This is so true that though they meet death at every turn, although they see their relatives die, although they attend their burial, still the most difficult thing for them to believe in is the reality of death. They see death; they do not believe in it. They regard it as only an episode, an episode on the road of the immortal life of man.

Nor do they doubt, at least openly, that they have lived before and will live again. At death, for instance, any display of fear is literally unforgivable. I recall one occasion when I was summoned to say good-bye to the dying Kowyeeshak, young Okomiut wife of Natakok and mother of two. With impassive face, each member of the camp indifferently shook her limp hand. But she suddenly roused herself and cried out against her family, recounting their sins and arguing bitterly that it was they, not she, who should be taken. Her husband was disgusted. He reprimanded her, and then Ohnainewk, head-man of the camp, silenced her with a cutting rebuke. As I stepped outside the tent, a relative began to chant a death song which begins, 'Say, tell me now, was life so nice on earth?'

Such an outburst, Ohnainewk volunteered, was a shameful exception, and it certainly differed markedly from other deaths which I witnessed. Here the natives meet the final passage of this life's voyage with calm resignation. Usually the sick person lies shivering in a corner, exhausted and coughing. His family and neighbours enter and leave the tent, from all outward appearances completely indifferent to his suffering. They seem to suppress not only an awareness of death, but the entire sense of tragedy. Unnoticed, his requests ignored, his questions unanswered, the sick man lies in silence, a stoic fatalist resigned to dying, awaiting his end, hoping and fearing nothing. Finally it is over. 'The breath has gone. It is over.' The entire camp soon assembles in the tent, and a low wailing of Christian hymns begins. After they leave, some to fashion a cross or prepare the grave, but most to go about their labours, a lone relative remains behind to chant the old songs. It is characteristic of these songs that they take a resigned, even light, attitude toward death. I recorded only one which revealed any suggestion of fear or rebellion:

> Who comes?
> Is it the hound of the dawn approaching?
> Away,
> Or I will harness you to my team.

Such exceptions occur. Generally, however, it is not death that is feared, but the ghosts of the dead who may bring dire calamity on the heads of the living. So the body is quickly buried, usually within a few hours after death. Mittens and boots worn by those who carry it to the grave are discarded, and sundry taboos, their number dependent upon each individual's relation to the deceased (and degree of acculturation), are observed for several days following the funeral. It is especially forbidden, for example, to use any edged instrument, such as a knife or needle, for the spirit still hovers about and might suffer injury. Such taboos are designed not to help the deceased in his spiritual travels, but to protect the living. In the case of Catholic converts who die with the priest beside them, viaticum and extreme unction are administered, but in all other cases no rites exist to ensure the appropriate state of the deceased after death or to give him the final spiritual easing-out of life.

Although white influence has done little to shake the Aivilik's faith in the immortality of the human soul, in one sense Christian theology has disturbed them. Rather than being reassured, Ohnainewk was puzzled by missionary efforts to present irrefutable proof of something he had no more questioned than the coming of tomorrow or the changing of the seasons. He saw no need to argue the point, for to his mind, the burden of proof had always lain on the opposite side. If anything was in need of proof it was not the fact of immortality, but the fact of death. And his entire belief system would never admit these proofs. It denied the very possibility of death. The dominant theme of his whole mythology was a constant and obstinate negation of the phenomenon of death. In the language of allegory and metaphor it affirmed life after death, the immortality of the spirit, the possibility of communion between living and dead. It gave sense to life and solved the contradictions and conflicts with the transience of human existence on earth.

But the missionary had unknowingly hinted at the subtle but significant difference separating these two philosophies. Ohnainewk sensed this difference and sought my assurance. I admitted that there were many white men who regarded death as the great darkness and silence from which none returned, and who believed that only by realistically admitting the fact of death could one realize the fullness of life. Exasperated, openly contemptuous of my presence, he turned away. But again and again during the forthcoming months it was he who raised the question, insisting that the dead live. Didn't the white man believe in communication with the spirits of the dead? Had not the white man heard voices not of the living? Seeds of doubt had been scattered and were taking root in his mind.

Missionaries have also taught him that the true home of man's immortal soul is elsewhere and that his life is, rightly regarded, a preparation and training for the next. This new time perspective, with its external focus for the life pattern, promises him, if he treats the present as a prelude to eternity, an early translation to that eternity at death. The Catholic priest guarantees as well the resurrection of the physical body and depicts its future home in vague but glowing terms. And finally the Oblate father

59

insists that the familiar world of things, including human bodies, moving about in space and changing in time, will someday be transformed. He speaks of the Last Day and the Second Coming of Christ as events marking the termination of the earthly order with the reappearance of the Crucified One not as Redeemer but Judge.

Thus we see that the doctrine of reincarnation on the one hand and of resurrection on the other is the chief difference between these two religions. To Aivilik adherents of reincarnation, this present life is not the first and last; it is but one of an infinite series, without absolute beginning or end. Opposed to this is the view of the Oblate father who rejects reincarnation and admits two lives only, one here in the natural body and one here-after in the body of the resurrection. In this latter doctrine the first or present life determines forever the character of the second or future, and the same body serves in both. No longer is the soul offered a series of new lives like the succession of seasons. Now it is promised eternity in a heavenly home. No longer are the Aivilik confronted with an endless series of reincarnations—new sufferings ceaselessly assumed, new trials, new pain—but deliverance from time. Time continues always to be time, but the Aivilik are told that they can pass out of time, escape the cycle and find eternal rest and happiness.

In all this the natives find only confused corroboration of cyclic reincarnation. The more subtle distinctions either escape them or are dismissed. I do not believe that Aivilik converts really understand Christianity's key point—the Divine Redeemer—for, not admitting death, they need no culture-hero to conquer it. Nor do they understand how this momentous conquest could be effected by charity and sufferance. But on the important issue of immortality both religions are at one. In August of 1950 I heard the lay catechist, Kidlapik, chant the Christian liturgy before the body of the deceased Kowyeeshak: 'Life is changed, Life is not taken away.'

Edmund Carpenter

> Can you not distinguish the sense, prain,
> from the sound, bray? . . . Get yourself
> psychoanolised!

The novel came of age with the development of Cartesian views of time and space; its death is implicit in the return to multi-dimensional thinking. James Joyce, bringing into artistic perspective the multiverses of modern thought, provided key techniques that opened up the post-Newtonian world for artists. His contribution to esthetics, as Eliot observed, was analogous to the Einsteinian revolution in physics. In *Ulysses* time and space are not treated as abstract guiding lines for the action of the whole novel, but as relations within a structure. *Finnegans Wake* extends this method by treating language 'phonoscopically'. Both deal with small space-time units—*Ulysses* with one day in one city, *Finnegans Wake* with one night in one house. At a theoretical level he abandoned 'the pinch in time of the ideal' in an attempt to 'roll away the reel world', while at a practical level he provided a 'verbivocovisual presentement'. He firmly centred his art within the bounds of the individual personality—the 'naked I'.

The poles of interpretation of these works are marked by the comments of two painter-critics: Frank Budgen saw them as great landscape works—verbal paintings—but Wyndham Lewis condemned both for their lack of spatial orientation and their compatibility with the Bergsonian notion of time-flux. But the goal of the critic's quest should not be the identification of these works with some doctrinaire position, but rather the analysis of their realistic organization. Picture Joyce planning the 'Wandering Rocks' section of *Ulysses* with a map of Dublin, a stop-watch and streetcar time-tables; throughout, the emphasis is on the relations of man to the real world. Joyce condenses all human experience to the form of the human body. In the *Wake* the action takes place in the body of the giant Tim Finnegan: Anna Livia Plurabelle (ALP), the river, is the blood stream, man's temporal flux, while Humphrey Climpton Earwicker (HCE alias Here Comes Everybody), the rock, is a phallic, stuttering, inseminating principle. In *Ulysses* each section is structured about an organ of the body and its characteristic rhythm. Both works emphasize the horizontal and vertical aspects of the body symbolism resolving by amalgamation the quarrel between the supporters of a doctrine of correspondences (Swedenborg, Blake, etc.) and of a doctrine of synaesthesia (the *symbolistes*). For as Joyce emphasizes the vertical element of the *Wake*—'the flasks above are as the tasks below', he also develops the horizontal movement of 'Little Anny Ruiny' (ALP) in the body of the giant, Tim Finnegan. In the structural chart that he used in preparing *Ulysses*, books 9 and 10, (corresponding to the 'Scylla and Charybdis' and 'Wandering Rocks' sections of the *Odyssey*) are devoted to literature and mechanics, executed in dialectic and labyrinthine techniques respectively. This combination forms the core of both books, for it is the interplay of brain and bloodstream, rock and water, the labyrinth of cognition and the dialectics of opposition, that creates universal movement. Time and space are treated under the microcosmos of one body. Both works achieve their epiphany in the human body: in *Ulysses* the climactic moment is the union of Bloom and Stephen at Bloom's home; the *Wake* reaches its climax as the night world dissolves with the impact of daylight on the sleepers.

The work of art for Joyce, as the body metaphor suggests, plays its role in this structuring of knowledge by providing an anthropology—a type of knowledge and insight into man and his cultural artifacts. The tension between the position of art as dealing with artifacts (things made and manipulated by man) and the romantic view of art as natural philosophy, is developed by making the artist of the night world an 'alshemist'. Throughout the *Wake* run thematic references to Swift and Sterne as extreme representatives of the timeless neo-classical synthesis achieved by Jonson and Pope. What Pope did in the *Dunciad* was to combine 'the stern poise for a swift pounce', working on the principle that 'samething rivisible in nightim, may be involted into the zeroic couplet'. Pope's *Essay on Man*, for example, is an attempt to provide a comic portrait of man's mind in act—a dynamic map in which the contours are changing and shifting from a series of fixed points. Joyce's interest, like Pope's, is in providing dynamic models for the changes taking place within the sensibility of man in the contemporary world. In the *Wake*, he described his method as presenting 'the map of the soul's groupography'. The metaphor is relevant because human communication occurs by verbal spatialization, man having 'learned to speak from hand to mouth till he could talk earish with his eyes shut'. Thus, there is a language of gestures which depends on mutual participation beginning at the sub-verbal level where one employs 'the handtouch that is speech without words' and moving to an awareness of the self where it can be seen that we 'agree to every word as soon as half-uttered, command me! your servant, good, I revere you, how, my seer? be drinking that! quite truth, gratias, I'm youish, see wha'm hearing?' Joyce's linguistic method is vivisective, portraying the whole community in action through his 'verbivocovisual presentement': the dynamic model in art. His overlayering technique is a spatial-temporal union of image and memory, of dialect usage and historical usage. It is a technique that includes the observer in his observations and carries with it the corollary that at the level of observation and model-building, art is not unlike science. The choice of terms such as 'vivisective' is not accidental, for Joyce employs working models of society in action as the basis of art, following his own advice that 'sifted science will do your arts good'.

By introducing conscious comedy and observing a close rapport of mind and body Joyce moved beyond communication viewed as a phatic communion with the verbal universe—participation in the word—to a doctrine that included in the word the total structure of the body. Joyce had a high regard for the dialectical, informational element in verbal communication as well as the emotive, participational element. His view of the word was to provide precise information about emotions and the operations of the mind. Modern communication engineers have discovered in the physical sphere that communication of information begins with uncertainty—the maximum uncertainty, the maximum potentiality of communication. Joyce applied this fact to the esthetic sphere. Like Pope, his work depends on continual peripeteia, but unlike Pope he departs from the conventional form of the printed language. *Finnegans Wake*, to be successfully understood, must be both read orally and followed on the printed page at the same time, for its puns operate both at the 'verbi' and 'voco' levels of the 'verbivocovisual presentement'. Joyce reached this stage of awareness by studying the technical effects of modern communication media while simultaneously translating their grammar, dialectics and rhetoric into traditional terms. 'Some of my puns are trivial and some are quadrivial'.[1]

Since art is a problem of communication with the human observer, Joyce in the *Wake* treated the trivium (grammar, dialectics and rhetoric) and quadrivium (music, astronomy, geometry, arithmetic), as communication studies. Comedy provided him with a means of 'reamalgamerging' the two levels and exploiting their similarities as well as their incongruities, but also with a means of providing continual surprise, intensifying the work at an information level. Joyce's work is totally freed from the idealism that lurks behind Pound and Eliot. The naive spatialization of Cartesianism is treated as figment of an attempted 'ideareal' history of the Viconian 'commodius vicus of recirculation' or Hegelian 'phonemanon' types: 'Sink deep or touch not the Cartesian spring!' for it is depth analysis that the Cartesian world generally lacks, thus failing to achieve a technique of digesting the totality of human experience in art. Unlike Hegel, Joyce did not see the comedy of ideas as a deeper form of tragedy, but derived the highest art forms from the comic. He described the *Wake* as a 'museyroom' and a gigantic, all-embracing 'funferall'. It is both funeral and wake, the exuberant celebration of the rites of revivification: 'You take Joe Hanny's tip for it. Postmartem is the goods. Jollification a tight second. Toborrow and toburrow and tobarrow!'

Joyce's notebooks reflect his interest in comedy as 'the perfect manner of art', for even tragedy participates in the nature of comic art so far as it leads to joy—the end of desire: 'All art which excites in us feelings of joy is so far comic and according as the feeling of joy is excited by whatever is substantial or accidental in human fortunes that art is to be judged more or less excellent.'

Comedy in the Joycean world is concerned solely with a glory in existence itself. The epiphany, which gives a metaphysical dimension to cloacal occurrences of everyday life, is the foundation stone—those 'sudden spiritual manifestations, whether in vulgarity of speech or gesture or in a memorable phase of mind itself'. The term 'epiphany' is relevant at many levels suggesting primarily a manifestation of the intellectual word begetting joy rather than desire. It is a literary technique that provides a means of seeing things with 'new eyes', permitting the artist to com-

---

[1] H. M. McLuhan, 'James Joyce: Trivial and Quadrivial.' *Thought*, Summer, 1953.

municate the verity of objects by manifesting their peculiar whatness or *quidditas*—their mode of existence. Juxtaposition or dislocation and over-layering—oral, visual and verbal—are the technical means of handling the epiphany, sharpening the focus of an object and placing it in a new setting. By juxtaposition of the seemingly incongruous Joyce arrests the movement of the mind through the cloacal labyrinth of daily existence, forcing it to focus on the ordinary and commonplace world as seen with 'eyes'. The process by which the epiphany is achieved occurs in three stages, according to Joyce:

First we recognize the object is one integral thing, then we recognize it is an organized composite structure, a thing in fact; finally when the relation of parts is exquisite, when the parts are adjusted to the special point, we recognize that it is that thing which it is. Its soul, its whatness, leaps to us from the vestment of appearance. The soul of the commonest object, the structure of which is so adjusted, seems to us radiant. The object achieves its epiphany.

Although some critics suggest a radical shift in position from the early view of the epiphany, Joyce's work is consistent right up to the point at the conclusion of the *Wake* where HCE is addressed as 'How culious an epiphany'. While he does not mention Aristotle and Aquinas with any frequency in the *Wake*, it is because it is a world that is 'thomistically drunk' and where 'truth is a bacchanalian revel, where not a soul is sober' (Hegel). He maintains a metaphysical realism describing the seeking of correspondences as 'O felicitous culpability! sweet bad cess to you for an archetypt!' For example, he applied Yeats' insight that poetry comes out of conflict with ourselves by dramatizing the conflict within the Self. In the *Wake* Shem and Shaun, the twin sons of HCE and ALP, are ultimately the artist and his daimon. Contrary to the tendency to identify Joyce with Shem and his brother with Shaun, Joyce, in a deeper sense, as Everyman, is both Shem and Shaun. Shem is the Penman, but Shaun is the Post of the Apocalypse who carries the Word recorded as a letter down through the history of man. Shem has a bardic memory—'the rite words by the rote order'—and is a time-binding force, while Shaun lives in an ad-world of one-day rhetoric and is a space-binding force. In such a world, Vico's ideal eternal history of man, with its quest for the True Homer, could become one of the central counter-plots to the story of an old Irish barroom ballad applied to the actual discovery of the remains of an archeological giant. In the ballad the sad fall of hod-carrier Tim Finnegan and his remarkable rebirth at his wake when some whiskey (Gaelic, *usqueabaugh*, literally, elixir of life) falls on him, becomes a means by which all cultural and historical existence can be 'reamalgamerged' into a work of art. His use of Vico, as his use of Homer was, structural and comic. Just as Bruno and Hegel provided him with the material for the continual dialectical battles between twin pairs: Shem-Shaun, Kev-Dolph, the Mookse and the Gripes, Cain-Abel, artist-cop, etc., so Vico provided him with a means of structuring the relation between parents and sons, written and oral language, family and nation. None of them, however, completely escape the satiric focus of the dream-world, for the *Wake* is the reverse of the *Dunciad*, exposing the night-world of the introvert at work and ending with the break of day. In the new-day world, the artist, Shem, has become like Shaun, and the administrator, Shaun, has become like Shem. The structure of the work is such that Shem and Shaun appear on the surface and are 'reamalgamerged' into the total community of redemption—the one man—the sleeping giant, Tim Finnegan. For the artist this symbol is valid because only in terms of the sense apparatus of one man does communication take place. It is the vivisection of this body of existence that marks Joyce's presentation;[1] like modern anthropology he discovered the roots for this analysis in the language and kinship structure of his society:

The modern spirit is vivisective. Vivisection is the most modern process that one can conceive. The ancient method investigated law with the lantern of justice, morality with the lantern of revelation, art with the lantern of tradition. But all these lanterns have magical properties: they transform and disfigure. The modern method examines its territory by the light of day. It examines the entire community in action and reconstructs the spectacle of redemption.

The contrast between the 'magic lantern' and the day-time world is the contrast between the ancient and modern. When Joyce uses 'modern' he has in mind a technical sense—the sense in which the scholastic-Aristotelian tradition is regarded as modern and the older Platonic tradition, ancient. In the *Wake* he applies the 'vivisective' method of Aristotle and the day-time world to the night phenomenon of depth analysis and idealism. It is the 'allnight newseryreel' of the magic lantern world of Vico, idealism and the anti-scholastic tradition. While this world contains within itself archetypes gleaned from the processes of cognition of the everyday world, Joyce had little sympathy for any romantic universal symbolism:

No esthetic theory . . . is of any value which investigates with the aid of the lantern of tradition. What we symbolize in black, the Chinaman may symbolize is yellow: each has his own tradition. Greek beauty

[1] H. M. McLuhan, 'Joyce, Aquinas, and the Poetic Process.' Renascence, 4: 1, 1951.

laughs at Coptic beauty and the American Indian derides them both. It is almost impossible to reconcile all traditions whereas it is by no means impossible to find the justification of every kind of beauty that has been adored on earth by an examination into the mechanism of esthetic apprehension whether it be dressed in red, white, yellow, or black. We have no reason for thinking that the Chinaman has a different system of digestion from that which we have though our diets are quite dissimilar. The apprehensive faculty must be scrutinized.

This vivisective technique is applied in the *Wake*, 'in the states of suspensive exanimation', where 'the panaroma of all flores of speech' occur in an 'auctual futule preteriting unstant'. The *Wake*, then, is literally a 'crossexamination' employing kinship structure and language as the keys to culture. Joyce's technique is like Shakespeare's in *Hamlet*, which he described as 'an earsighted view of old hopeinhaven with all the ingredient and egregiunt whights and ways to which in the curse of his persistence the course of his tory will had been having recourses'. The *Wake* is a 'recorse'—an 'ordovico and viricordo'—advancing the Hegelian and *symboliste* insight that the process of creation is the retracing of the moment of illumination by realizing that the mind in act is the total sensual and apprehensive equipment in act. On the basis of this discovery Joyce grounded his technique in the vulgarities of speech and gesture and the memorable phases of the mind. Throughout his life he collected epiphanies, as Flaubert had collected *idées reçus*. The whole technique of the *Wake* with its new language develops from this basic insight. Joyce's realism, no matter how far it may have transcended the immediate, was founded on literal and exact observation. His puns are rooted in the peculiarities of the language itself: 'yung and easily freudened', 'there's no police like Holmes', etc.

Behind this activity was a theory of language and communication that is familiar to students of the social sciences—language as mental gesture: 'So why, pray, sign anything as long as every word, letter, penstroke, paperspace is a perfect signature of its own? A true friend is known much more easily, and better into the bargain, by his personal touch, habits of full or undress, movements, responses to appeals for charity than by his footwear say.'

The doctrine of the word as signature of being runs throughout the entire Joyce canon, but Joyce achieves a synthesis in his final work that closes the gap between the written and the oral tradition. Because of his sensitivity to the loss of the written tradition he provided a new language for creative purposes. It is the goal of Yeats' quest and the answer to

Mallarmé's condemnation of literature, for it is not in itself a literary language. The *Wake* lacks a style in the conventional sense for it orchestrates *all* styles as gestures in the universal dance. In *Stephen Hero* Joyce suggested that there should be an art of gesture: 'I don't mean an art of gesture in the sense that the elocution professor understands the word. For him gesture is an emphasis. I mean a rhythm.' Gesture as rhythm is the road to the *Wake*, for all words are gestures and gestures themselves are *analogues* of words *in their operation*. To Joyce all motion was part of a meaningful pattern related to the learning process. But these patterns went further: they provided rhythms related to words that could be used creatively. Eliot has pointed out that the discovery of a new rhythm is the most important contribution a poet can make to his craft; Joyce extended this further by relating his rhythm to the organic activity of the body itself. Music theorists, such as Curt Sachs, have suggested that many rhythms begin from precise bodily movements—walking, the heart beat, etc.

If language is rooted in gesture, it is obvious that the rhythm of language is closely connected with the body and its internal communication systems. Significant gestures arouse analogous patterns in both speaker and receiver owing to their co-presence in a common social or physical milieu. In experience we internalize the external conversation of gestures. Joyce, then, has in *Ulysses* and the *Wake*, a method by which the communication between his characters and the world of the book is an analogue of the communication between the book and the world of reality, for the basic principle of Joycean comedy is 'I'm yoush . . . my shemblabe! My freer'.

Joyce can explain the problem in the much smoother terms of the process of apprehension, since he is approaching the problem from an artistic point of view and does not have to set up any pragmatic structure of observation. This line of speculation leads the world of the social sciences and the world of Joyce to results that are startlingly similar. For example, G. H. Mead suggests that 'the institutions of society . . . are nothing but ways of throwing on the social screen . . . in enlarged fashion the complexities existing inside the central nervous system, and they must, of course, express functionally the operation of this system'. He further suggests that the hand is the implemental stage in human activity from which the mind develops. While this does not totally agree in intent with Joyce's view that the hand is the tool of tools, just as the mind is the form of forms, the significance of the analogy is apparent: the hand as basis of gesture is at one and the same time a tool and a form. Since the hand and the form both call up a two-edged relationship in interpersonal communication, it is not surprising to discover Mead suggesting that there is a strong participational element in human communication: 'In the human group . . . there is not only this kind of communication [informational], but also that in which the person who so used the gesture and so communicates assumes the attitude of the other individual as well as calling it out in the other.'

The human cognitive process, therefore, is capable of participational as well as informational communication. If, as Mead suggests, the cognitive process is the internalization and inner dramatization by the individual of the external conversation, then Joyce's analysis is an extension with a difference. He adopts Aquinas' principle that 'Art in its work imitates nature.' It is in the recognition of the fact that the process of nature and the process of art are analogues that the entire esthetic is based.

Joyce's realism is susceptible of analysis from the pragmatic and behaviouristic points of view, but in action it extends beyond any such static analyses. That is why *Ulysses* can be classified as a realistic and intensely symbolic work. The mass communcation media (particularly the press) and the form of the modern city provided Joyce with epiphanies that are always rooted in the commonplace. *Finnegans Wake* is a treatment of this problem from another angle. Joyce formed an epic from the mass media by knowing what to select and how to handle the selection in the internalization of conversation in the dreaming giant, Finnegan. Throughout the *Wake* run asides such as 'if you are looking for the bilder deep your ear on the movietone!' or describing the letter, the exegesis of which is a mode in miniature of the exegesis of the *Wake* 'This nonday diary, this allnights newseryreel. My dear sir! In this wireless age any owl rooster can peck up bostoons' or describing the Dublin of the washerwomen: 'a phantom city phaked of philm pholk'. This technique of the *Wake* is an attempt to merge the onslaught of a new oral tradition with a written tradition that is ultimately based on the oral tradition. In such a method the great clue that Joyce discovered was the nature of language as a key to the labyrinth of human cognition. As much is indicated in the *Wake* among opinions concerning the fall and its nature: 'Sylvia Silence, the girl detective (*"Meminerva"*, but by now one hears turtlings all over Doveland!) when supplied with informations as to the several facets of the case in her cozydozy bachelure's flat, quite overlooking John a'Dreams mews, leaned back in her really truly easy chair to query restfully through her vowelthreaded syllabelles: Have you evew thought, wepowtew, that sheew gweatness was his twagedy?'

The term 'detective' suggests the method for retracing the labyrinth of 'vowelthreaded syllabelles'. The musical motif is indicative of the manner in which the *Wake* is constructed. It is a work of Meminerva: memory, the time-binder, and nerves, instantaneous sensual response leading to spatial reconstruction, fused in Minerva, the figure of mental arts and wisdom. Typical of the encyclopedic method of the *Wake* are the correlations between the two main figures—HCE and his wife ALP. As Marshall McLuhan writes, 'H.C.E. is mountain, male and active. A.L.P. is river, female and passive. But ALP equals mountain and historically "H" is interfused with "A" and "A" is both ox-face and plough, first of arts and letters so that dramatically the roles of HCE and ALP are often interchangeable.'[1] One could go on to suggest that ALP, for example, is both mountain and mole hill, for the 'alp' in Irish is also a small salamander-like creature and HCE is an 'old parr' (drinker of Scotch, a young salmon, and an old man). Not only is the structure of the letters themselves employed as gestures, intermixed with verbal play, but the love chase of HCE after ALP is presented in the cinematic terms of a Sonja Heine ice-carnival with a maximum of metamorphosis. The tendency of criticism accustomed to the flat perspectives of univocity has been to emphasize one aspect of the work—it is described as a book for the ear, a book of word play, a book of metamorphoses, a great work of landscape art, etc. These forms, however, are all adapted to previous modes of communication, while the *Wake* is adapted to overlayerings within the self that are characteristic of modern culture.

The *Wake* works simultaneously through a series of dialectical oppositions in existence and their communal participation in all forms of existence. The brothers, Shem and Shaun, are opposites yet components of all human experience. In the Inquest of Yawn (Shaun asleep) by the Four old men, the inquiries regarding the brother, Shem, always return to a confusion of the two. Anagrams are used as a technical device to point up the conflict and reconciliation that the two brothers represent. The questioner at one point states: 'Hood maketh not frere. The voice is the voice of jokeup, I fear. Are you imitation Roma now or Amor now.' Under inquisition Shaun is gradually becoming Shem, 'my shemblable. My freer!' for both are aspects of HCE or Here Comes Everybody—Shem, the I, and Shaun, the me. Joyce, in spite of the similarities with Shem, openly associates himself with HCE in the same section: 'Speak to the Right! Rotacist ca canny! He caun ne'er be bothered but maun e'er be waked. If there is a future in every past that is present *Quis est qui non novit quinnigan* and *Qui quae quot at Quinnigan's Quake!* Stump! His producers are they not his consumers? Your exagmination round his factification for incanimation of a warping process. Declaim!'

[1] *Ibid*, 1953, p. 85.

The reference to *Our Exagmination Round his Factification for Incani- mation of Work in Progress* (a title Joyce provided for a volume of studies on the *Wake* by the *transition* group) relates Joyce to HCE, the Every- men of his drama. This passage not only satirizes the efforts of the night- minded *transition* group to comprehend the *Wake*, but provides an im- portant clue to Joyce's communication process—'His producers are they not his consumers?' At one level it suggests that the *transition* writers provide Joyce with his material as well as consuming it, but at a deeper level it suggests that the communication networks of society filter to the artist his material and at the same time he produces artifacts for the com- munication networks of his society. Sergei Eisenstein recognized in *Fin- negans Wake* 'the limit in reconstructing the reflection and refraction of reality in the consciousness and feelings of man', which Joyce achieved by 'a special dual level method of writing: unfolding the display of events simultaneously with the particular manner in which those events pass through the consciousness and feelings, the associations and emotions of one of his chief characters!' When Eisenstein suggested that 'the price paid is the entire dissolution of the very foundation of literary diction, the entire decomposition of the literary method itself', he failed to grasp Joyce's complex use of the oral and visual *as well as the verbal* aspects of language. Joyce is not trying to approximate a cinematic form in litera- ture, but attempting to bring the standard of craftsmanship in written and oral composition to the level where it can transfer values and insights from the mass media into literature. The critical problem is accentuated by the emphasis that Eisenstein places on an 'inner speech' which, while inalienable from that which is 'enriched by sensual thinking', is divorced from the oral and written tradition of language. What Joyce saw, how- ever, was the sensual character of the very forms of writing (apparent to a manuscript culture) and vocal expression, which formed networks in themselves. The word in Joyce is not inner, it is both printed and spoken. The *Wake* imprints its meaning on the memory of the reader just as its rhythm affects his ear, his blood stream and his emotions.

Joyce continues the neo-classical tradition of wit in his attempt to por- tray the 'souls' groupography' in a comic mode. The effect aimed at is the inclusion and participation of the individual in the work as a whole— an effect that Pope and Ben Jonson had attempted. Joyce has the advan- tage of a more complex language enriched by a greater variety of art forms, but his problem was common with theirs—to steer a mean between the extremes of romanticism (enthusiasm) and rationalism. It has hardly been noticed that he shares their interests in unity: his works confine themselves to moments of time and points of space; they deal with every- day occurrences and present a comic view of mental activity. When

Joyce appears during the inquest of Yawn, he divulges the roots of his 'communionistic' technique. It is the 'handtouch' of 'Bygmester Finnegan of the Stuttering Hand', for the stutter of HCE breaks the flow of ALP and begins the transference of information, just as the 'zeroic couplet' broke the flow of Renaissance lyricism to 'charge' language with meaning. Joyce's work shows an increased sensitivity to written language which has been partially reduced back to a flux. His techniques of arresting eye and ear are an attempt to push the dynamic model in the arts to a point where a more complete participation on the part of the producer-consumer-reader is possible. Though dealing with the magic lantern world, he is attempting the careful and precise analysis of vivisection. The movement of the *Wake* is towards day—'my coming forth from darkness'. accomplished through the gift of language, 'Be thy mouth given unto thee! For why do you lack a link of luck to poise a pont of perfect peace?' The satire implicit in the title is a key to the resolution of the work—for Joyce's favorite phrase was 'Wait till Finnegan Wakes!'

Donald Theall

Although in recent years a vast amount has been written about social classes, remarkably few attempts have been made to trace the origin and distribution of social systems which involve the division of the members of a community into classes. Such references to the subject as I have found in historical or anthropological works are incidental and almost accidental.

Nearly all the modern writers who have referred to the subject have assumed that class divisions have arisen only as the result of conquest. Thus Herbert Spencer thought that class distinctions do not exist where life is permanently peaceful, but that they are initiated by war through the formation of a slave class, and Westermarck believed that 'castes are frequently, if not always, the consequences of foreign conquest and sub-jugation, the conquerors becoming the nobility and the subjugated the commonalty or slaves.' L. Landtman, in his book *The Origin of the Inequality of the Social Classes*, which though useful can hardly be said to deserve its title, cites seven other writers to the same effect.

Recently Professor Ralph Linton has expressed a similar view: 'Most of the world's aristocracies have arisen through conquest. In a surprising number of cases the conquerors have been less numerous and less culturally advanced than the people they conquered. Such invaders brought with them the integrated culture and conscious solidarity of the uncivilised tribe. They rarely made any attempt to change the culture of the conquered, being content to rule and exploit them. In the states formed in this way the aristocrats formed one society and the commoners another, each with its distinctive culture. The class struggle was thus really a struggle between peoples.' He gives no examples, so it is difficult to guess what he has in mind, but he is clearly describing not a class system but the coexistence of two linguistic groups in the same country. He later says that the dispersal of the conquerors leads to their rapid fusion with the conquered, and cites the Normans as an example. This seems to contradict what he said before in *The Study of Man*, pp. 111–2, 246.

It seems clear that it was the Normans whom Spencer and at least some of the others who put forward this theory had in mind. The theory is simple enough—the Normans came over and conquered the Saxons. The Normans then became the nobility and the Saxons the commoners. That is how class distinctions arose in England, and that is how they have always arisen.

This theory, though beautiful in its simplicity, is completely fallacious. It would be absurd to suppose that all the foot soldiers, grooms, cooks and so forth who accompanied the Conquerer became feudal barons and knights as soon as Hastings was won, and Professor Douglas has shown (in *History*, Sept., 1943) that all the Normans who are known to have been enfeoffed by him were already noblemen in France. We know, moreover that a form of the feudal system existed in England before the Conquest, and that the chief change which took place was the substitution of Norman barons for Saxon thanes.

We may suppose that the Saxons when they invaded England enslaved many of the Britons, but in so doing they were merely extending the system of their home country. We know that the Germanic tribes consisted of jarls, carls and thralls, freemen and slaves, before ever they invaded the Roman Empire or crossed the North Sea. It is very doubtful if any people has made slaves of foreigners unless they were already familiar with the idea of slavery; such ideas do not spring up suddenly after a victory.

In spite of the baselessness of this theory, no doubts arose as to its validity, and it was extended to Greece and Rome. The Spartans, we were told, 'represented historically the small band of Dorians who conquered a home for themselves in the Peloponnese in prehistoric times' (W. A. Dunning, *A History of Political Theories*, p. 7). This is obviously untrue, for the Messenians, whom the Spartans conquered and enslaved, were also Dorians.

For Rome Sir James Frazer and others have supposed that the plebeians were the original inhabitants and the patricians their conquerors, but Warde Fowler on the other hand supposed that the patricians were the original inhabitants and the plebeians outsiders whom the patricians allowed to settle in the city.

Full of the racial theory of class origins, our scholars were delighted to find that in India the castes are known as 'colours', and the colour of the Brahmans is white and of the artizans black. Here was clear proof that a white race of Brahmans had conquered a black race of earlier inhabitants. So pleased were they, as Hocart points out, that they failed to notice that there were four castes each with its colour. The royal colour was red, and that of the caste of farmers and merchants yellow. For the racial theory to be valid there would have not only to be a black race of conquered and a white race of conquerors, but three races of conquerors, a red race who became kings, a white race who became priests, and a yellow race who became farmers and merchants. This would not do at all, so when the fact that there were four colours was realised, it was quietly ignored.

The theorists seem never to have glanced towards Venice, where a system which divided the people into nobles and commoners existed for a thousand years. The original nobles are said to have come from Heraclea, and to have formed part of the early settlers, but exactly who they were is not at all clear. It is certain, however, that they did not owe their position to conquest. Though most theorists have postulated conquest as the origin of social classes, other theories have been put forward. Several writers have suggested that nobles are the descendants of those who raised themselves, or were raised by kings, to positions of power. Hobhouse and his collaborators went so far as to say that 'the mere extension of regular industry makes for social differentiation, since the effects of energy and thrift become cumulative. Hence we have the partial rise of the nobility and the more extensive development of a servile or semi-servile class' (*Social Institutions of the Simpler Peoples*, p. 254). One might be able to explain in this way systems such as our own, in which the division between classes is pretty flexible, or those in force in some tribes by which a man can rise in rank by giving feasts, but among many tribes, as in Rome and among the Hindus, the division between the castes or classes is, at least in theory, absolutely fixed, and it is this rigidity which has to be explained.

The explanation which I shall adopt is that of the late A. M. Hocart set out in his book *Caste* and other writings. It is based on the fact that fixed caste or class distinctions, wherever they exist, are always religious, that is to say that the different castes or classes play different parts in the ritual. The Roman patricians were a priestly caste, and long after they had lost the sole right to the consulship and other magistracies, they retained the chief priesthoods; the chief priests had not merely to be the sons of patricians, but of patricians who had gone through a sacred marriage rite with patrician women. In the same way a Brahman is not merely a descendant of Brahmans; he must have gone through the rites which make him one of the 'twice-born'. G. Dumézil has shown in *Naissance de Rome* that the Romans once had a caste system similar to that of the Hindus, and that the plebeians originally corresponded to the farmer caste.

The religious nature of the caste system is clear from the Indian evidence. Men of the barber and washerman castes, both low castes, perform religious functions at weddings and funerals, and the barber is said to be 'like a priest on the cremation ground'. Brahmans cannot officiate on the cremation ground, because they must have no contact with death. The fact that the rites are so divided affords evidence that Brahman and barber were originally of the same race or tribe.

Stronger evidence comes from Fiji, where the people are divided into nobles and commoners. The nobles behave as it is thought nobles should behave, that is they are quiet and dignified, whereas the commoners are rough and noisy, but every noble has a common father and every commoner has a noble father.

It seems, then, that some prehistoric people became divided into two moieties, which developed a sacramental relationship to each other, that is to say that they initiated each other, married each other, and buried each other. In a sense they were as gods to each other, as the Fijian moieties were till their conversion to Christianity. Incidentally this emphasizes the correctness of the view of the incest taboo which I took in my *Jocasta's Crime*; incest is or was simply a breach of the rule that members of one moiety must marry members of the other.

Not only did human beings come to be divided into two moieties, but everything came to be ritually divided into two moieties, as in China it

76

is still so divided, and each human moiety came to represent ritually one half of the world. One moiety represented, among many other things, sky, summer, light and life, while the other represented earth, winter, darkness and death. Such divisions still persist among many peoples, especially the American Indians.

Hocart was inclined to suppose that at one time the moieties changed over, that is to say that the team which represented light, etc., in one year represented darkness, etc., in the next. By this he would explain the fact that the Persian words for 'god' and 'demon' are transposed in Sanskrit. It may be noted that in Hindu representations of the Churning of the Sea of Milk the gods and demons appear as two tug-of-war teams exactly similar in dress and appearance.

In any case it seems, according to Hocart, that the half of nature which included darkness and death was not originally regarded as the worse half. Those who represent this half must originally have acted, and in some cases still act, voluntarily. The idea of death as an evil is by no means universal; many people have died, and even allowed themselves to be killed, quite cheerfully.

Hocart's general theory of diffusion is that such surprising developments as the division of a tribe into two moieties, each with ritual control over half the phenomena of nature, could not occur more than once, but that such a system, to whomever it was diffused, would tend to change in similar directions owing to qualities inherent in the system itself. One is that the moieties would tend to become stabilised in their functions, and another that the representatives of the more active phenomena, such as light and life, would tend to become more important than those representing the more passive phenomena. Once this has happened the first moiety becomes the gods, the representatives of light and life, and the second the giants or demons, the representatives of darkness and death; and this though the two moieties still intermarry, as did the gods and Titans in Greece and the gods and giants in Scandinavia.

Finally the gods, or the representatives of the gods, that is to say the kings and nobles as they have now become, become so superior to the other moiety that they will no longer marry into it. This was happening in Fiji, as by hypothesis it had happened in India, at Rome and elsewhere, and when this happens you have your system of social classes complete.

This explanation may seem highly theoretical, and so it is, but highly theoretical explanations may be true. Of course it will seem untrue to

77

those who suppose that you can reach the explanation of savage customs by diving deep into the savage mind. Savages do not differ in this respect from the civilised, and it would be obviously impossible to explain the jury system, for example, by diving into the jurors' minds. Its function has no connection with its origin, but if it had not originated as it did, it could not have been adapted to its present function. Much the same applies to all the customs of the civilised, and in all probability to all the customs of savages.

We now find that some peoples have fully developed class or caste systems; some have partly developed ones; some have clear traces of systems now lost, and some have neither system nor traces of it. To postulate the similar working of the human mind and the functional necessity for such systems explains nothing. The only way to explain the origin of social classes is to follow them, and all traces of them, back till they point in the direction of a theory which will cover them all.

Raglan

IT HAPPENED IN HISTORY

To psychological states in which one or another motive predominates, there correspond in Veblen's system different societies and different periods of history. Briefly, Veblen's picture of prehistoric culture was that in the beginning there was savagery, the kind of society characteristic of Neolithic times: small, peaceful, sedentary, industrious, and protected by matriarchal goddesses who stood for just such attitudes of a Demeter. Women were equal to men. Veblen's evidence for the existence of such a Golden Age was, he half-confessed, scanty; it was partly derived not from ethnology but from psychology by way of analogy between primitives and children. However, Veblen, like Kropotkin, was presenting a useful corrective to the prevalent competitive versions of Social Darwinism of his time.

The 'fall' from savagery comes about, according to Veblen, for any one of a number of reasons, most of them involving an increase in wealth; but it may not in Veblen's view come at all—as the Eskimo and Pueblo bear witness.[1] In contrast to Marx, Veblen can be commendably un-

[1] I am inclined to agree with those skeptical ethnologists, Dorothy Eggan, Esther Goldfrank, John W. Bennett, and others, who have recently shown, e.g., by dream analysis, that some of the cultures Veblen thought were survivals of peaceful savagedom — such as the Pueblo Indian tribes — are not for the most part such happily peaceable people.

dogmatic on this point. The disruption of savagery and the shift to the next and 'higher' stage of barbarism is marked by the development of patriarchal religions whose fierce gods symbolize the new order of status and dominance: in 'The Blond and the Aryan Culture', Veblen identifies maternal, peaceful institutions with an original agricultural way of life, and patriarchal, military institutions with a later nomadic way. The three good instincts which gave savagery its tone must now share hegemony with the quasi-instinct of predatory emulation.

Barbarism itself passes through two stages, roughly equivalent, in European history, to the Dark Ages and feudalism respectively, and is in turn succeeded by the 'handicraft era' of early modern times (this designation was one of several concepts in economic history that Veblen seems to have taken from Werner Sombart; analogous stages, regarded as steps in a naively progressive series, can be found in Fourier and in Lewis H. Morgan). Veblen conceives the handicraft era as a period in which man's instinctual heritage, never wholly extinct in the underlying population which happily remains more savage than barbarian, again comes to the fore and takes the lead in shaping institutions.

For Veblen, as for Marx and Engels, technology was the prime mover in these transitions from stage to stage. True, technology was mediated through the social relations of production, but these were bound sooner or later to catch up with technology. Veblen, like Marx, interpreted socialism as an effort on the part of the rest of the culture to catch up with the machine-made industrial revolution. Moreover, Veblen was in some respects more technology-minded than Marx, who was notably inept at things mechanical. The former saw invention as self-generated by the instinct of workmanship, with occasional unintended assists from idle curiosity. From this standpoint, what matters in history is not men's consciousness, their alienation or their effort to remove it by concerted action, but simply work in accordance with instinctual drives. All else is waste, an anachronism to be eliminated sooner or later.

William Fielding Ogburn has since made the concept of 'cultural lag' familiar, and indeed Americans are often more than ready to grant that their religious, political, and other 'peripheral' doings are behindhand in comparison with economic and technical advance. The very term 'lag', which Veblen uses, implies a value-judgment in spite of itself, since to delay, linger, and wait is, in the American idiom, a sign not of sound conservative judgment but of backwardness. Yet Veblen repeatedly disclaims making such a value-judgment: he insists that he is merely speaking from an economic point of view and that from some other point of view, such as an aesthetic one, one might value precisely what was laggard. Much of *The Theory of the Leisure Class* is in fact devoted to a penetrating examination of the snob appeal of the outdated and the antique—of what is economically useless—as compared with the negative prestige carried by knowledge of the new, the useful, the mechanical. The leisure class itself, Veblen argues, is a laggard class, enabled by its wealth to remain in the backwash of economic development, hence a brake upon the wheels of progress.

For in spite of his disclaimers and in spite of his skepticism, Veblen does ally himself, more or less unequivocally, with the progress-minded thinking of the 19th century rationalist. He envisages a society cleansed by the machine and its presumptive accompanying cast of thought of all ritual, reliquary, and rite. The problem of how such a society, if conceivable at all, would hold together never seems to bother him. Or perhaps it is more accurate to say that Veblen was so concerned with war and invidious distinction as disrupters of society that he wanted men held together by the strongest ties of adaptation to the human and technological environment, with peaceful and unemulative labour as the be-all and end-all of life. Against the flaunting egocentrism of the Gilded Age, he opposed a group-oriented but still individualistic workmanlike dutifulness. Take, for example, his attitude towards the belief in luck, to which he devotes some brilliant passages in *The Theory of the Leisure Class*. In his rationalist view that the march of technology would extirpate the belief in luck, because a true scientific determinism and such a belief could not coincide, he overlooked the possibility that the belief in luck is one of the cushions which allows technology to be accepted by men whose jobs and skills it so drastically rearranges. In ruling out the belief in luck as superstitious, Veblen assumed a more predictable lot for individuals than an industrial system can assure them. Moreover, he did not carry his own thinking about 'contamination' of instincts quite to the point of understanding the compartmentalizations that allow beliefs in magic and science, ritual and technology, to exist in the same individual. Veblen seems to have taken for granted a biologically grounded social solidarity resting on the instinct of workmanship and the allied parental bent, but the notion, so clear to Durkheim, that religious rituals might express and renew social solidarity and hence become the source of economic energies and scientific advance was quite alien to Veblen's economic thinking.[1]

---

[1] Among economists and political scientists this spirit, though chastened, is still alive. One economist friend of mine told a Standard Oil official: 'Why don't you break up your company into smaller units; small businessmen make more money than big ones' — as if businessmen were in business mainly to make money, and not to make friends, find challenge or an easy life, or many other goals in the complex motivations of the business bureaucrat. An agronomist recently wrote a biting critique of the 'false values' by which farmers are taught by the

Nevertheless, he qualifies the simplistic concept of lag in two significant respects. In the first place, his notion that basic human nature is peaceable, only overlaid by a short-lived experience with pecuniary and barbarian predation, implies that certain kinds of lag or regression to this earlier, more 'natural' substratum will actually constitute a social advance. This leads him to an ambivalent view of Christianity: on the one hand, as a patriarchal religion of futile subservience to extravagant earthly representatives of a leisure-laden heavenly hierarchy; on the other hand, as a religion of brotherhood and abnegation at odds with pecuniary culture. Indeed, the leisure class itself plays a similarly ambivalent role. In the main, it is the fortress of conservatism, predation, and organized futility—the combatants in the economic arena struggle for the invidious honor of becoming as futile as their 'betters'. But by its very nature as a backwater, the leisure class serves to protect survivals of the non-invidious, non-predatory aspects of life. Its women, the most sheltered, are the most eager to exchange a life of fatuous vicarious idleness for workmanlike activity and social usefulness; it is their reversion which makes them reformers. Thus, it is only survivals of the recent past which Veblen considers genuinely laggard, and as soon as one reverts to the primitive savage culture one comes into contact with those Ur-human traits which are at the same time the face of the Utopian future.

Veblen's second qualification of the theory of lag is related to his notion that technology is the first aspect of culture to be borrowed in a diffusion process. This gives an advantage to a latecoming (laggard?) society, which could borrow the fruit of another society's technological work without taking along the encrustation of irrelevant and interfering habits which had grown up around the technology in its place of origin. This important idea Veblen once put as follows (*The Instinct of Workmanship*, pp. 135–6):

In the origination and indigenous working-out of any given technological factor . . . elements of imputed anthropomorphism are likely to be comprised in the habitual apprehension of these factors, and so find lodgment in the technological routine that has to do with them; the

---

agricultural colleges and stock shows 'to "judge" animals by fancy points — "web, fluff and quills of feathers", with other like details — and have encouraged a spirit of speculation and gambling in prizes and prices which is inconsistent with the careful development of the inheritance of useful qualities in the animals so valued . . . ' E. Parmalee Prentice, 'Food for America, 1980 — The Supply of Animal Proteins. The Agricultural Colleges.' *Political Science Quarterly*, 58:481, 1951. This energetic latter-day Veblen does not fully appreciate that neither self-interest nor national interest can spur agricultural productivity without the 'gamemanship' of emulation and the prize-giving pressure of county committees. For the argument that 'waste' is one of the bases of American economic advance, see my article 'Some Relationships between Technical Progress and Social Progress.' *Explorations in Entrepreneurial History*, 6, 1954.

result being, chiefly a limitation on their uses and on the ways and means by which they are utilised, together with a margin of lost motion in the way of magical and religious observances presumed to be intrinsic to the due working of such factors . . . Now, when any given technological or decorative element crosses the frontier between one culture and another, in the course of borrowing, it is likely to happen that it will come into the new culture stripped of most or all of its anthropomorphic or spiritual virtues and limitation . . . ; since the borrowing is likely to be made from motives of workmanlike expediency, and the putative spiritual attributes of the facts involved are not obvious to men who have not been trained to impute them.

Veblen had observed how his father, coming as an immigrant to the United States, had perforce left behind a good many habitual agrarian practices of the Norwegian village, while accepting eagerly the developing machine technology of the American wheat belt. Moreoever, his father accepted this technology without learning Yankee words and ways —much as Thorstein Veblen himself became rapidly acculturated to the international sciences of philosophy, philology, and economics without adopting the complex of genteel customs maintained by the Yankee guardians of the higher learning.

Much in the same way, Veblen regarded German and Japanese imperialism as the product of a borrowing of English machine technology without English empiricism, libertarianism, and wasteful consumption. These predatory empires, still socially and idealogically feudal, having borrowed technology 'clean', won an advantage over the Western democracies whose productivity had already been dissipated in an emulative race for idle and luxurious living. This advantage, however, would only be temporary; sooner or later, the machine would not only derange German and Japanese feudalism but also—a curious inversion of the 'lag' theory—drag in its wake the very wasteful consumption practices that surrounded it in its Anglo-Saxon home of origin. Hence Veblen advises Japan (in 1915) to strike fast if it wishes to conquer and in *Imperial Germany and the Industrial Revolution* (also published in 1915) he suggests that Germany may have struck too late.

There is much that is paradoxical in all this for Veblen's own theories. If Germans and Japanese are now the hard-working people who have not yet learned how to act like dilettante gentlemen, should this not also make them peaceable, as other industrious folk have been throughout history? Veblen's not wholly satisfactory answer is that the dynasts have adopted technology but have not yet been domesticated by it, and when hard pressed, here as elsewhere, he falls back on racial explanations. The fact is that, while Veblen's instinct of workmanship can be read as his puritanical paean to hard work, he only intermittently thought men lived by work alone (witness his concept of idle curiosity) and hence he did not feel compelled to admire the industrial late-comers for their vaunted 'efficiency'. Rather, despite or even perhaps because of their obedient workmanship, he regarded them as barbarians—so much so that passages of *Imperial Germany* might have been written for Lord Northcliffe's agency by an Oxford don.

To be sure, Veblen's ill-disguised and quasi-racial dislike of the Germans does not explain, except in small part, why Veblen liked the English and especially the French despite the obsolescence of their technology and the ardent wastefulness their leisure classes had attained through centuries of practice (Dorfman states in his *Thorstein Veblen and His America* that the last intellectual project Veblen planned was to go to England in order to find out how such decency and kindliness could flourish in an imperialist state). We are brought back, not only to the ambiguities lurking in Veblen's concept of lag, but also to those lurking in his major concept of workmanship, with its character both as an end—which permits a judgment of the beneficence of a social system as a whole—and as a means—which can only be judged in terms of efficiency.

All these subtleties in Veblen's thought, however, were to be submerged by the time of the Russian Revolution, after which the Soviets stand out as justified both by socialist ends and ruthless, 'no nonsense' means.

SOCIALIST DARWINISM

In Veblen's mind, Darwinism was the suitable philosophy for the coldly impersonal experience of factory production, where men draw, not so much on the fruits of their individual labour, as on a pool of machinery, human capacities, and technological resource provided them by the society as a whole. By Darwinism emphasis on behaviour conducive to the welfare of the species, Veblen wanted to emphasize that the accumulated industrial arts should not be appropriated by one part of the species as against the rest (including all the dead who had made a 'bequest' of their skills); there was no more 'right' to do this than for a fish to appropriate the water in which it swam. Much of Veblen's work was devoted to belittling the Captains of Industry who thought themselves responsible for American productivity, whereas they merely engrossed the instinct of workmanship of the race, charged mankind for

84

what, as a body, it already 'owned', and wasted what others had produced in a frenzy of extravagant, if usually vicarious, display.

So often does Veblen harp on this theme that it seems fair to say that the conflict between workmanship and wastemanship is almost obsessive with him. In order to be moderately sympathetic with his nearly exclusive concern with economic production, and the passionate hatred for luxury that his irony cannot hide, we must go back to Rolvaag, Dreiser, Norris, and other turn of the century writers to remind ourselves that America was once a rich, neglectful country which permitted some people to starve and encouraged others to throw their money around. If we read him literally, it would appear that he did want man to live by bread alone, provided Consumers' Research had studied the ingredients and no middle man had made a profit on the loaf.

This concentration on scarcity is what gives economics the name of the 'gloomy science', and in Veblen's case it gives his system, to use his own slang against him, a certain one-eyedness. So exclusive an attention to activities beneficial to the species as a whole must leave out of view the whole range of more differentiated and individualized human motives. Of course, Veblen was commendably attempting to reinstate work and sympathy as natural human motives, much as D. H. Lawrence strove to restore to sex its rightful importance. But both men confused the alleged naive dominance of these motives among primitive tribes with the necessarily more subtle, 'contaminated' part they can play in modern societies. Surely the middle-class citizen against whom both Veblen and Lawrence raged is more than half right in cherishing his exemptions from the round of procreating and maintaining the species. Dress and polite manners, which Veblen mocked, can be, like that 'mental' love which Lawrence mentally scorned, a means of establishing personal identity; although of course they can be and often are adaptations to conventional expectations, as Veblen and Lawrence claimed. We have already drawn attention to the fact that Veblen himself ducks away from utilitarianism in the field closest to home, that of university research and instruction, and stands out for the life of learning as an end in itself. (He gets around the fact that instruction is a socially useful activity by welcoming it only as a necessary complement to research, in that it stimulates the instructor and trains up future researchers.) Indeed, Veblen's whole treatment of the instinct of idle curiosity may be seen as something of a protest against the insistent pragmatism implicit in the instinct of workmanship and the unremitting condemnation of waste. Leaving aside what shelter it may have offered him in dealing with his efficient and impersonal father, we can see that this 'tender-minded' motive held for Veblen a salutary corrective to the exclusively 'tough-minded' workaday preoccupations of the world around him. Yet by simultaneously enjoining the worker not to mourn his lost craftsmanship but to make his peace with machine production, Veblen was prescribing for others what he, as an idly curious academic craftsman, refused to accept for himself.

This is indeed a basic paradox for a man whose whole bent of thought and life was to deny any distinction to persons or among persons. Veblen did not want anyone to make anything of *his* person, which would have tied him down to *being*, to being a person, as against making something of his work, from which he thought he could disengage himself. So, too, he obviously thought that the university professor bore the same relation to his means of production—laboratories, journals, books—that the factory worker supposedly did to his, that is, an impersonal, detached, self-disregarding, unostentatious, nearly invisible connection. Certainly he has penetratingly satirized the false pretensions of the educated. Yet it is again paradoxical that Veblen, who made the term 'common man' his trademark, time and again expresses contempt for common sense, which he thought invariably lagged behind the facts of life: no iconoclast of his day was surer that the received opinions of the multitude were wrong. Perhaps the paradox can best be reconciled by recalling Veblen's view that ultimately the productivity of the machine depends on dis-interested scientific theory—yet in trying to get rid of all aristocratic and privileged elements in thought and scholarship, he ended up entrusting theory to hard-bitten engineers and a few statistically-minded economic consultants, no likely vessel.

THE BIOLOGY OF HOPE

In all this, it is important to emphasize once more that Veblen's system of social science rests almost as much on biology as on history. This is true of the evolutionism which Veblen took from Darwin and also of Veblen's only occasionally skeptical reliance on the concepts of instinct and race. In the 1950's we need not labour over the limitations in Veb-len's particular handling of the instinct-habit methodology. Likewise, most of what Veblen said on the subject of race is now beside the point. As he himself observes, this theory could be equally well stated in terms of learned habits, and yet covert assumptions with respect to race often crop up in Veblen's work and enable him to avoid some puzzling questions about his distinctions between classes, nations, and periods of history. There are times when his talk of race and instinct, in combina-tion with his ascetic Puritanism, his desire to prune back culture to its

86

imagined beginnings in Savagery, his hatred for advertisers and other middlemen of goods or ideas, makes him sound like a sexless D. H. Lawrence or an unpoetic Ezra Pound. When, late in life, he stated that the next generation of economists could do without theory, or when he laughed at Malinowski's work which was then appearing, he was in effect turning his back on the very intellectual pursuits which had once excited him; he is almost ready, with the Nazis, to say: 'When I hear the word "culture", I reach for my revolver.'

However, all this talk, as with any thinker, needs to be put into a context. Compared with much of the writing on race in his lifetime, Veblen's treatment emphasizes nurture more than nature. Most of the time, Veblen is closer to the progressive biologistically-grounded assumptions of Lester Ward than to the Social Darwinists who assumed that their race, their kind, were the most fit to survive. And again and again he insisted that mixed races, hybrids, stood a better chance than 'pure' ones, especially if, like the emancipated Jews, they also bore a mixed cultural inheritance. Finally, it is hard to blame a man who had suffered as much as Veblen had in the cause of scholarship if he lapses occasionally into anti-intellectualism, in his own complicated form of midwest Philistinism.

It is important for Veblen's system that his emphasis on race and instinct at times led him to see institutions virtually as excrescences, with the main dramatic tensions in society not located in institutions, in roles, or in motives, but among the instincts, and between them and life as a whole. He was a conservationalist in spirit, like some of the neo-Malthusians today, preoccupied with biological subsistence as the fundamental human problem. Hence he tended to be unsympathetic to the institutions which men have built and inherited to give stability, channeling, and interpretation to life—especially, of course, when these seemed to get in the way of subsistence. And since Veblen recognized that institutions often create the needs they serve, he concluded that they were largely exploitative. Thus he saw at the end of the human road a society devoted to industrial workmanship, free of anthropomorphic illusion, of emulation, waste, and war—a society which did not give other meaning to the universe than that blind play of cumulative forces studied by Darwin; a society in which men admitted their insignificance, their kinship with other animals, and their helplessness in the slow working out of the evolutionary drift. As a society without lag and friction, in which men served each other because instinctually bound to do so, not only the state but all other institutions would wither away.

It is of a piece with this biologistic thinking that Veblen never seems to have asked himself how species-serving workmanship could be so readily contaminated by the desire for approval, nor why it is that emulation often results in workmanlike behaviour. His system does not include a social instinct (along the lines of gregariousness rather than solicitude), nor does he try to explain how the very nature of group life may lead a culture to prefer other values to the workmanship which this descendant of peasant Lutherans took too readily for granted. One senses that Veblen, in his methodology as in his life, sought to disregard those aspects of human nature which make men vulnerable to the judgments of their fellows—and this despite that fact that his writings abound in illustrations of such vulnerabilities.[1]

One result is that, as against Freud's instinct system, with its irreconcilable conflict between love and destructiveness and its contradictory and excessive demands on love itself, Veblen's is an optimistic system, at least in the long run—optimistic, that is, in terms of one who asks of life only that it be peaceable and provident; as we have seen, the three instincts he regarded as native to men were all beneficent. Until the end of the first World War, Veblen seems to have felt that somehow man will strive to right the balance of motives to the greater use of his own good sense and constructive rather than destructive propensities. While a King of France may let himself be roasted to death because he could not himself perform the menial office of displacing his royal body from before the fire, in general the common man—and much more surely, the common woman—is spared such distortions of workmanship and allowed to lead a life of slightly less strenuous absurdities. In this prewar period Veblen believed that the gradual recrudescence of whole and natural ends, the slow erosion of futility as the social consequence of the machine process, and the patient labors of idle curiosity, might bring things out all well in the end; revolution was not required, but only a free play for the instinctual impetus inherited from Savagery.

VEBLEN: ANTI-INSTITUTIONAL ECONOMIST

This strand of qualified optimism in Veblen reminds us that he never made contact, so far as his writings show, with the pessimistic theories

---

[1] See, e.g., *Absentee Ownership*, pp. 115-117: 'Men are moved by many impulses and driven by many instinctive dispositions. Among these abiding dispositions are a strong bent to admire and defer to persons of achievement and distinct'on, as well as a workmanlike disposition to find merit in any work that serves the common good . . . It is in these cases a matter of distinction, of course, with no hint of achievement, except such achievement as a loyal deference is bound to impute . . . Men like to believe that the personages whom they so admire by force of conventional routine are also of some use, as well as of great distinction — that they even somehow contribute, or at least conduce, to the material well-being at large. Which is presumably to be set down as one of the wonders wrought by the instinct of workmanship, which will not let men be content without some colorable serviceability in the personages which they so create out of nothing-in-particular.' It seems pretty clear in such passages that Veblen is not the prisoner of his instinct-theory, but is using it as an ironical and polemical device.

of society that were being developed by his great European contemporaries: Max Weber, with his emphasis on the 'iron cage' of modern industrialism and bureaucracy; or Pareto, with his cynical notion of the 'circulation of elites'; or Michels, with his analogous 'iron law of oligarchy'. The concept of bureaucracy which, under the influence of these men (and others, such as Mosca and Bentley), has become part of the working equipment of modern social science, remained for Veblen—as for many laymen today—simply an epithet.[1] His thought moves characteristically from a concern with individual motives or 'instincts' to the largest aggregates, such as 'the underlying population' or 'the vested interests'. In between lies his type-characters: the Captains of this and that; the Engineers; the denizens of country towns. For this so-called 'institutional economist', institutions seem not to have had a very full-bodied existence—and when they did, he spent his time attacking them for being institutions.

To be sure, Veblen and his disciples sometimes use the term 'institution' to refer to such features of the economy as the pricing mechanisms, the corporation, or the state of the industrial arts; and when they urge economists to study institutions they mean to divert them from 'abstract' theorems of supply and demand while focussing them upon such behavioural data as price in particular markets, advertising techniques, and other practices conducive to monopoly. In that sense, the Veblenians are perhaps not improperly designated 'institutionalists'. Even so, however, this behaviouristic empiricism is not to be equated with the tenderness towards institutions in general of some modern anthropologists and sociologists influenced by Durkheim or Malinowski: the latter reject most forms of 19th century rationalism whereas the Veblenians, more explicitly rebellious and less tolerant of going concerns just because they go, move within those forms. For instance Veblen's closest study of an institution—*The Higher Learning*—is for the most part obsessed with the idea that only the president and the board of trustees, the administration, were saboteurs of scholarly ideals; he tended not to see, within the faculty itself, any of the vested interests of 'field' or method, any of the bureaucratic tendencies in recruitment or in judgments as to what was and what was not to be counted as 'research'.

THE REDEFINITION OF 'RESEARCH'

Yet it is just at this point, in expanding our conventional definitions—especially, perhaps, those of economists—as to what is 'research', that

---

[1] In his essay, 'Some Neglected Points in the Theory of Socialism,' Veblen does take account of Spencer's condemnation of socialism as bureaucratic, but he answers the charge by saying (1) that since capitalism is so wasteful, socialism can afford to be somewhat inefficient, and (2) that there are other alternatives, such as the possibility of a constitutional economy

Veblen made one of his most significant long-run contributions. Scholarship is always falling into nepotism in the topics it considers worth sponsoring. To an extraordinary extent Veblen studied matters which had been thought too vulgar or too trivial for notice. Just to consider leisure was a step forward in an age of production. Thus, while there were other men in the universities in his day who had a better sense, for example, of the place of leisure in the coming America of abundance —Simon Patten is outstanding in this respect—no one studied the nuances of leisure-class behaviour with Veblen's intensity. Who but Freud would have thought much could be made of the meanings of carrying a walking stick, a topic to which some sarcastic passages of *The Theory of the Leisure Class* are devoted? What American, other than a few sociologists studying the American Negro, would have thought to trace the way in which a servant class spreads leisure-class styles among the underlying population at large?

Moreover, Veblen's ironic detachment from all the 'good causes' saved him from concentration on the matters his colleagues defined as 'problems'. They did not think such agencies as the YMCA constituted a problem but only lack of support for them—Veblen considered that these agencies supported a devout animism, a brutal sportsmanship, an honorific patronage of the poor, and were therefore a problem for a mechanistic industrial age. To be sure, Veblen did not confine himself to finding significance in the esoteric or the disreputable, which would have simply established another snobbish hierarchy of research in place of the one he was undermining.

Veblen to some extent shared the spirit of Zola and his American followers, and also the spirit of W. I. Thomas and other sociologists of the 'Chicago School' who were plunging with fascination into the study of the life of the city, its immigrant swarms, its sexual deviations, its vagabond occupations. The turn of the century was the period of the great surveying expeditions by which literature and sociology took stock of the assorted peoples whom industrialisation and urbanisation had thrown together. Yet there are great differences between Veblen and these contemporaries. In the first place, most of them, whatever manifestoes of 'naturalism' might constitute their charter of work, were reform-minded. This is as true of Jack London, who combined a Darwinian premise with a vaguely socialistic conclusion, as of most of the social workers, the sociologists, and the muckrakers. In comparison,

analogous to a constitutional democracy, to a regime of contract or of status. It seems to me from this argument that Veblen never met head-on (nor, for that matter, did Spencer and other laissez-faire advocates) the contention that all large-scale societies will inevitably be 'bureaucratic', will suffer from hardening of the institutional arteries — and hence greatly resemble each other, whatever the label.

Veblen's reform-mindedness was far more sublimated. In the second place, Veblen was too withdrawn, too 'scholarly' in the classical sense, to enjoy first-hand contact with the objects of study: nothing could be more alien to him than the gusto of a Chicago novelist doing field-work in a shabby bar. Whereas W. I. Thomas published a book of essays on *Sex and Society* in 1907 and remained preoccupied with sexual life in other works, Veblen made place for a parental bent but not for a sexual instinct and the theme of sex is notably absent from his writings, save in a late, fond disquisition on Scandinavian illegitimacy rates. And whereas Thomas late in life learned Yiddish so that he could read the advice columns in the Jewish *Daily Forward*—columns which he found rich in implication as to the shifts in attitude undergone by East-side immigrants—Veblen preferred to continue learning the dead languages, including Sanskrit, and to translate Scandinavian sagas.[1]

It appears, then, that Veblen's term, 'idle curiosity', goes far to describe his own focus of attention. It is 'idle' in the sense of refusal to be committed to those 'great issues' that his contemporaries took most seriously, in the sense of having nothing of the eager beaver about it, and in the sense of not giving an account of itself to any vested interest whether academic or popular. It is certainly not the curiosity of the privileged writer or anthropologist who, half-guiltily and half-adventurously, discovers poverty and alien cultures. It is the curiosity of a bystander, who casts a cold eye, rather than of a rescue party or castigating moralist. It is playful, lively, inquisitive, unimpressed. That in Veblen's case it turned out to direct his attention to waste, trusts, socialism, imperialism, and many other unremittingly exigent issues, only indicates that he was human and that ivory towers are built by human hands for inescapably human purposes. Likewise, that Veblen's passionate moral sense sharped his idly curious eye is also not to be wondered at; our play and dreaming express as well as relieve our workaday anxieties and inhibitions. And yet there is a real if impalpable freedom in play, which transcends the very human condition that shapes it—much as Veblen's concept of idle curiosity transcends his otherwise biological and economic determinism. In the play of his irony, Veblen found a form for the manifold tensions in him—between his morality of reform and his morality of science, between his detachment and his fear and hatred of

---

[1] Those social scientists who have a single-track commitment to field-work may read this as an implied criticism of Veblen for 'arm-chair theorizing'; those humanists who have a disdain for the contemporary and for 'fact-grubbing' may read this as implied praise; it is not intended as either. As an advocate of idle curiosity, I believe that the methods scholars use should be suited both to the problems studied and to the researchers' personal gifts and temperaments, and I see the task of graduate education as aiding the individual student to expand his roster of abilities in accordance with increasing awareness as to what his gift and temperament is. Veblen's students, such as Wesley C. Mitchell and Hoxie, were often stimulated by him to explorations he himself shied away from.

bullying and injustice, between his detestation of waste and his passive acceptance of Darwinian pessimism. In my judgment, his irony is as superior to the naturalists' frequent grimness as Charlie Chaplin's pessimism is superior to that of soap opera.

But having used this word 'superior', I bring myself up with a startled realisation that Veblen would have rejected any such rank or distinction —other than one premised on his morality of waste. Plainly, I do not go along with him there but feel that some things are more worthwhile, more beautiful, more desirable than others. However, as a charter for research, the assertion that soap opera may be as significant as Chaplin cannot be gainsaid, and when anyone studies soap opera and other devalued products of popular culture he is making use of a freedom Veblen helped win: to proceed (as this journal seeks to do) without reference to the boundaries between departments or between 'important' subjects and 'trivial' ones.

David Riesman

(*This is the second of two instalments of Dr. Riesman's article on Veblen.*)

In the pirate's wardroom, the dinner service is of solid silver, stamped with the arms of Castile and Leon. The serving dishes are Sung porcelain. On the walls, panelled in English oak, are a handsome Dutch painting, a pair of crossed duelling pistols that formerly belonged to a French count, a Malay *kris*, and an Inca breastplate in pure soft gold. Everything is of the best, for the pirate captain has natural good taste and an eye for quality. Nothing matches anything else, however, for it has all been stolen piecemeal, in most cases immediately following on the murder of the previous owner.

In my own dining room, where there is neither solid silver nor gold, an Indian miniature from the Rajput Hills jostles an Azande *shongo*, or throwing knife, on the wall, and the shelves are shared uneasily by a group of Australian *churingas*, a terracotta ithyphallic *Silenos* from ancient Thebes, an Iroquois turtle rattle, a collection of Japanese *netsukes*, a Gaboon ship harp, and a Corsican vendetta knife. Although these have all been obtained peaceably, by gift, trade, or purchase, I cannot see that my dining room differs significantly in kind from the pirate's wardroom, or either from André Malraux's 'museum without walls', the organizing metaphor of his new art book,[1] which simply raises our small acts of cultural piracy to the level of an aesthetic principle. 'In fact our resuscitations are selective' he writes, 'and although we have ransacked the ends of the earth, we have not taken over all the arts that came to light.' These are the pirate's verbs, and the pirate, too, is selective, more selective in fact than Malraux.

The Voices of Silence is a book about art styles, in their collective relations to cultures and their individual relations to artists. It was begun in 1936, some of it appeared in English in *Verve* as early as 1938 (then as now excellently translated by Stuart Gilbert), a penultimate version was published in three volumes as *The Psychology of Art* from 1947 to 1950, and now, extensively revised and amplified, these become the four books of the new thick (and presumably final) volume.

The present book seems to me to have four principal arguments, somewhat related to each other. The first is the concept of the 'museum without walls', the present availability of all the world's arts that we owe to photography. This permits us to see a picture in a context of *all* the artist's work, which gives it 'a new significance'. This abundance then produces a new selectivity, as we can discover those works most uniquely the artist's, in which everything not his characteristic style is stripped away, and reduce our consideration to these, a process Malraux calls making 'a true anthology'. All modern painting should be treated 'anthologically', Malraux says, adding innocently, 'more or less'. The museum without walls not only gives us this anthology drawn from an artist's entire work, but gives us an art style in its entirety, from which we can similarly make significant selections. Having then anthologized the best work of the best artists, the best examples of the best styles, we can settle happily in our wall-less museum (or wardroom) and appreciate them all. 'I do not know of a single great modern painter who does not respond both to certain works by savages and to Poussin' Malraux writes, in a sentence that hardly needs the additional parenthetical reservation, 'if in differing degrees.'

The book's second argument is a pluralism that starts from Malraux's definition of art as 'That whereby forms are transmuted into style.' Any forms, so long as some authentic transmutation occurs. 'Far from being eclectic and taking pleasure in the diversity of forms, our modern pluralism stems from the discovery of the elements that even the most seemingly disparate works of art have in common,' he writes. Invidious aesthetic categories like 'retrograde', 'barbarian', 'primitive', go out the

---

[1] *The Voices of Silence*, by André Malraux; Doubleday; p. 661; $25.

window. Celtic coins are not clumsy imitations of the work of Macedonian *toreutai*, but a major style of their own, the work of Great Masters, and they may only be called 'barbarian' in quotes. Similarly, Gothic statues are not botched classical statues, African heads are not failed realistic portrayals. Prehistoric cave paintings are not only 'a highly developed style', but behind their forms 'we surmise other forms'.

From this follows a third argument, which we may call 'neo-evolutionary', that widely-differing cultures have a comparable if not identical development. Malraux writes: 'The reason why the life-story of Gandharan art has special interest for the sculptor lies precisely in this fact that, by-passing the intermediate stages of Romanesque and Gothic, it came into line with our Renaissance.' One of the book's repeated insistences is that styles are not different ways of 'seeing', but aesthetic conventions with histories. Any emphasis on individual expression as a determinant is rejected; Malraux has little use for terms like 'instinctive', 'inspiration', or 'the unconscious'. Art styles are born, marry, beget, and die, and the artist's 'uniqueness' is only an anecdote in this great biography.

From the sequence of cultural piracy, pluralism, and evolution, Malraux somehow derives a fourth point that is probably the book's principal theme (it gives it its title), the moral importance of art. 'When man faces destiny' through art, 'destiny ends and man comes into his own.' The arts we value are religious ones, although we do not share their religions; they express 'man's ability to escape from chaos, even though the way of escape lies through blood and darkness'; they are 'voices of the abyss', of 'the dark places of man's heart'. The aesthetic impulse is creative, it is 'the desire to build up a world apart and self-contained, existing in its own right'; it represents 'humanization' in 'the deepest, certainly the most enigmatic, sense of the word'. 'Every masterpiece, implicitly or openly, tells of a human victory over the blind force of destiny'; art speaks 'the immemorial language of Man the conqueror'; 'All art is a revolt against man's fate.'

Malraux argues these theses with a great variety of techniques, shifting imperturbably from close technical criticism of the lines of a Rheims sculpture, to the study of the sources of Van Megeeren's Vermeer forgeries, to an illustrated history of El Greco's development, to a biographical anecdote about Renoir. There must be few types of art scholarship and criticism that do not find a place somewhere in this vast book. His principal device, however, is dichotomy, the creation of opposed poles of imagery, similar to those in G. Wilson Knight's Shakespeare studies. 'Provided we have art, not culture, in mind' he writes, 'the

95

African mask and Poussin, the ancestor and Michelangelo are seen to be not adversaries, but polarities.' On the one hand are 'the forms of all that belongs essentially to the human', on the other, 'all the forms that crush or baffle man'. In the first cluster are 'the radiant archetypes': instinct, pleasure, gesture, harmony, the human, uniqueness, specific events, and free will. In the other cluster are 'the tragic archetypes': ritual, destiny, hieratic immobility, paralysis, the eternal, nature, attributes, and fatalism.

These polarities are not entirely fixed, in that the ingredients of the second cluster can be transmuted into the first, negations become affirmations, by the mysterious powers of art (or Malraux's dialectic). 'Our renaissance of the art of savages is more than a rebirth of fatalism' Malraux writes, negating his negation. 'I name that man an artist who *creates* forms' he proclaims boldly, but his personal taste seems to be for the creators of the more humanistic forms. At times, particularly in regard to the French moderns, he is extremely all-embracing; at others, like a pictorial Yvor Winters, he reduces Venetian Baroque to nine great pictures and names them. The greatest artists for Malraux seem to be Giotto, Rembrandt, and Goya, painters of a markedly humanistic bent, but the seven full-page reproductions that interrupt the text after page 582, and seem to represent Malraux's quintessential anthology, include works by only three European artists, and those three surprising: Vermeer, Piero della Francesca, and Gruenewald.

Even at its most pluralist, Malraux's framework omits a good many art styles and a great deal of art. He argues for a pure plastic art that does not require the social content of Goya or Rembrandt—'the depiction of a world devoid of value can be magnificently justified by an artist who treats *painting itself* as the supreme value'—but these are not the works he seems most to admire. 'The paintings of the Pygmies fail to interest us' he writes; 'perhaps, indeed, total savagery is incompatible with art.' Malraux rejects styles that 'pander' to what he calls 'delectation' as furiously as did the young Stephen Dedalus of *The Portrait*, and he dismisses them similarly as either 'sentimental' or 'licentious'. 'No mode of plastic expression is foreign to this universal language' Malraux writes, but surely some are for him, and not only the kinetic arts of delectation. Certain kinds of pictorial stasis do not seem to interest him at all, whether represented by Greek black-figure pottery, Bahuana ivory pendants, or Mondrian.

Malraux persistently treats 'ritual and ceremonial symbolism' as a kind of Byzantinism that petrifies the human values of his first cluster, although in practice these elements, whenever he is aware of them, seem to augment a work's meaning and interest for him. Thus he values New Ireland soft-wood carvings of ancestors, which, he understands: 'form the court of the Great Primordial Ancestor, the sculptures in the house of worship suggest him, music is his voice, the festivals converge on him and the dance mimes his gestures as it mimes the tribe's heroic past, the epiphanies of the sun, the moon and death, the fertility of the soil, life-giving rain, the rhythms of the firmament.' He has no similar sense of the relationship of myth and ritual to Hopi *kachina* figures; they are only 'household gods', and it is significant that a photograph of three of them together is the book's only loveless illustration. On the other hand, in a Celtic coin 'the engravers seem harking back, across the chaos of prehistory, to the totemic boar'; Georges de Latour's painting 'partakes of the nature of the Mystery-Play, and has the slow rhythms of a rite'.

In these cases, both significantly French, myth and rite become 'history', and as such Malraux can handle them. History is an important value, but always ambivalent: 'The link between history and art often seems so tenuous'; 'Though this creative process has a place in history, it is independent of history'; capital-H 'History' is in fact our modern equivalent for the Eternal. If the experience of this reader can be taken as typical, a lower-case history is equally involved, the history of experience or familiarity. Thus, of the pictures Malraux reproduces in color, works like El Greco's *View of Toledo* now seem boring, while the exciting works are by unfamiliar painters like Latour and Takanobu, or painters not previously taken seriously (until Malraux pointed out their formal organizations) like Chardin. This capacity to enlarge the reader's horizon is probably the book's greatest value, but its relation to history seems defiantly negative.

The principal opponent Malraux argues against, as W. M. Frohock points out in his able *André Malraux and the Tragic Imagination*, is Oswald Spengler. Frohock shows that *The Voices of Silence* and the latest novel, *Les Noyers de l'Altenburg*, share the same question, 'whether it is possible for man to be considered a permanent, continuously identical identity', and debate it against the same opponent, what the art book calls 'the German theory of cultures', represented in the novel by the anthropologist Moellberg (apparently based on Frobenius). To an American reader, the book's argument seems pointed less at Spengler than at a man whose imposition of German philosophy on American thinking we tend to overlook, Franz Boas. We have adopted Hegel's cynical ethical relativism in the form of Boas' cultural pluralism, and Spengler's theory of closed cultures (modified into Wissler's 'culture areas') as Boas' restriction of 'dynamics' to the record of diffusion and acculturation, rather than polygenesis and evolution. If, as Malraux argues, man is a continuity, culture an evolution, and art an absolute, then Boas must be unwritten and Tylor and Frazer restored, a process we can see already at work in a new anthology, *Primitive Heritage*, compiled by that reliable bellwether, Margaret Mead.

Another implication of considerable importance in the book is the odd guerrilla warfare conducted against modern abstract painting. There are, Malraux writes, 'certain deep-rooted collective emotions, which modern art has chosen to ignore.' Something else of value may be substituted—'in a Braque still life the peach no longer has a bloom, the picture has it'—but it is not ultimately adequate. In Malraux's view, *a* style is coming into being now, 'perhaps the greatest style the West has ever sponsored', which 'seems to belong to some religion of which it is not aware'. It is, he makes clear, a convention of expressive representation, not of abstraction; 'a style', not 'a calligraphy'. 'Were our culture to be restricted solely' he writes, 'to our response (lively though it is) to forms and colors, and their vivid expression in contemporary art—surely the name of "culture" could hardly be applied to it.' By this time, Malraux has almost completely undermined the book's earlier definition: 'Modern art is, rather, the annexation of forms by means of an inner pattern or schema, which may or may not take the shape of objects, but of which, in any case, figures and objects are no more than the expression.'

The Voices of Silence is full of genuine insights: that 'Rembrandt was the first great master whose sitters sometimes dreaded seeing their portraits', that Dostoevsky has much in common with Byzantine art, that the Middle Ages involve 'apotheosis taking the place of incarnation', and many more. It is at the same time a tissue of contradictions: 'an art which breaks up into ideograms is regressive' and the 'triumph of the sign is a sign of death', but all great art before Christianity had been 'a system of signs', the Gandhara carvings make an important rediscovery of 'symbolic representation', and all true styles are *'significations'*.

The book is full of moving rhetoric: the Buddhist vision sees the world as 'two homeless children clasping hands in a dead city, loud with the tedium of apes and the heavy flight of peacocks'; 'those monsters of the abyss which the psychoanalyst fishes for with nets, and politics or war, with dynamite'; and its conclusion (at least in English) tolls the authentic Brownian bell: 'Survival is not measurable by duration, and death is not assured of its victory, when challenged by a dialogue echoing down the ages.' In all this beauty and eloquence, however, there is a good deal of oracular nonsense: 'for the artist is by nature secretive and likes to mystify', 'Seldom is a Gothic head more beautiful than when broken', 'the true hero of every fairy story is the fairy', 'certain African statues, not one curve of whose noses could have been varied by the image-maker without the risk of his being put to death by order of the witch-doctor', and the discussion of Freud and the Freudian doctrine of wish-fulfillment is shamefully ignorant and foolish.

A reference to primitive Christianity as 'that oriental night-world of blood and doom-fraught stars', to later Christianity as a time when 'value was being disintegrated into a plurality of values', to the taste of Augustan Rome as 'Second Empire in France', and to Rome in general as soulless, suggest that the author of *The Conquerors* and *Man's Fate* is still at war with a large part of the Western heritage. He nevertheless believes 'that, for three hundred years, the world has not producd a single work of art comparable with the supreme works of the West', that 'what is challenged in our culture is challenged by the *past* of other cultures', and that the arts of other cultures, their 'idols', could not have been appreciated by ours until the present period of enlightenment. We are thus left 'sole heir' of the world's bequest, and finally identified as the new Rome— our tastelessness and soullessness tactfully unmentioned—welcoming to our Pantheon 'the gods of the defeated'.

This Pantheon is, of course, our familiar pirate's wardroom, and here we might pause to note who Malraux speaks for with his omnipresent 'we' and 'us'. Sometimes it is the Western world, sometimes an undefined community of the spirit, sometimes an elite consisting of unnamed modern painters and sculptors, sometimes his readers, and very frequently, I think, only M. Malraux. What *actual* agreement can be presumed? We are all, for example, cultural pluralists (the pirate was a founding father of cultural pluralism), and surely we do not need Malraux to tell us that the time after the fall of Rome was not *really* 'dark', nor that Africans (except Pygmies) are not *really* 'savages'. But how many of us accept the full implications of our belief, and insist that if Celtic coins and Benin bronzes are comparable to the arts of Greece, then Gaul and Benin had high civilizations comparable to Greece's, and that all previous hierarchies of culture have been foolishly based on literacy alone? And if we believe that certain civilizations are high, then we believe that certain others are low, and we are not cultural pluralists at all. We may even admit to the possession of some ethical absolute from which we can criticize traits in other configurations (would female circumcision in Kenya be an art style, or Buchenwald lampshades?)

99

If the 'primitive' works of art we choose to adopt are not a meaningful part of our own culture, but are not meaningless in our culture either, then most of our previous thinking in this area has been oversimple. Malraux writes 'for us today the mask or the ancestor is no more a magical or a numinous object than a medieval Virgin is *the* Virgin.' But neither are our contemporary serious arts magical or numinous, in just this sense. What we need, it seems to me, is a conception of magic as inherent in formal organization, equally present in Picasso's lithographed bulls and the bulls of the Altamira caves, in Klee's *Around the Fish* as in the Australian bark drawing it so much resembles. I think the key to this approach is the word Malraux is so wary of, the word 'ritual', and that to attain it he need only extend the way he talks about Latour's painting to cover less representational hieratic organizations.

If we talk of art in terms of symbolic actions that are individual modern equivalents for collective older rites, then a modern poem or picture can once again be discussed as fertility magic, making the metaphoric crops grow in some meaningful sense. This approach sees the work of art, not in narrowly configurational terms, but as functional in a context it carries along with it, out of place and time. In these terms, 'culture areas' becomes merely one more outmoded museum category. A thing of beauty is once again that old chestnut, a joy forever, and its origin is irrelevant, because it retains in its formal organization a magical capacity to act on us and initiate us into its rites. At which the pirate chuckles, and goes off to capture a Japanese ship that might be carrying a first-rate Takanobu.

Stanley Edgar Hyman

INTRODUCTION

Self-awareness as a Generic Human Trait

One of the distinguishing features of human adjustment, as compared with that of animals lower in the evolutionary scale, rests upon the fact that the human adult, in the course of ontogenetic development, has learned to discriminate himself as an object in a world of objects other than himself. Self-awareness is a psychological constant, one basic facet of human nature and the human personality.[1] As one psychologist has said, '. . . everyone, with the possible exception of infants, some philosophers, and some psychopaths, is aware of one's self.'[2]

Self-awareness in man cannot be taken as an isolated psychological phenomenon, however, if we are to understand the full range and depth of its human significance. For it is becoming increasingly apparent that this peculiarly human phenomenon is the focus of complex, and functionally

---

[1] Cf. Erich Fromm, *Man for Himself*, 1947, pp. 39-40. In the characterization of Patrick Mullahy, *Oedipus: Myth and Complex*, 1945, p. 241, 'The key problem of psychology for Fromm is the specific kind of relatedness of the individual towards the world and to himself.'
[2] Isidor Chein, 'The Awareness of Self and the Structure of the Ego.' *Psychological Review* 51, 1944, p. 305.

dependent, sets of linguistic and cultural variables that enter into the personal adjustment of human beings as members of particular societies. At the same time, it seems necessary to assume self-awareness as one of the prerequisite psychological conditions for the functioning of any human social order, no matter what linguistic and culture patterns prevail. If such be the case, the phenomenon of self-awareness in our species is as integral a part of a human socio-cultural mode of adaptation as it is of a distinctive human level of psychological structuralization.

It is likewise evident that, as one of the consequences of self-awareness, man has reflected upon his own nature as well as the nature of the world perceived as other than self. He has been able, moreover, to articulate and express through symbolic means explicit notions that embrace this polarity. Thus ideas of this order, in concrete and conceptual form have become an intrinsic part of the cultural heritage of all human societies. It is possible, therefore, to investigate concepts of the self and its nature, as well as those linguistic and cultural variables that facilitate the emergence of the self as a perceptible object. In addition to investigations that are oriented in a traditional psychological or psychiatric frame of reference, concomitant inquiries oriented in cross-cultural perspective, should widen as well as deepen our understanding of a distinctive human attribute.[1]

The nature of the self, considered with reference to its conceptual content, is a culturally identifiable variable. Just as different peoples entertain various beliefs about the nature of the universe, they likewise differ in their ideas about the nature of the self. And, just as we have discovered that notions about the nature of the beings and powers existent in the universe involve assumptions that are directly relevant to an understanding of the behaviour of the individual in a given society, we must likewise assume that the individual's self-image and his interpretation of his own experience cannot be divorced from the concept of the self that is characteristic of his society. For such concepts are the major means by which different cultures promote self-orientation in the kind of meaningful terms that make self-awareness of functional importance in the maintenance of a human social order. In so far as the needs and goals of the individual are at the level of self-awareness, they are structured with reference to the kind of self-image that is consonant with other basic

---

[1] In *The Perception of the Visual World*, 1950, p. 226, James J. Gibson emphasizes the fact that 'perceiving the environment includes the ego as part of the total process. In order to localize any object there must be a point of reference. An impression of "there" implies an impression of "here", and neither could exist without the other.' He then goes on to remark that although 'the definition of the ego is a problem with which psychologists and philosophers have struggled without much success, the concept of a self, by whatever term it is called, is necessary for any scientific theory of personality, of social behavior, or abnormal behavior, or of ethical behavior.'

orientations that prepare the self for action in a culturally constituted world. In his discussion of 'The Primitive World View', Redfield points out that the concept of 'world-view' differs from culture, ethos, mode of thought and national character. It implies 'certain human universals'. Among other things it assumes 'that in every society all men are conscious of self. Self is the axis of world view. Everyone distinguishes himself from all else. . . . It is the picture the members of a society have of the properties and characters upon their stage of action. While "national character" refers to the way these people look to the outsider looking in on them, "world view" refers to the way the world looks to that people, looking out. Of all that is connoted by "culture", "world view" attends especially to the way a man, in a particular society, sees himself in relation to all else. It is the properties of existence as distinguished from and related to the self. It is, in short, a man's idea of the universe. It is that organization of ideas which answers to a man the questions: Where am I? Among whom do I move? What are my relations to things?'[1]

As I have pointed out elsewhere, 'As a result of self-objectification human societies become social orders of conscious selves, in contrast with the societies of other primates where the development of ego-centered processes as part of the psychological structure of the individual do not become salient. In fact, when viewed from the standpoint of this peculiarity of man, cultures may be said to be elaborate systems of meaning which, in an animal capable of self-awareness, implement a type of adaptation which makes the role of the human being intelligible to himself with reference to an articulated universe and to his fellow men.'[2]

Historical Perspective

Although man's self-awareness has long provided philosophers with an intriguing problem for speculation and psychologists have played fast and loose with it over several generations, anthropologists have paid comparatively little attention to the relevant ethnographic facts. It was recognized, of course, that concepts of the 'soul' manifested considerable variability in content from one culture to another and a considerable body of data was put on record.[3] But concepts of the soul were seen primarily in their relation to religion and magic rather than in a psychological frame of reference, relevant to the generic fact of man's self-awareness on the one hand, and the content of a culturally constituted

[1] Robert Redfield, 'The Primitive World View.' *Proceedings of the American Philosophical Society*, 46, 1952, p. 30; cf. *The Primitive World and Its Transformations*, 1953, pp. 86, 91.
[2] A. Irving Hallowell, 'Personality Structure and the Evolution of Man.' *American Anthropologist*, 52, 1950, p. 169.
[3] An early survey by A. E. Crawley, *The Idea of the Soul*, 1900, now seems completely antiquated from a psychological point of view.

self-image, on the other.[1] When Wissler[2] set forth what he called the 'universal pattern of culture' the absence of any concept of self in this pattern was not an oversight but an historically significant omission. Art, social organization, even war, were included, and of course, religion. The implication is plain. Whereas, among other things, concepts of the deity or other spiritual beings, are assumed without any question to be an integral part of man's characteristic cultural adjustment of life, the concepts that man entertains about his *own* nature, exemplified in concepts of self, appear not to deserve any emphasis at all, to say nothing of an equal ranking with the other cultural categories included.[3] Subsequently, Murdock[4] listed a more specific series of items which he described as 'common denominators of culture',[5] saying, 'they occur in every culture known to history or ethnology.' It is interesting to note that while 'soul concepts' are to be found in this list, self-concepts are not. Traditional concepts of self, however, play the same kind of pragmatic role in the psychological adjustment of the individual to his world as do other classes of concepts and culturally derived means. Just as concepts of spiritual beings, for example, help to structuralize the vital part of the universe that is other than self and orient the individual in cosmic perspective, in the same way a concept of self not only facilitates self-orientation but enables the individual to comprehend the nature of his own being and, by inference, the nature of other selves with whom he interacts. Since concepts of this category define the most typical and permanent attributes of a phenomenal class of objects among which the personal self finds itself included, their importance in any culture is obvious.

It must be recalled, however, that it is only within the last few decades that anthropologists have manifested any vital interest in the relation betwen culture variability, the psychological structure of the individual and his differential behaviour. Besides this, there were other obstacles

---

[1] It is perhaps of some historical significance that an article published in 1916 which did concern itself with 'Primitive Notions of the "Self".' *American Journal of Psychology*, 27: 171-202, was written by Arthur J. Todd, a sociologist, and published in a psychological journal. A few years later Geza Roheim published a series of articles on 'Das Selbst.' *Imago*, 7: 1-39. 142-179, 310-348, 453-504, 1921, in which he interpreted the material reported from a wide range of cultures according to psychoanalytic principles. These were among the contributions for which Roheim was awarded the Freud prize in 1921. But they did not effect the main stream of anthropological thought.
[2] Clark Wissler, *Man and Culture*, 1923.
[3] It is worth noting, therefore, that as early as 1937 and thereafter Lawrence K. Frank repeatedly referred to concepts of the self as an intrinsic aspect of all cultures. In an article on 'The Task of General Education' he wrote: 'In any culture, we find that the basic conceptions that underlie the whole framework of man's life are concerned with the nature of the universe, man's place therein, his relations to his society or group life, and to other individuals, and finally his conception of human nature and of the self.' See the collection of Frank's papers published under the title *Society as the Patient*, 1948, p. 215, and likewise pp. 152, 162, 226, 277, 290.
[4] George P. Murdock, 'Common Denominators of Culture.' in Ralph Linton, ed., *The Science of Man and the World Crisis*, 1945.
[5] John Gillin, *The Ways of Men*, 1948, p. 196, repeats Murdock's items without emendation.

which interfered with the development of any serious interest in question focussed upon such a topic as the concept of self. One of these was the fact that self-awareness has been minimized or even denied as an observable phenomenon among primitive peoples. At this period all sorts of attempts were made to differentiate the mind, the thinking or the mentality of 'early' man or 'primitive' peoples from 'civilized' (European) peoples. One point of differentiation was made to turn upon the status of self-awareness in the evolution of the human mind. Self-awareness was undeveloped in primitive man as compared with civilized man.[1] This interpretation of certain ethnographic facts still crops up, for instance in the statement of H. Kelsen that, 'Hand in hand with the predominance of the emotional over the rational tendency in the soul of primitive man goes a remarkable lack of ego-consciousness, a lack of any developed experience of his self.'[2]

Paul Radin, in his *Primitive Man as Philosopher* (1927) takes quite the opposite point of view. He raises the question: 'How does primitive man regard the ego?' But he goes on to point out that 'Few ethnologists have ever attempted to obtain from a native any systematized account of their own theory. It has in fact, been generally contended that they have none. As a result our material consists of isolated statements on different aspects of the Ego and we are perforce compelled to weld them into a consistent or inconsistent whole—as the case may be—in order to see their complete bearings. This unfortunately cannot be helped.'[3]

In 1938 Marcel Mauss[4] took as the subject of his Huxley lecture 'Une catégorie de l'esprit humain: la notion de personne, celle de "moi".' He points out that, while we have here 'une de ces idées que nous croyons innées,' an investigation is needed of how it was 'lentement née et grandie au cours de longs siècles et à travers de nombreuses vicissitudes, tellement qu'elle est encore, aujourd'hui même, flottante, délicate, précieuse, et a élaborer davantage.' While everyone finds 'l'idée de "personne", l'idée du "moi"' natural enough and, besides this, 'au fond de sa

---

[1] See, e.g., C. J. Bittner, *The Development of the Concept of the Social Nature of the Self*, doctoral dissertation printed by the author, Iowa City, 1932, p. 10, who cites Durkheim, Baldwin, and Levy-Bruhl as among those 'who assert that primitive man is devoid of self-consciousness, and that he fails to distinguish between subject and object, between things in consciousness and out of consciousness, between self and other.' But Levy-Bruhl actually represents a more qualified view.
[2] Hans Kelsen, *Society and Nature*, 1943, p. 6. The ethnographic evidence adduced in support of this statement is not convincing, quite apart from any possible evolutionary implications.
[3] Paul Radin, *Primitive Man as Philosopher*, 1927, pp. 259, 260. In his chapter on 'The Nature of the Ego and of Human Personality' Radin deals with the Maori, Oglala Sioux, and the Batak. It is interesting to note that the Maori are cited by Kelsen, *op. cit.*, p. 11, to make the point that, since the pronominal use of 'I' may have an extended use that includes the tribal group, they 'lack ego-consciousness'.
[4] Marcel Mauss, 'Une categorie de L'esprit humain: la notion de personne celle de "moi".' Huxley Lecture, 1938. *Journal of the Royal Anthropological Institute*, 68: 263-281, 1938. Reprinted in *Sociologie et Anthropologie*, Bibliotheque de Sociologie Contemporaine, Presses Universitaires de France, 1950.

conscience, toute équipée au fond de la morale qui s'en déduit', at the same time 'il s'agit de substituer à cette naïve vue de son histoire, et de son actuelle valeur, une vue plus précise.'

While Mauss excludes a psychological approach as irrelevant to his immediate concern, he assumes that 'il est évident, surtout pour nous, qu'il n'y a jamais eu d'être humain qui n'ait eu le sens, non seulement de son corps, mais aussi de son individualitè spirituelle et corporelle à la fois.' What interests Mauss is the concept of the self as 'un subjet d'histoire sociale. Comment, au cours des siècles, à travers de nombreuses sociétés, s'est lentement élaboré, non pas le sens du "moi", mais la notion, le concept que les hommes des divers temps s'en sont crées? Ce que je veux vous montrer, c'est la série des formes que ce concept a revêtues dans la vie des hommes des sociétés, d'après leurs droits, leurs religions, leurs coûtumes, leurs structures sociales et leurs mentalités.' Mauss characterizes his lecture as 'un plan de travail.' It remains fragmentary, but nevertheless suggestive, especially in regard to the need for further historical elucidation of the concept of the self in western culture.

More recently, a few anthropologists have become interested in the self as a topic. Dorothy Lee has published the most sophisticated analysis of the concept of self among a non-literate people yet to appear, but her approach is essentially a linguistic analysis.[1] At the meetings of the American Association for the Advancement of Science (1949) Marian W. Smith read a paper on 'Varrying Concepts of Ego Extension', later published in *Psychiatry*.[2] And now, in contrast with earlier editions, the *Outline of Cultural Materials* includes an item called 'Ethnopsychology'[3] under which we find 'concepts of the self, of human nature, of motivation, of personality', so that, in the future, we should have more detailed inquiries into such topics.

There is an additional reason why anthropologists of an earlier generation could hardly have been expected to concern themselves with concepts of the self, except at a purely descriptive cross-cultural level. If they had turned to their psychological colleagues for enlightenment, the latter would probably have discouraged, rather than encouraged, them. Despite the fact that William James had dealt with the 'empirical self', and there had emerged from the work of J. M. Baldwin, C. H. Cooley and particularly G. H. Mead, the hypothesis that the self is a social product, Sargent points out that 'between about 1910 and 1940 most psycho-

---

[1] Dorothy Lee, 'Notes on the Conception of the Self among the Wintu Indians.' *Journal of Abnormal and Social Psychology*, 45:3, 1950.
[2] Marian W. Smith, 'Different Cultural Concepts of Past, Present, and Future. A study of Ego Extension.' *Psychiatry*, 15: 395-400, 1952.
[3] George P. Murdock, Cellan S. Ford, *et al*, 'Outline of Cultural Materials.' *Behavior Science Outlines*, 1, 3rd ed., Human Relations Area Files, 1950, item 828, section 82, 'Ideas about Nature and Man.'

logists preferred not to mention "ego" or "self" in their writings'[1] But, following G. W. Allport's address to the Eastern Psychological Association in 1943 on 'The Ego in Contemporary Psychology' this subject once again emerged as completely reputable and has proved to be a topic of expanding interest in psychological circles. It is in some of the current textbooks in social psychology as well as elsewhere that we find the most systematic discussions of the self.[2]

So far as psychoanalytic theories are concerned, it is likewise of some historic interest to note that it was only in the early 1920's that 'Freud finally formulated a theory of the total personality, and the ego with its function of reality testing became the Ego of the Ego, Superego and Id.'[3] This shift in interest from the libido to the activities of the ego was signalized with the publication of *The Ego and the Id.*[4] This occurred during the period when psychologists were still uninterested in questions relating to the self but when, on the other hand, some anthropologists were becoming vitally interested in personality structure and its dynamics in relation to variability in cultural patterns.[5]

Since the major purpose of this paper is to clear the ground for a more effective handling of cross-cultural data that seem relevant to a deeper understanding of the role of self-awareness in man as *culturally constituted* in different societies, I am not directly concerned with questions of personality dynamics as such. The discussion is deliberately couched at another level which, for want of a better term but without implying too many theoretical implications, might best be called 'phenomenological'. What I wish to indicate specifically is the need for some frame of reference by means of which it may be possible, in the first instance,

---

[1] S. Stanfield Sargent, *Social Psychology*, 1950, ch. 1; cf., Percival M. Symonds, *Dynamic Psychology*, 1949, ch. 20. For additional material on Baldwin see Vahan D. Sewny, *The Social Theory of James Mark Baldwin*, 1945, ch. 2, 'The Individual: Social Origin of the Self and Society.' Some of the deeper historical roots of thinking about the social nature of the self have been reviewed in Bittner, *op. cit.*
[2] Since this paper was completed in the summer of 1951, with the expectation that it would appear shortly in Vol. 4 of *Psychoanalysis and the Social Sciences*, under the general editorship of the late Dr. Geza Roheim, I have not attempted to include all relevant articles and books in the bibliography that have appeared since that date. But, as examples of a trend of interest in varying aspects of the subject dealt with by other than anthropologists, the following items are cited here: Percival M. Symonds, *The Ego and the Self*, 1951; Carl R. Rogers, *Client-Centered Therapy*, 1951; David P. Ausubel, *Ego Development and the Personality Disorders. A Developmental Approach to Psychopathology*, 1952; Harold Palmer, *The Philosophy of Psychiatry*, 1952; Soloman E. Asch, *Social Psychology*, 1952, ch. 10; Risieri Frondidi, *The Nature of the Self*, 1953.
[3] Clara Thompson, *Psychoanalysis: Evolution and Development*, 1950, p. 61.
[4] *Ibid*, p. 63. The publication date of Freud's book was 1923; the English translation appeared in 1927.
[5] See Clyde Kluckhohn, 'The Influence of Psychiatry on Anthropology in America during the Past One Hundred Years.' in J. K. Hall, G. Zilboorg and H. A. Bunker, eds., *One Hundred Years of American Psychiatry*, 1944. He points out that up to 1920, 'The dominant currents in American anthropology . . . were descriptive and historical . . . indeed, most anthropologists of the period of 1920 seem almost apologetic when they incidentally allude to individual variations. Anthropology was focused upon the standard, the average, the abstracted culture patterns. It is hardly too much to say that the prevalent trend of American anthropology was "anti-psychological".'

to view the individual in another society in terms of the psychological perspective which his culture constitutes for him and which is the integral focus of his activities, rather than to content ourselves with the perspective of an outside observer who may even pride himself on his 'objectivity'. In this way I believe we can also discern more clearly than otherwise some of the common functions that all cultures play in building up and re-enforcing self-awareness in the individual through certain basic orientations, despite wide differences in actual culture patterns.

Terminology

Before going on to a discussion of the assumptions and hypotheses that underlie the frame of reference I have in mind, it will be necessary to say a few words about terminology. It is impossible at the present time to escape entirely from the dilemma presented by the absence of any standardized usage. The only way to cut this Gordian knot is constantly to bear in mind the actual data that can be described on a phenomenological level (as, e.g., self-awareness, self-perception, self-reference by means of language, self-conception). While some writers use the terms 'self' and 'ego' as synonymous, others do not. I have chosen the term 'self' as more convenient for several reasons. In psychoanalytic usage 'ego' is used to refer to one aspect of the total personality as construed in terms of an explicit theory of personality development and functioning. To use this term in cross-cultural perspective would be confusing since it could not possibly carry the same connotation. I believe it is best to reserve this term as well as superego for technical use in a psychodynamic context. Besides this, where both the terms 'ego' and 'self' are used by some writers, 'self' is the more inclusive term. At the same time, 'self' is not ordinarily used as a synonym for 'the total personality'. This latter term, furthermore, has now assumed a more or less sophisticated usage as part of a technical psychological vocabulary however it may still be used in common speech. From the standpoint of cross-cultural inquiry it seems to me much better to make the concepts of 'self' a point of departure, rather than concepts of 'ego' or 'personality'. The term 'self', in short, does seem to connote a concept that remains closer to the phenomenological facts that reflect man's self-awareness as a generic psychological attribute. It retains the reflexive connotation that is indicated when we say that a human individual becomes an object to himself, that he identifies himself as an object among other objects in his world, that he can conceive himself not only as a whole but in terms of different parts, that he can converse with himself, and so on. Murphy's definition of the self as 'the individual as known to the individual' exemplifies this essential emphasis upon the 'reflexive mood'. It is quite true, of course, that the self known to the individual may not represent a 'true' picture from an objective point of view. But this assumes another perspective and indicates the point at which technical constructs such as ego, super-ego, etc., are necessary in order to help make analysis intelligible in *psychodynamic* terms. In cross-cultural perspective, on the other hand, and at the level of phenomenological description, the fact remains that human beings do function in terms of concepts of self which, in part, are culturally derived.

In this perspective we can seek answers to such questions as: By what cultural means is self-awareness built up in different societies? How do individuals view themselves in terms of the self that they know? What are the cultural as well as the idiosyncratic factors in their self image? What is the time span involved in the continuity of the self as culturally defined? What relation is there between varying self-concepts and differential behaviour? What is the relation of the self as culturally constituted to the needs and goals of the individual as culturally defined?

If it is possible to view the self as culturally constituted and known to the individual in the same frame of reference as we view the culturally constituted world in which the individual must act, this preliminary step may enable us to apprehend with greater clarity both the essential role of culture in relation to a generic human attribute and to define with more precision some of the constant and variable factors that structuralize the psychological field of behaviour for the individual in different societies.

GENERAL ASSUMPTIONS AND HYPOTHESES

Awareness of self is not given at birth. 'Like all other objects of experience, the self grows out of the matrix of indefiniteness which exists at the first perceptual level. It comes gradually into being as the process of differentiation goes on within the perceptual field . . . there is also considerable evidence to show that the body in all its forms is at first as strange, as unfamiliar, as unorganized as are any other perceived objects. For many months, much of it is not recognized as self.'[1] But, in the course of the socialization process self-awareness does eventually emerge so that, as Murphy says, 'one of the most important things the child ever learns as a result of social contacts is that he is a person, a self.'[2] Consequently there is a conceptual as well as a perceptual aspect of self-awareness to be taken account of in the mature individual. Self-conceptualization in a significant meaningful form undoubtedly comes later[3]

---
[1] Gardner Murphy, *Personality: A Biosocial Approach to Origins and Structure*, 1947, p. 480.
[2] Gardner Murphy, L. B. Murphy, and T. M. Newcomb, *Experimental Social Psychology: An Interpretation of Research upon the Socialization of the Individual*, rev. ed., 1937, p. 207.
[3] Symonds, *op. cit.*, 1949, pp. 71-72.

when, through mastery of speech and other aspects of his culture, the nature of the self as culturally defined becomes an integral part of the implicit assumptions that become the basis for the activities of the individual and the interpretation of his experience.

The foregoing aspects of ontogenetic development in man are, of course, universal. And since human experience occurs in a social milieu, in the sense that intimate and continuing contacts with other human beings are the major sources which mediate the influences that mould the development of the child, the self has often been referred to as a 'social product'. It might be more accurately characterized as, in part, a *cultural product*. For the acquisition and use of a particular language, the specific content that is given to an articulated world of objects that is built up *pari passu* with self-awareness and the integration of personal experience with a concept of the nature of the self as traditionally viewed, are among the necessary conditions that make possible the emergence and functioning of human awareness as a generic aspect of human personality structure. At the same time, such cultural constituents give a variable colouring to this unique psychological attribute of man.

Furthermore, the pre-eminent role which cultural factors play in the experience of self-awareness in man, highlights a related problem which only needs mention in passing. The cultural factors referred to are dependent, in turn, upon a mode of social living that requires the functioning of complicated representative processes and the existence of extrinsic symbolic systems[1] These mediate social and personal adjustment in a way that is only characteristic of man. Consequently, it seems reasonable to infer that, among other primates and the lower animals, not only the conditions that make self-conceptualization possible are lacking but, in some animals, even those conditions which in the child (and possibly in some of the anthropoid apes) permit the rudiments of a body image to develop out of perceptual experience. As Parr[2] has pointed out 'an animal without appendages cannot touch himself and thus cannot through feeling become acquainted with his own body. Though long, sinuous creatures such as snakes or eels—or long-necked ostriches and giraffes— can turn around and see a large proportion of their bodies, a more rigid animal, like the mackeral, cannot see itself at all. There are, of course, mirrors in nature and an animal may occasionally chance upon his reflection; yet he lacks the powers of deduction to realize that the reflection is a counterpart of himself. This relative ignorance of self has its social implications. Having no adequate

[1] Hallowell, 1950, *op. cit.*
[2] A. E. Parr, 'On Self-recognition and Social Reaction in Relation to Biomechanics, with a Note on Terminology.' *Ecology*, 18, 1937, pp. 321 ff.

concept of his own body, an animal can have no clear conviction that his associates are of his kind. He does not consciously recognize his companions or even his offspring as being "birds of a feather"; his mate may be only a foreign object that has a special allure.'

For a differentiated sense of self-awareness to emerge it must be possible for the individual to react to himself as an empirical object, to identify himself and refer to himself in contradistinction to other selves and things, to represent himself to himself, to appraise himself, etc. Such reflexive processes imply conceptualization and the use of symbolic means of representation and reference. Unlike some of the lower vertebrates referred to by Parr, the human individual, through language and reflective thought is able to integrate perceptions of his own body and his personal experiences with a meaningful concept of self that is the common property of other members of his society.

While common roots of a rudimentary sense of self-awareness that lie at an unconscious level in man may be paralleled in some of the higher apes it is only under the conditions characteristic of human adjustment that self-awareness becomes differentiated and assumes a functional importance in the maintainance of a social mode of life. For I believe that we must assume that the functioning of any human society is inconceivable without self-awareness, reinforced and culturally constituted by traditional beliefs about the nature of the self.

This hypothesis receives support from the universal fact that, as compared with the societies of animals lower in the scale of organic evolution, any human society is not only constituted as a social order but as a moral order as well. A moral order being one that is characterized by the fact that not only norms of conduct exist but organized or unorganized social sanctions to reinforce them, an inevitable conclusion must be drawn. The members of such an order are expected to assume moral responsibility for their conduct. Such an assumption, in turn, implies self-awareness of one's own conduct, self-appraisal of one's conduct with reference to socially recognized standards of value, some volitional control of one's own behaviour, choice of alternative lines of conduct, etc. Assumptions like these, of course, cannot be made in the case of insect societies, or the societies of infra-human primates. Without the development of self-awareness, as an intrinsic part of the socialization process, and without a concept of self that permits attitudes directed towards the self as an object to emerge and crystallize, we would not have some of the essential conditions necessary for the functioning of a human society.

Self-awareness is also basic to the discrimination and learning of the multiple roles which are required of the individual in human societies. He must have some awareness of his statuses in the social structure with reference to sex, age, etc., in order to fit into the total patterns of social interaction that maintains the socio-economic system as a going concern. If he were not aware of his roles he would not be in a position to appraise his own conduct in terms of traditional values and social sanctions.

The psychological implications of the development of self-awareness cannot be fully appreciated, however, without reference to a relative fact of equal importance. This is the concomitant emergence in the socialization process of the awareness of a contrasting world of articulated objects, experienced as 'other-than-self'. If this were not so, the human individual would be destined to remain at an infantile stage of psychological development. For this level is precisely one in which objects of an external world have not yet become clearly articulated in experience and where the beginnings of ego-centred processes have not yet developed to the point where the subject is able to perceive himself as an object in a universe that likewise contains objects other than himself. And, just as cultural factors are constitutive in the development of self-awareness, the structuralization of a world of objects other than self becomes organized, in part, in cultural terms. This is due to the fact that perception in man, as is now more evident than ever before, does not present the human being with a 'picture' of an 'objective' world which, in all its attributes, is 'there' only waiting to be perceived and completely unaffected by the experience, concepts, attitudes, needs and purposes of the perceiver. Perception is 'never an absolute revelation of "what is".'[1] On the other hand, this does not imply any denial of the existence of an objectively definable order of phenomena existentially extraneous to the human individual or even the human species. It has been stated, for example, that, 'There is some perceptual level at which exists absolute objectivity; that is, a one-to-one correspondence between experience and reality.'[2] But a satisfactory definition of this level for man as a whole is obscured by the fact that the psychological field in which human behaviour takes place is always culturally constituted and human responses are never reducible *in their entirety* to stimuli derived from an 'objective' or surrounding world of objects in the physical or geographical sense. For the world of human awareness is mediated by various symbolic devices which, through learning and experience on the part of individuals establish the concepts, discriminations, classificatory patterns, and attitudes by means of which perceptual experience is

---

[1] W. H. Ittelson and F. P. Kilpatrick, 'Experiments in Perception.' *Scientific American*, 185: 50-55, 1951; cf. A. Irving Hallowell, 'Cultural Factors in the Structuralization of Perception.' in J. H. Rohrer and M. Sherif, eds., *Social Psychology at the Crossroads*, 1951.
[2] Ittelson and Kilpatrick, *op. cit.*

personally integrated. In this way assumptions about the nature of the universe become, as it were, *a priori* constituents in the perceptual process itself. Language, of course, plays a major role both in terms of its structural characteristics as well as the potentialities inherent in narrative discourse (myths, tales, anecdotes, etc.) for the symbolic presentation of events. The graphic and plastic arts may likewise reinforce the same order through visual representation, etc.[1]

If we accept the hypothesis that awareness of self as an empirical object and awareness of objects other than self are a coordinate result of maturation and socialization in man, and that both involve cultural constituents, then we can go a step further. This categorical distinction and the polarity it implies becomes one of the fundamental axes along which the psychological field of the human individual is structured for action in every culture. This phenomenon may be thought of as generic. Where differential cultural factors enter the picture is in the varied patterns which the environmental field may take when viewed from the standpoint of the self. Since the self is also partly a cultural product the field of behaviour that is appropriate for the activities of *particular* selves in *their* world of culturally defined objects is not by any means precisely coordinate with any absolute polarity of subjectivity—objectivity that is definable.

Failure to recognize this fact appears to be the main reason why some of the descriptive data on non-literate peoples has, from the time of Tylor on, frequently been interpreted as an indication that they were unable to distinguish clearly between the 'subjective' and the 'objective'. In the *Early History of Mankind*, Tylor, for example, spoke of the life of primitive man as resembling 'a long dream'.[2] And in his *Primitive Culture*[3] he generalized to the effect that, 'Even in healthy waking life, the savage or barbarian has never learned to make that *rigid distinction* between imagination and reality, to enforce which is one of the main results of scientific education. Still less, when disordered in body and mind he sees around him phantom human forms, can he distrust the evidence of his very senses. Thus it comes to pass that throughout the lower civilization men believe, with the most vivid and intense belief, in the objective reality of the human spectres which they see in sickness, exhaustion, or excitement.' (Italics mine)

While even some early critics of Tylor, for instance Crawley,[4] found themselves unable fully to accept his statement, the major ground of the objection rested on common sense. Man's very existence depends

---

1 Hallowell, 1950, *op. cit.*; 1951, *op. cit.*
2 E. B. Tylor, *Researches into the Early History of Mankind*, 1878, p. 137, 1st ed. 1865.
3 E. B. Tylor, *Primitive Culture*, 1, 1st Amer. ed., 1874, p. 445.
4 Crawley, *op. cit.*, pp. 15-16.

113

on making *some* distinction between 'objective' and 'subjective'. He cannot nourish himself in a dream world. While this is true enough, the issue remains over-simplified if we leave it there. For this common sense answer itself assumes that there must of necessity be some easily recognized, if not sharply definable 'line' that differentiates the polar categories at issue. But it is the precise locus of this 'line' that presents a problem that has not even been satisfactorily settled by philosophers or psychologists![1]

If we take a fresh look at the ethnographic data it is quite true that the 'line' between what *we* call objectivity-subjectivity may appear somewhat blurred. This is partly due to the fact that subjectivity-objectivity cannot be adequately conceived in simple 'linear' terms but only with reference to the total pattern of the psychological field. The 'line' that we think should always be drawn precisely 'here' may not be drawn sharply at all, although it may appear somewhere else as a recognizable boundary. I believe that the basic principle involved has been stated by MacLeod. He points out that, 'subjectivity and objectivity are properties of an organized perceptual field in which points of reference are selves (subjects) and objects, and the degree of articulation in this dimension may vary greatly.' In our discussion here the 'degree of articulation' in self-object relations may be construed in terms of a structure and content definable by reference to the cultural factors directly relevant to the psychological field of the individual. By thus approaching the matter we can apprehend the actual behavioural environment of the self. Instead of making any *a priori* distinction between 'subjectivity' and 'objectivity' a matter of primary concern, on the assumption that data assignable to such categories are readily separable in the experience of individuals in other cultures, it will be assumed that, in so far as such a distinction has a meaningful character, it will receive a varying emphasis that is only intelligible in terms of the total patterning of the behaviour field of the individual. For it must not be forgotten that the empirical self and the empirical world of surrounding objects have both emerged out of a common process of maturation, socialization, and personal experience. An intelligible behavioural environment has been constituted for the individual that bears an intimate relation to the kind of being he knows himself to be and it is in this behavioural environment that he is motivated to act.

---

[1] See, e.g., Robert B. MacLeod, 'The Phenomenological Approach to Social Psychology.' *Psychological Review*, 54, 1947, p. 200. He introduces his discussion of 'the self as phenomenal datum' with a brief resume of the subjectivity-objectivity problem as viewed by philosophers and then goes on to remark: 'In recent psychology, the problem has been more frequently stated in terms of degrees of dependence on the organism — with the same resultant confusion. It becomes speedily clear that any act or experience of an organism is dependent on the organism, and that any attempt to differentiate exactly between the contributions of the organism and those of the environment is doomed. Thus, in the traditional sense, all psychological data become "subjective".'

The Behavioural Environment of Man

The concept of behavioural environment must be clearly distinguished from a concept of environment construed as being 'external' to the individual, with properties that are definable independently of the selectively determined responses that the socialization process in man always imposes. The 'objective', 'geographical' or 'physical' environment as thus conceived stands in contrast with the behavioural environment.[1] It has a limited usefulness even in the observation of animals at the subhuman level. On the other hand, the concept of behavioural environment takes account of the properties and adaptational needs of the organism in interaction with the external world as constituting the actual behavioural field in terms of which the activities of the animal are more thoroughly intelligible. Capacity or incapacity for colour vision, for instance, defines an aspect of the behavioural environment that may radically differentiate one species from another irrespective of the properties of an external world described 'objectively'. The order of psychological reality in which the animal acts is, in the first instance, a function of its organic properties as much as it is a function of the properties of the objective environment as they impinge on the organism. This is why G. H. Mead[2] insisted long ago that the organism 'determines the environment. . . . . . , the organism, then, is in a sense responsible for its environment.'

This is eminently true of man both in his unique potentialities as an

---

[1] While this distinction is by now familiar enough, there is no uniformity in the contrasting terms employed. With reference to the study of animal behavior the contrasting terms employed by J. von Uexküll, *Theoretical Biology*, 1926, appear in the English translation of his book as 'world' and 'surrounding world'; in K. Koffka, *Principles of Gestalt Psychology*, 1935, the parallel terms are 'geographical environment' and 'behavioral environment'; in Andras Angyal, 'The Experience of the Body-Self in Schizophrenia.' *Archives of Neurology and Psychiatry*, 35: 1029-1053, 1936, and *Foundations for a Science of Personality*, 1941, 'external world' and 'environment' ('The external world can be called environment only when and insofar as it is in interaction with the organism', p. 97); in Kurt Lewin, *Principles of Typological Psychology*, 1936, 'objective environment' or 'foreign hull' of the 'Life Span' and 'psychological environment' or 'environment'; Kurt Goldstein, *Human Nature in the Light of Psychopathology*, 1940, says: 'Each organism has its own characteristic milieu, that is, the milieu that is appropriate to the nature of the organism', p. 88; R. Stagner, *The Psychology of Personality*, 2nd ed., 1948, uses the term 'behavioral environment', pp. 95, 136; and Henry A. Murray, *et al*, *Explorations in Personality*, 1938, p. 166, makes reference to the problem; David Krech and Richard S. Crutchfield, *Theory and Problems of Social Psychology*, 1948, p. 38, 'the real environment of a person is that environment which would be described by an objective observer; the psychological environment is that which would be described by the experiencing person himself . . . The very same physical environment can result in radically different psychological environments for two different persons.' Philosophers have dealt with this problem too. See, e.g., Grace A. deLaguna's penetrating book on *Speech, Its Function and Development*, 1927, and John Dewey and Arthur F. Bentley, *Knowing and the Known*, 1949, pp. 271-272, where they touch upon this question at a high level of abstraction.

[2] George H. Mead, *Mind, Self and Society*, 1934, pp. 130, 100, 'Nature — the external world — is objectively there, in opposition to our experience of it, or in opposition to the individual thinker himself. Although external objects are there independent of the experiencing individual, nevertheless, they possess certain characteristics by virtue of their relation to his experiencing or to his mind, which they would not otherwise possess or apart from those relations. These characteristics are their meanings for him, or in general, for us. The distinction between physical objects or physical reality and the mental or self-conscious experience of those objects or that reality — the distinction between external or internal experience — lies in the fact that the latter is concerned with or constituted by meanings . . . ', p. 131.

organic species, and the differential behavioural environments that are created for human individuals reared in different cultural settings. Human adjustment, on the whole, cannot be simply explained as responses engendered by factors attributable to a physical environment constituted for the individual in the socialization process. It may even be argued that human potentialities and a cultural mode of life *precludes* any reductive interpretations focused upon the outside physical world alone. Even the 'natural resources' of any human society only become 'resources' when, in a particular culture, the knowledge and technology necessary for their exploitation is developed. The same principle applies to classes of objects such as the 'heavenly bodies' that we label as 'natural' and which, following scientific procedures of observation, we find located in physical space and subject to mechanical laws. But the sun, moon, thunder, wind are not 'natural' phenomena in this sense in the culturally constituted behavioural environment of all peoples. Our contemporary categorization is derived from highly specialized scientific investigations and a mode of reasoning that is *only* typical of recent phases of western culture. It is sometimes forgotten in comparing other cultures with our own that: 'From the time of Thales down through the period we broadly call "the Renaissance", a majority of philosophers taught and most men believed that the world was *animate*. It lived and flourished as did man, and like man, was susceptible of decay, even of death.' It was only during the 17th century that 'this conception gave way to the idea of the world as *mechanism*—a world machine, no longer animate, but mechanically responsive to the "laws of Nature"[1] Consequently, while the 'objective' properties of 'natural' objects upon which we are accustomed to center our scientific attention may be equally perceptible in certain respects to individuals whose behavioural environment is structured differently from ours, at the same time such properties may be much less salient for them.

Evidence from human cultures everywhere also indicates that man typically responds to objects in his *behavioural environment* that to the sophisticated mind are symbolically constituted, i.e., spiritual beings of various classes. Such objects, clearly conceptualized and reified, may occupy a high rank in the behavioural environment although from a sophisticated Western point of view they are sharply distinguishable from the natural objects of the physical environment. However, the nature of such objects is no more fictitious, in a psychological sense, than the concept of the self. Consequently, culturally reified objects in the

---

[1] Marjorie Hope Nicolson, *The Breaking of the Circle. Studies in the Effect of the 'New Science' upon Seventeenth Century Poetry*, 1950, p. xviii; cf. R. G. Collingwood, *Idea of Nature*, 1945, and the remarks of J. H. Randall, 'The Nature of Naturalism.' in Yervant H. Krikorian, ed., *Naturalism and the Human Spirit*, 1944, especially pp. 355-356.

behavioural environment may have functions that can be shown to be directly related to the needs, motivations and goals of the self. Symbolically represented, such objects are integral parts of the psychological field of the individual and must be considered as relevant variables because they can be shown to affect actual behaviour.[1]

Consequently, I believe it both preferable and clarifying for us to speak of the environment in which man lives as a culturally constituted behavioural environment, rather than to say that man lives in a 'social' or 'cultural' environment, without further analysis. This is particularly the case if we seek for deeper behavioural understanding. It is of considerable importance in this connection to note that the same assumptions that have invalidated the usefulness of the concept of 'objective' or 'physical' environment find their logical parallels in the naive use of such terms as 'social' or 'cultural' environment. For it is likewise assumed that a social or cultural environment can be defined in terms of properties or structures that are, in the first instance, conceived independently of the individuals they are said to environ. Without further analysis it is implied, if not explicitly stated, that this environment, as described by some objective observer, is the actual environment to which the individual responds. This leads to what MacLeod has called the 'sociological bias' which, he points out, is somewhat analagous to the 'Stimulus-Receptor bias' that once prevailed very widely in the study of perception. 'This bias in its most common form', writes MacLeod, 'involves the acceptance of the structures and processes of society as defined by the sociologist as the true coordinates for the specification of behavior and experience. From this point of view, e.g., the church or the political party in which the individual possesses membership, is regarded as an institution of society, possessing the manifold properties and functions which a many-sided sociological investigation reveals, rather than as the church or political party as it is apprehended and reacted to by the individual. The process of social adjustment, of socialization or of attitude formation thus becomes defined in terms of a set of norms which have reality for the scientific observer, but not necessarily for the individual concerned.'[2]

The traditional approach of cultural anthropology, having as one of its primary goals a reliable account of differential modes of life found among

[1] It is unnecessary to invoke any novel principle to cover such data among 'primitive' peoples. Referring to an even broader range of phenomena MacLeod, 1947, op. cit., points out that, 'Purely fictitious objects, events and relationships can be just as truly determinants of our behavior as are those which are anchored in physical reality.'
[2] MacLeod, 1947, op. cit., pp. 198-199; cf. the systematic attempt by Roger C. Barker and Herbert F. Wright, 'The Psychological Habitat of Raymond Birch.' in J. H. Rohrer and M. Sherif, eds., Social Psychology at the Crossroads, 1951, and Methods in Psychological Ecology, 1951, to measure the parameters of psychological laws for different conditions of life in their studies in ecological psychology.

the peoples of the world, has not been directly concerned with the behaviour of individuals. It has been culture-centered, rather than behaviour-centered. In consequence, it has been found convenient to organize the presentation of the descriptive ethnographic data collected in terms of a more or less conventional series of topics: language, religion, technology, social organization, etc. No matter how reliable such data are, or whatever their value for comparative and analytic studies of *culture*, of necessity the material is presented from the standpoint of an outside observer. Presented to us in this form, these cultural data do not easily permit us to apprehend, in an integral fashion, the most significant and meaningful aspects of the world of the individual as experienced by him and in terms of which he thinks, is motivated to act, and satisfies his needs. The language of a people, as objectively described and analyzed in terms of its formal categories, is not the language that exists for the individual who uses it as a means of communication, in reflective thought, as a mode of verbal self-expression, etc. He may, indeed, be quite unconscious of its objective characteristics. It is an integral part of himself and his world. It is neither 'objective' nor 'subjective'. The same holds true, in principle, for other cultural phenomena when viewed from the standpoint of the individual within his cultural setting. Because culture can be objectively described and, for certain purposes, treated as if it were a *sui generis* phenomenon, it is sometimes implied, or even argued that it is in fact phenomenologically autonomous.[1] To do so is to misunderstand totally the basic conditions of human psychological adjustment. Any inner-outer dichotomy, with the human skin as a boundary, is psychologically irrelevant. As Murray points out with reference to this problem considered ontogenetically— 'much of what is now *inside* the organism was once *outside*. For these reasons, the organism and its milieu must be considered together, a single creature—environment interaction being a convenient short unit for psychology.'[2]

[1] Leslie A. White, 'Ethnological Theory.' in Roy Woods Sellars, V. T. McGill, Marvin Faber, eds., *Philosophy of the Future*, 1949, p. 368, says that culture is ' . . . a specific and concrete mechanism employed by a particular animal organism in adjusting to its environment. It is the mechanism that articulates man with the earth and cosmos. It is therefore something describable in zoological, material, mechanical terms. Yet we have only to browse through the literature to discover how often it is conceived otherwise.' And in 'The Individual and the Culture Process.' in *Centennial, American Association for the Advancement of Science*, 1950, p. 75, 'Culture is . . . a thermo-dynamic system in a mechanical sense. Culture grows in all its aspects — ideological, sociological, and technological when and as the amount of energy harnessed per capita per year is increased, and as the means of expending this energy are improved. Culture is thus a dynamic system capable of growth.' And *ibid*, p. 80, 'Relative to the culture process the individual is neither creator nor determinant, he is merely a catalyst and a vehicle of expression.' For a contrary view, see David Bidney, 'Human Nature and the Cultural Process.' *American Anthropologist*, 49: 375-396, 1947, and Melford E. Spiro, 'Culture and Personality: The Natural History of a False Dichotomy.' *Psychiatry*, 14: 19-46, 1951.
[2] Murray, *op. cit.*, p. 40. More recently E. C. Tolman (see Talcott Parsons and Edward A. Shils, eds., *Toward a General Theory of Action*, 1951, has remarked that 'psychology is in large part a study of the internalization of society and of culture within the individual human actor.' Cf. T. M. Newcomb, *Social Psychology*, 1950, p. 6, with respect to the same point and the more elaborated exposition by Spiro, *op. cit.*

The concept of behavioural environment enables us to take cognizance of this fact, to appraise and re-order culturally given data in order to bring into focus the actual structure of the psychological field of the individual. At the same time it enables us to approximate more closely to an 'inside' view of a culture, the kind of naive orientation we unconsciously assume towards our own culture, but which is so difficult to achieve in the case of another. More specifically, viewing a culture from the 'inside' can best be achieved if we organize our data in a manner that permits us, as far as possible, to assume the outlook of the self in its behavioural environment.

BASIC ORIENTATIONS PROVIDED BY CULTURE

From this standpoint culture may be said to play a constitutive role in the psychological adjustment of the individual to his world. The human individual must be provided, among other things, with certain basic orientations in order to act intelligibly in the world he apprehends. Such orientations are basic in the sense that they are peculiar to a human level of adjustment. They all appear to revolve around man's capacity for self-awareness. If it be assumed that the functioning of *human* societies depends upon this psychological fact, among others, it is not difficult to understand why all human cultures must provide the individual with basic orientations that are among the necessary conditions for the development, reinforcement and effective functioning of self-awareness. It is these orientations, it seems to me, that may be said to structure the core of the behavioural environment of the self in any culture. Whereas cultural means and content may vary widely, common instrumental functions can be discerned.

1 Self-Orientation

Animals below man, for instance, even though they may be highly capable of acting in a complex behavioural environment that includes many classes of objects other than themselves, including other animals of their species, do not have to become self-oriented, in order to function adequately in a social group. On the other hand, one of the common functions of culture is to provide various means of self-orientation for the human being.

It is quite generally recognized that language plays an essential role in this self-orientation. But only certain features of language have been emphasized, to the exclusion of others, while the generic function of all languages in providing linguistic means of self-orientation, has not been sufficiently stressed.

119

Despite wide variations in linguistic structure Boas called attention years ago to the fact that, 'the three personal pronouns—I, thou, and he—occur in all human languages' and emphasized that, 'the underlying idea of these pronouns is the clear distinction between the self as speaker, the person or object spoken to, and that spoken of.'[1] If this be accepted, we have an unequivocal indication that languages all have a common socio-psychological function. They provide the human individual with a linguistic means of self-other orientation in all contexts of inter-personal verbal communications.

Although we do not have parallel investigation in other societies, in western culture we have had a number of studies which indicate the mastery of our system of personal and possessive pronouns at a very early age. According to Gesell,[2] for example, the child begins to use self-reference words—mine, me, you and I, in that order, at two years, whereas at eighteen months 'self' and 'not self' are not clearly differentiated.

As compared with the mastery of a pronominal system we know very little about the acquisition and use of kinship terms ontogenetically. In many non-literate societies such terms are among the major linguistic means that orient the individual in a self-other dimension in relation to his roles in the social order.

Then there is the universal phenomenon of personal names. These are related to self-orientation in so far as they are personal and unique. They serve as a linguistic device for self-identification and unequivocal identification of the self by others. The fact that, in some cultures, the individual knows his name although it may not be customary for him to use it freely for self-identification indicates the need for more detailed studies of the variable aspect of personal naming in relation to self-orientation. But it seems to me that the ubiquitous fact of personal naming must be considered to be in the same functional category as the pronominal pattern.[3]

In this connection it would also be interesting to know more about the role which personal names play in the sexual orientation of the self. Certainly in many cultures, although how widely spread the custom is I do not know, the panel of names available for boys is not the same for girls. Names are sex-linked. Under these circumstances knowing one's

[1] Franz Boas, The Mind of Primitive Man, 1911, rev. ed., 1938.
[2] A. Gesell, The Psychology of Early Growth, 1938.
[3] Muzafer Sherif, The Psychology of Social Norms, 1936, p. 174, quotes W. McDougall as saying that one's name 'becomes a handle by the aid of which he gets hold of himself and acquires facility in thinking and speaking of himself as an agent, a striver, a desirer, a refuser.'

own name is equivalent to knowing one's own sex. Awareness of one's sexual status is likewise implied in the use of certain kinship terms in many cultures. So, in acquiring the proper use of kinship terms the child likewise becomes sexually oriented. There are other aspects of language that should be considered in relation to self-orientation but these illustrations must suffice.[1]

Whatever the idiosyncratic content of the self-image may be and whatever weight it may be given in psychodynamic analysis, the content of the self-image is, in part, a culturally constituted variable.[2] While one of the constant functions of all cultures, therefore, is to provide a concept of self along with other means that promote self-orientation, the individuals of a given society are self-oriented in terms of a provincial content of the self-image.

This by no means implies that we must expect to find a single linguistic term or a concept even roughly equivalent to 'self' to 'ego' or 'soul' in all cultures. The absence of any such single term and the correlative fact that the self-image may present subtleties foreign to our mode of thinking is one of the reasons such a topic, approached from outside a culture, poses some inherent difficulties. On the other hand, there are analogies familiar to the anthropologist. Art, religion and law, for example, have been investigated in societies in which abstract terms for such phenomena do not exist. It also has been found, that too rigid *a priori* definitions and concepts, consciously or unconsciously modeled after those of our own intellectual tradition, may even lead to a denial that comparable phenomena exist in other cultures, only because the phenomena observed fail to meet all the requirements of the definitions and concepts employed by the observer. In any case, we must not expect to find concepts of the self among non-literate peoples clearly articulated for us. To a certain extent it is necessary to approach the whole subject naively, to pursue it obliquely from different angles, to attack the conceptual core of the problem in terms of its pragmatic implications and in the full light of related concepts in a single cultural matrix. We already

---

1 George A. Pettitt, 'Primitive Education in North America.' *Univ. of Calif. Publ. in Amer. Arch and Ethn.*, 13, 1946, ch. 6, has discussed other functions of names among the North American Indians, such as 'stimulating self-development and achievement through ridicule, as a type of prestige reward for specific achievements or general good behavior and popularity; as the principle medium for transference of ready-made personalities.'
2 Donald Snygg and Arthur W. Combs, *Individual Behavior: A new Frame of Reference for Psychology*, 1949, p. 82, appear to be among the few who have given this fact explicit recognition. They write: 'To this point we have spoken of the development of the phenomenal self only in terms of the child's reactions to his physical surroundings. As a matter of fact, the culture into which the individual is born is a far more potent factor in the development of the phenomenal self. While the child is born into a world of physical objects, even these are subjected to the particular interpretations of the culture so that the phenomenal self becomes overwhelmingly the product of the culture. For most of us, the phenomenal self we develop is a direct outgrowth of the cultural matrix of our parents and early guardians.'

know from available data, for instance, that such concepts as reincarnation, metamorphosis, and the notion that, under certain circumstances the 'soul' may leave the body, must be relevant to variations in the self-image which different peoples have. But we know much less about the way in which such concepts become psychologically significant for the individual in relation to his motivations, goals and life adjustment.

2 Object-Orientation

A *second* function of all cultures is the orientation of the self to a diversified world of objects in its behavioural environment, discriminated, classified and conceptualized with respect to attributes which are culturally constituted and symbolically mediated through language. The role of language in object-orientation is as vital as in self-orientation. The late Ernst Cassirer laid special emphasis upon this point. 'Language', he said, 'does not enter a world of completed objective perceptions only to add to individually given and clearly delimited objects, one in relation to the other, "names" which will be purely external and arbitrary signs; rather, it is itself a mediator in the formation of objects. It is, in a sense, the mediator par excellence, the most important and most precise instrument for the conquest and the construction of a true world of objects.'[1] It is this objectifying function of speech that enables man to live and act in an articulated world of objects that is psychologically incomparable with that of any other creature.

Object orientation likewise provides the ground for an intelligible interpretation of events in the behavioural environment on the basis of traditional assumptions regarding the nature and attributes of the objects involved, and implicit or explicit dogmas regarding the 'causes' of events. A cosmic and metaphysical orientation of the self supplies a conceptual framework for action in an orderly rather than a chaotic universe. It is not necessary, of course, that the individual be aware of the underlying metaphysical principles involved, any more than it is necessary that he be aware of the grammatical principles of the language that he speaks. But the former are as open to investigation as the latter. It is for this reason that considerable confusion has been created by the application of the natural-supernatural category to non-literate peoples in approaching their religion or world view.[2] This dichotomy simply reflects the outcome

---

[1] Ernst Cassirer, 'Le Langage et la construction du monde des objets.' *Journal de la Psychologie Normale et Pathologique*, 30, 1932, p. 23, reprinted in H. Delacroix, et al., *La Psychologie du Language*, 1933.
[2] David Bidney, *Theoretical Anthropology*, 1953, pp. 165-166, emphasizes the point that the fact that 'natives do differentiate between secular, everyday experience and sacred, superhuman tales and traditions about gods and spirits, since they have special terms to designate the different categories of narrative and tradition . . . does not mean that they distinguish clearly between the sphere of the natural and that of the supernatural, since gods and spirits are just as much a part of the order of 'nature' as are men and animals. The dichotomy of the natural and supernatural implies a scientific epistemology and critical, metaphysical sophistication which must not be assumed without reliable evidence.'

of metaphysical speculation in latter-day thought in western culture. Instead of assuming *a priori* that this dichotomy is really meaningful in other cultures, it might be more profitable to discover the metaphysical principles that actually exist. At any rate, if we assume the outlook of the self as culturally oriented in a behavioural environment with cosmic dimensions and implicit metaphysical principles, a great deal of what is ordinarily described as 'religion' is seen to involve the attitudes, needs, goals, and affective experience of the self in interaction with certain classes of objects in the behavioural environment. These classes of objects are typically *other* selves—spiritual beings, deities, ancestors. The relation of the self to them may, indeed, be characterized by the same patterns that apply to interpersonal relations with other human beings. Among other things, the individual must be quite as aware of his status in relation to other-than-human beings, as he is with respect to his human associates. He must learn to play his proper role in response to their roles as culturally defined.

In other words, the 'social' relations of the *self* when considered in its *total* behavioural environment may be far more inclusive than ordinarily conceived. The self in its relations with other selves may transcend the boundaries of social life as objectively defined.[1] This is a fact of some psychological importance since it is relevant to the needs, motivations and goals of individuals under certain circumstances. At the same time, the social relations of the self in the more inclusive sense, may not be directly relevant in a sociological frame of reference where the aim of the observer is to define the lineaments of 'social structure' in the usual sense. Nevertheless, it should not be overlooked that the social structure, defined as a result of such investigations, is not the phenomenon apprehended by the self. Nor may it represent the most salient aspects, for the individual, of the greater society of selves apprehended in the behavioural environment. In some cultures the social orientation of the self may be so constituted that relations with deceased ancestors or other-than-human selves become much more crucial for an understanding of the most vital needs and goals of the individual, than do interpersonal relations with other human beings.

3 Spatio-temporal Orientation

Since the self must be prepared for action, a *third* basic orientation that all cultures must provide is some kind of spatio-temporal[2] frame of

---

[1] From a psychological point of view this is by no means a peculiarity of primitive peoples. Krech and Crutchfield, *op. cit.*, p. 471, point out that 'our social world does not consist only of "real" people but also characters of literature, history and fable.'
[2] Gibson, *op. cit.*, p. 157, emphasizes the fact that 'the abstractions which we call space and time are not as distinct as they have been assumed to be, for space cannot be apprehended except in time.'

reference. Animals other than man have to find their way about in space but they do not have to be oriented in an acquired schema that involves the conscious use of culturally constituted reference points and the awareness of one's position in space.[1] Just as a culture provides the means that enable the individual to identify himself and to define his position with reference to his behaviour in a scheme of social relations, it likewise provides him with the means for defining his position in a spatial frame of reference that transcends immediate perceptual experience.[2] Getting lost or becoming spatially disoriented is apt to be an emotionally distressing situation for an individual in any culture.[3] The capacity to move freely and intelligently from place to place, to conceptualize the spatial location of one's destination and to be able to reach it, as well as to be able to return back home, is a commonplace of everyday human living.

Just as personal names mediate self-identification and personal reference, in the same way names for places and significant topographical features are a universal linguistic means for discriminating and representing stabilized points in space which enables the self to achieve spatial orientation. Place names become focal points in the organized directional schema made available to the individual through knowledge and experi-

---

1 The remarkable spatial mobility and directional orientation of bees described by Von Frisch, for example, in no way depends upon the self-awareness and self-reference that we assume in man. The mechanics of their spatial orientation are of a completely different order. G. Revez, 'The Problem of Space with Particular Emphasis on Specific Sensory Space.' *American Journal of Psychology*, 50: 429-444, 1937, p. 434n, points out that 'although the experience of space and perception of objects or animals seems to agree with that of our own, the theory of a general phenomenal agreement between animal and human perception is highly disputable from a logical and theoretical angle . . . Because of lack of language and ideas, all animals must have a different space concept . . . their objects must be perceived in a fundamentally different configuration and order than ours . . . This must be the case regardless of their particular stage of evolutionary development and their biological relationship to man.' Muzafer Sherif and Hadley Cantril, *The Psychology of Ego-Involvement*, 1947, pp. 93-94, while accepting William Stern's emphasis upon the fact that 'the personal world of every individual becomes centered around himself', and that 'in making judgments of "space" and "time" the individual inevitably uses himself as a central point of reference', do not emphasize the dependence of the individual upon cultural means in order to achieve spatio-temporal orientation.
2 With reference to locomotion, Gibson, *op. cit.*, pp. 229-230, differentiates a simple type, which is 'oriented directly toward the goal' and where 'the body movement is a function of optical stimulation which yields the perception of a visual world with the goal-object in it' from a more advanced form which involves the 'act of going to an object or place beyond the range of vision.' In the latter case 'one must know both where he is going and where he is now. It requires, over and above the visual world, a frame of reference or a typographical schema. The individual must perceive the space which surrounds him on all sides . . . and must also apprehend the world beyond the visible scene — the layout of the building, of the city and its streets, of the region, and of the country with its highways and cities. He is then said to be oriented in space — actually, in a series of more and more inclusive spaces of which the most general is the astronomical universe. The conception of an objective world, independent of the standpoint of any observer, rests upon this type of orientation.' Thus, a culturally constituted orientation in a world of objects other than self must be integrated with a spatial orientation of the self that provides a frame of reference for activities in this world. Redfield, 1952, *op. cit.*, p. 31, remarks: 'I suppose that every world view includes some spatial and temporal dimensions, some conceptions of place and past and future. Man is necessarily oriented to a universe of extension and duration.'
3 The anxiety that may be precipitated by spatial disorientation is dramatically illustrated by the Balinese cases cited by Jane Belo, 'The Balinese Temper.' *Character and Personality*, 4: 120-146, 1935, reprinted in Douglas C. Haring, ed., *Personal Character and Cultural Milieu*, rev. ed., 1948. I have discussed the cultural constituents of spatial orientation among the Ojibwa in a chapter that will appear in a volume of my selected papers, *Culture and Experience*, to be published in 1954 by the University of Pennsylvania Press.

ence. Such stable points of reference are not only a guide to action; once known, they can be mentally manipulated in relational terms at a more abstract level, as in maps, for example. Place names likewise become integrated with the temporal orientation of the self. For self-awareness implies that the individual not only knows where he *is*, but where he *was* at some previous moment in time, or where he expects to be in the *future*. The identification of the self with a given locus—be it a dwelling, a camp, a village, or what not—also depends upon the linguistic discrimination of place. Other selves, living or dead, and selves of an other-than-human category likewise can be assigned a characteristic spatial locale through the device of place-naming. Place-naming is another common denominator of cultures.

Orientation in time is coordinate with spatial orientation and, however simple the means or crude the temporal intervals discriminated may be, the self is temporally as well as spatially oriented in all cultures.[1] Temporal disorientation is abnormal in any culture if judged in relation to the traditional temporal schema.[2] Of course in a culture without names for days of the week self-orientation in time is not possible in terms of this particular schema. On the other hand, if 'moons' are named it is assumed that the individual knows his 'moons'.

What we know all too little about is the earliest phase of temporal orientation in the child—a sensed relationship of experienced events in time—at a period before traditional cultural concepts are learned and consciously employed, and even before a concept of self is fully developed. L. K. Frank directed attention to this problem many years ago, indicating among other things how what we have here called motivational and normative orientations become integrated with the beginnings of temporal orientation and a growing sense of self at an early age:

Here then begins the characteristically human career of man who, not content to be ruled by hunger and other physiological functions, transforms them so that hunger becomes appetite, bladder and rectal pressures become occasions for modesty, cleanliness, etc. and later sex becomes love. This transformation of naive behavior into conduct involves the acceptance of values, or, more specifically, necessitates value be-

[1] Murdock, 1945, *op. cit.*, lists calendars among the common denominators of culture, and Kenneth E. Bok, *The Acceptance of Histories: Toward a Perspective for Social Science*, MS, writes: The historical-mindedness of men as a trait that distinguishes them from other animals and the fact that no society can function without reference to the past are points that are reiterated in current literature.'
[2] In our culture temporal orientation is of diagnostic value in mental disorders. A person so disoriented as to be unable to give the year, month, or day of the week, is almost sure to be a case of amentia, senility, or to be psychotic. See, e.g., G. H. Kirby, *Guides for History Taking and Clinical Examination of Psychiatric Cases*, 1921, p. 69, and Paul Schilder, 'Image and Appearance of the Human Body.' *Psychological Monographs*, 4, 1935.

havior and time perspectives wherein we see the individual responding to present, immediate situation-events (intraorganic or environmental) as point-events in a sequence the later or more remote components of which are the focus of that conduct . . . If we let A represent one of the immediately impinging situation-events facing an individual, either within his organism or in the environment, it is clear that A is the first of a sequence A, B, C, D . . . N. When the infant responds naively to A (physiological need) by a physiological process (evacuation) he behaves organically and directly. As training in toilet habits proceeds, he learns to recognize A (the internal pressure) as a preparatory signal or behavior cue, not a stimulus to immediate releasing behavior; the bladder pressure A now becomes the first term in a sequence A, B, C, D . . . N, leading to the appropriate later term N which may be the household toilet. This response to A in terms of its consequences then becomes the prototype of value behavior with an almost infinite regression toward the future, for again we see that N (voiding at a specified place, in privacy, and keeping the clothes dry) is itself a first term or A in another sequence of holding or earning the much needed security of parental approval and love and a wider social approval and acceptance by teachers, schoolmates, and so on.

What looks like a simple, childish achievement of control and elimination assumes, upon reflection, a large significance for understanding human conduct and the question of values within a time perspective. As will be realized the various time perspectives of a culture give the dimenisons of the values that are operating in the lives of those living in that culture by specifying the conduct that must be observed in response to each situation, wherein that immediate situation is to be seen as instrumental to a more remote or deferred situation.[1]

The deeper psychological implications of the relation between temporal orientation and the emergence and functioning of self-awareness in the human being is nowhere more clearly apparent than in the integral connections between memory processes and the development of a feeling of self-identity. This integral relation is one of the necessary conditions required if any sense of *self-continuity* is to become salient. Human beings maintain awareness of self-continuity and personal identity in time through the recall of past experiences that are identified with the self-image. If I cannot remember, or recall at will, experiences of an hour ago, or yesterday, or last year that I readily identify as *my* experiences, I cannot maintain an awareness of self-continuity in time. At the lowest functional level, however, recall neither implies volition nor any capacity

---

[1] Frank, *op. cit.*, pp. 341-342.

to organize the memory images of past events in any temporal schema. Even if we should grant animals below man a very high capacity for recall, without some symbolically based and culturally derived means, it is impossible to organize *what* is recalled in relation to a temporal schema on the one hand and a self-image on the other. Consequently, in order for a sense of self-continuity to become a functionally significant factor in self-awareness, the human individual must be temporally oriented as well as self-oriented. If we wish to postulate a sense of self-continuity as a generic human trait, a culturally constituted temporal orientation must be assumed as a necessary condition. This seems to be a reasonable hypothesis in view of the fact that self-identification would have no functional value in the operation of a human social order if, at the same time, it was not given a temporal dimension. *Who* I am, both to myself and others, would have no stability. It would make it impossible to assume that patterns of interpersonal relations could operate in terms of a continuing personnel. From this standpoint, I believe it can be deduced that psychopathological phenomena that affect the maintenance of personal identity and continuity must of necessity be considered abnormal in any society.[1] For in order to play my designated roles I not only have to be aware of who I am today, but be able to relate my past actions to both past and future behavior. If I am unable to do this there is no way I can assume moral responsibility for my conduct. I am not quite the same person today as I was yesterday if the continuity of my experience is constricted through the impairment of memory or, as in the case of some individuals with 'multiple' personalities, different sets of memory images become functional as a 'new' personality manifests itself. Fugue states, in some instances, are unconsciously motivated devices for breaking the sense of self-continuity or disconnecting the self from past actions felt to be morally reprehensible.

There is still another important aspect of the relation between the temporal orientation of the self and the maintenance of self-continuity. This is the time-span of recalled experiences that become self-related. Cultural variables are involved here. What we find in certain instances is this: Not only is a continuity of self assumed, self-related experiences are given a retrospective temporal span that far transcends the limits beyond which we know reliable accounts of personal experience can be recalled. The earliest experiences of the human being cannot become self-related and recalled as such because the infant has not yet become

[1] See M. Abeles and P. Schilder, 'Psychogenic Loss of Personal Identity: Amnesia.' *Archives of Neurological Psychiatry*, 34: 587-604, 1935; G. W. Kisker and G. W. Knox, 'The Psychopathology of the Ego System.' *Journal of Nervous and Mental Diseases*, 46: 66-71, 1943; Sherif and Cantril, *op. cit.*, ch. 12, 'Breakdown of the Ego.'; and David Rappaport, *Emotions and Memory*, 1942, p. 197ff, according to whom Abeles and Schilder 'were the first to recognize that the loss of personal identity is a specific disturbance'.

an object to himself, nor has he incorporated any working temporal schema which makes possible the differentiation of experiences of this period from later ones. Besides this, past experience as recalled implies a spatial as well as a temporal frame of reference. Dudycha and Dudycha, as a result of systematic investigation, state that the 'average earliest memory is somewhere in the fourth year.'[1] But one of my Objibwa informants referred to memories in his mother's womb (spatial locale), and he knew *when* he would be born (consciousness of *future* time).[2]

We also are aware, from modern observation, of the distortion of early memories that can occur through repressive amnesia,[3] and the phenomena of pseudo-memory. One instance of the latter, in the form of *déjà vue*, turned up while I was collecting Rorschach protocols among the northern Ojibwa. Having been presented with Card I this subject hesitated a long while before he would say anything at all. Then he went into a long disquisition, the main point of which involved the statement that when he was a baby and still on a cradle board (i.e., long before he was able to talk) he had once looked up through the smoke hole of the wigwam and seen exactly what he now saw before him on the Rorschach card.

Facts such as these indicate plainly enough that self-related experience as recalled need not be true, in order to be psychologically significant for the individual or his associates. Since reliable knowledge regarding the vagaries of memory is such a recent acquisition in our own culture, it is easy to understand how, through the long span of human history, the door has been left wide open to varying emphases in different cultures upon the nature and the time span of past experiences that can be self-related.[4] Although less directly related to the self, there is the correlative problem of how far it is possible for any reliable knowledge of past historical events to exist in communities of non-literate peoples. Events of the past, whether connected with the self or not, cannot assume conceptual reality unless they are incorporated in the psychological field of present awareness. This is only made possible through symbolic means;

---

[1] G. J. Dudycha and M. M. Dudycha, 'Childhood Memories: A Review of the Literature.' *Psychological Bulletin*, 38, 1941, p. 681.
[2] The emphasis laid upon the recall of prenatal memories, memories at conception, and even memories of deaths in previous incarnations by those practicing dianetics, is an interesting anomaly in American culture. In one case a patient reported what her mother said while she was still an unborn foetus. See J. A. Winter, *A Doctor's Report on Dianetics. Theory and Therapy.* Intro. by Frederick Perls, M.D., 1952.
[3] Sometimes these may assume a symbolic form and be derived from actual events of a previous period even though the individual is not conscious of them as recalled memories. Freud discovered early in his investigations that what he first took to be authentic early memories were not so in fact.
[4] Further inquiries are needed. How widely prevalent in non-literate cultures is the idea that memories from early infancy or the pre-natal period can be recalled? What is their content and under what conditions is the individual motivated to recall them? Where the notion of reincarnation is present, answers to the same questions might be sought.

past events have to be represented in some fashion in order to become salient. Even though some temporal orientation that permits the ordering of past events in sequence may exist, with no written records or other checks, knowledge of such events can only be communicated through the recalled memories of individuals,[1] and the repetition of narratives that embody these. And, just as retrospective self-related experience may be culturally defined as reliable, even though it may date from the womb or earliest infancy, in the same way myth and legend may be accepted as 'history'. Thus a temporal dimension, transcending the life span of living individuals, can be given to significant events that pertain to the life histories of mythological as well as human figures of importance in the traditional beliefs of a people.

One common type of past experience that may become particularly important when integrated with certain concepts of the nature of the self is dreaming. Once we recognize the fact that self-awareness is a generic human trait, that a self-related experience of the past depends upon a memory process (recall) and that the human individual is, at the same time exposed to some culturally constituted self-image, there is nothing psychologically abstruse about the incorporation of dream experience into the category of self-related experiences. Self-awareness being as phenomenally real in dreams as in waking life there is no inherent discontinuity on this score. Assuming an autonomous soul separable from the body under certain conditions, as in sleep, it is possible to interpret dream experiences as personal experiences, even though in retrospect, the experiences undergone by the self in this phase may far transcend the self-related experiences of waking life in unusual spatial mobility, or in other ways. This by no means implies, however, that the individual ignores or is unaware of any distinction between self-related experience when awake and when asleep.[2] A sense of self-continuity conceptually integrated with a self-image, provides the necessary connecting link. Dream experiences become integrated through the same kind of memory process through which other experiences become self-related. But this integration of experience from both sources does mean that the content

---

[1] Oscar Oppenheimer, ' "I" and Time: A Study in Memory.' *Psychological Review*, 54, 1947, p. 223, points out that 'we are able to experience the past in a symbolic way because past is passed present. It is exactly the same as our present moment with the all-important qualification that it is not real. It could be real only if it was the present moment. There is no past as a reality, there is a past only as a hypothesis. Ah, to be sure, of high probability. The belief that things happened the way we visualized them in an act of memory is so strong in most cases that we do not consider the possibility of a mistake for a moment, and therefore we are shocked when in some cases we find out later that we were mistaken and things did not happen in the way we "remembered" them.'
[2] J. S. Lincoln, *The Dream in Primitive Cultures*, 1936, p. 28, e.g., remarks that 'Tylor and early anthropologists used to speak of the primitives' inability to distinguish dream and reality. Although cases of such confusion do occur, the description is not altogether accurate as a universal generalization . . . Most cases show that in spite of regarding the experiences of the dream as real, primitives do distinguish between dreams and the perceptions of waking experience, yet often the dream experience is regarded as having a greater value than an actual experience.'

of self-related experiences may, in different cultures, assume qualitatively distinctive attributes.

A dream of one of my Ojibwa informants will serve to document several of the foregoing points in a concrete form:

As I was going about hunting, with my gun in my hand, I came to a lake. A steep rock rose from the lake shore. I climbed up this rock to have a look across the lake. I thought I might sight a moose or some ducks. When I glanced down towards the water's edge again, I saw a man standing by the rock. He was leaning on his paddle. A canoe was drawn up to the shore and in the stern sat a woman. In front of her rested a cradle board with a baby in it. Over the baby's face was a piece of green mosquito netting. The man was a stranger to me but I went up to him. I noticed that he hung his head in a strange way. He said, 'You are the first man [human being] ever to see me. I want you to come and visit me.' So I jumped into this canoe. When I looked down I noticed that it was all of one piece. There were no ribs or anything of the sort, and there was no bark covering. I do not know what it was made of.

On the northwest side of the lake there was a very high steep rock. The man headed directly for this rock. With one stroke of the paddle we were across the lake. The man threw his paddle down as we landed on a flat shelf of rock almost level with the water. Behind this the rest of the rock rose steeply before us. But when his paddle touched the rock this part opened up. He pulled the canoe in and we entered a room in the rock. It was not dark there, although I could see no holes to let in any light. Before I sat down the man said, 'See, there is my father and my mother.' The hair of these old people was as white as a rabbit skin. I could not see a single black hair on their heads. After I had seated myself I had a chance to look around. I was amazed at all the articles I saw in the room—guns, knives, pans and other trade goods. Even the clothing these people wore must have come from a store. Yet I never remembered having seen this man at a trading post. I thought I would ask him, so I said, 'You told me that I was the first human being you had seen. Where, then, did you buy all of these articles I see?' To this he replied, 'Have you never heard people talking about *pagitcigun* [sacrifices]? These articles were given to us. That is how we got them.' Then he took me into another room and told me to look around. I saw the meat of all kinds of animals—moose, caribou, deer, ducks. I thought to myself. This man must be a wonderful hunter, if he has been able to store up all this meat. I thought it very strange that this man had never met any other Indians in all his travels. Of course, I did not know that

I was dreaming. Everything was the same as I had seen it with my eyes open. When I was ready to go I got up and shook hands with the man. He said, 'Anytime that you wish to see me, this is the place where you will find me.' He did not offer to open the door for me so I knew that I had to try and do this myself. I threw all the power of my mind into opening it and the rock lifted up. Then I woke up and knew that it was a dream. It was one of the first I ever had. [The narrator added that later he discovered a rocky eminence on one of the branches of the Berens River that corresponded exactly to the place he had visited in his dream.]

My informant W.B. narrated this dream as the equivalent of many other personal experiences he had related to me that were not dream experiences. The phenomenal reality of self-awareness is as evident here as in his other narratives, but he distinguished this narrative as a dream. It is noteworthy too that the behavioural environment of the dreamer is spatially continuous with that of waking life. This is unequivocal, not only because the narrator starts off by saying he was out hunting and because the topographical features of the country conform to ordinary experience, but particularly because of the comment in parenthesis at the very end. He recognized, later, when awake, the *exact spot* he had visited in the dream. He could go back there at anytime in *the future* and obtain the special kind of medicine that the *memengweciwak*, the beings he met, are famous for. Had he been a pagan, this is what he would have done, he told me. For he received a special blessing. This is the implication of what they told him on parting as well as the fact that he was able to 'will himself out' of their rocky abode. The fact that W.B. thought he could act in the future with reference to a dream experience of the past shows an implied temporal continuity of the self in a behavioural environment with a unified spatio-temporal frame of reference for *all* self-related experience. The anthropomorphic characters that appear in the dream are of particular interest because they are not human (*anicinabek*). Yet they are well-known inhabitants of the behavioural environment of the northern Ojibwa.

What is of special theoretical importance for our discussion here, is that whereas most non-human beings of the behavioural environment of the Ojibwa can *only* be met in dreams, it is otherwise with *memengweciwak*. These beings have been reputedly seen or heard singing outside of dream experiences by a number of Indians. This 'equivocal' status also demonstrates the unified structure of the behavioural environment of the Ojibwa. It is impossible to dichotomize it in our terms and make psychological sense from the anecdotal accounts of the Ojibwa themselves. *Memengweciwak* are not human beings (Indians), nor are they 'spirit-

131

ual' entities in the sense of being perceptually intangible beings dwelling in a spatial region remote from man. From the Ojibwa point of view they are inhabitants of the same terrestrial region as men and belong to the same class of perceptually apprehensible objects as a moose, a tree or a man. And, like them, they may be 'perceived' in dreams as well as in ordinary daily life.

Consonant with this conception of these beings anecdotes are told about Indians who sometimes have met *memengweciwak* while out hunting. One of these stories has an interesting climax. After following some *memengweciwak* to one of their rocky dwellings an Indian, according to his own account, attempted to follow them in. But the rocks closed as soon as *memengweciwak* had gone through. As the prow of his canoe bumped hard against the rocks, the Indian heard them laughing inside. On the other hand, an old man once told me that he had seen his father enter the rocks. What the Ojibwa say is that it is necessary to receive a blessing from *memengweciwak* in a dream first. This is the significance that W.B. attributed to his dream experience, although, being a Christian, he never took advantage of it to become a manao (i.e., an Indian doctor who uses Medicine obtained from *memengweciwak*).

It would be possible to demonstrate from other dream material, how the horizon of self-related experience is enormously broadened through the integration of this kind of symbolic activity with that of waking life. The range of mobility of the self in space and time may likewise be extended throughout the limits of the behavioural environment. In the world view of the Ojibwa human beings share such mobility with the non-human selves of their behavioural environment. This will be illustrated later. But the psychological fact that the individual actually does experience such phenomena (in dreams) is one of the main reasons why the events of mythological narratives assume an unquestioned reality in the minds of the Ojibwa. Experientially, the world of the self and the world of mythological personages is sensed as continuous; it is all part of the same whole. How far this is the case in other cultures is, I believe, open to empirical investigation.

In the past decade or so the 'personal document' approach in anthropology has begun to add a new dimension to ethnography.[1] A number

[1] Clyde Kluckhohn, 'The Personal Document in Anthropological Science.' in L. Gottschalk, C. Kluckhohn, R. Angell, *The Use of Personal Documents in History, Anthropology and Sociology*, Prepared for the Committee on Appraisal of Research, Social Science Research Council, 1945; and 'Needed Refinements in the Biographical Approach.' in S. Stanfeld Sargent and Marian W. Smith, eds., *Culture and Personality*, 1949. Georg Misch, *A History of Autobiography in Antiquity*, 1, p. 8, remarks that 'as a manifestation of man's knowledge of himself, autobiography has its basis in the fundamental — and enigmatical — psychological phenomena which we call consciousness of self and self-awareness . . . In a certain sense the history of autobiography is a history of human self-awareness.'

of autobiographies of individuals in non-literate societies have appeared. But one point has been overlooked. If concepts of the self and the kind of experiences that become self-related are culturally constituted, then the content of autobiographical data must likewise be considered in a variable framework. This content in some cultures will not be in accord with the kind of self-related experience that we consider auto-biographical in western culture. It may contain a great deal of the fantasy material that we exclude from autobiography and relegate to dreams or visions. The anthropologist may collect dreams, it is true; but such data may be separated from autobiographical data on an *a priori* basis and never considered as integrally related to a self-image. In recent years, the aim of collecting dreams has been principally inspired by their value for the analysis of personality dynamics.[1] At another level, how-ever, dreams or other fantasy data, may be considered relevant to auto-biography, if we consider that autobiography involves a retrospective account of the experiences of the self. It would be interesting to know what a systematic phrasing of autobiography with relation to the self-image of a culture might bring forth. One thing the investigator would then encourage would be the searching of the subject's memory and the recall of *all* experiences that were interpreted by him as self-related.

Temporal orientation is not only an important means through which past experience can be organized in a self-related manner; a temporal schema is directly related to future conduct, to contemplated action, to the destiny of the self. This implies the notion of self-continuity as one of the ubiquitous aspects of self-awareness. The self not only has a past and a present, but a long future existence. Murdock lists eschatology as a common denominator of culture. The self may be conceived to be im-mortal, indestructible or eternal. Such grandiose attributes of the self-image necessitate a spatio-temporal frame of reference since deceased selves, if they continue to exist, must exist somewhere. Frank says that:

It has been the great office of culture, and specifically of religion to provide the major time perspective of conduct by insisting upon the relative dimensions of the immediate present as seen in the focus of eternity. Culture, as transmitted by parents and other cultural agents, prevents man from acting impulsively and naively, as his needs, urges, and desires might dictate, and so compels him to regulate his conduct towards the opportunities around him, which he sees in the time perspec-tive of life after death or other forward reference. The Hindu belief in reincarnation and endless striving toward perfection is probably the most

---

[1] Geza Roheim, 'Dream Analysis and Field Work in Anthropology.' in *Psychoanalysis and the Social Sciences*, 1, 1947.

attenuated and compelling time perspective that sets every event and human action in this ever-receding perspective from which there is no escape. Each culture and each religion presents its own time perspective and emphasizes the necessity of patterning human conduct in its focus, so that one culture will repress and another foster sexual functioning, one will favor and another repress acquisitiveness, and so on. Thus asceticism, continence, and all other virtues may be viewed as responses to the dimensions imposed upon the presently religious, ethical time perspectives, many of which reduce the present to insignificance except as a preparation for the future in which this asceticism will be rewarded. To insist then upon time perspectives in human conduct is to recognize the ages old significance given to the future, but to bring that future into the manageable present and give it an operational meaning by showing that *the future is that name we give to the altered dimensions of the present.*[1]

To understand the orientation of the self in its culturally constituted behavioural environment, future time and a cosmographic dimension cannot be ignored.

4 Motivational Orientation

A fourth orientation with which a culture must provide the self may be characterized as motivational.[2] Motivational orientation is orientation of the self towards the objects of its behavioural environment with reference to the satisfaction of its needs. This is why the self must be groomed for action. The satisfaction of needs requires some kind of activity. A world of objects is not only discriminated; objects of different classes have specific attributes that must be taken into account in interaction with them; even the valence they have for the self is culturally constituted. Some classes of objects have highly positive attributes. Others may, on occasion, or even characteristically, be threatening to the security of the self. Consequently, any sort of activity must be given purposeful direction in order that the pursuit of appropriate goals may contribute to the needs of the self.[3] Since the motivational structure of individuals includes the entire range of needs, interests, wants and attributes that underlie the functioning of a human social order, a motivational orienta-

---

1 Frank, *op. cit.*, p. 345; cf. Smith, *op. cit.*
2 Hadley Cantril, *The Psychology of Social Movements*, 1941, pp. 45-46, 'For only by understanding the development of the ego can motivation be put into its proper *social* context, and only by understanding the relation of needs, derived drives, frames of reference, and attitudes to the ego can motivation be placed in its proper *personal* context. If we leave the ego out of account, our picture is inadequate and we deal only with some abstract or incomplete man.'
3 Krech and Crutchfield, *op. cit.*, p. 64, points out that 'Since the nature of the preferred goals depends largely upon the pattern of past experiences to which the individual has been exposed, it is to be expected that typical goals will differ from individual to individual and from culture to culture. The physical and social environment of the person limits and shapes the goals he may develop.' Stagner, *op. cit.*, devotes a chapter to 'a cultural interpretation of motivation'.

tion is as necessary for the maintenance and the persistence of traditional culture patterns as it is for the psychological adjustment of the individual.

Motives at the human level are peculiarly complex because they are essentially acquired rather than innately determined.[1] In consequence, their range and variety is very great. Many attempts to reduce human motives to constant biological attributes of the organism, or physiological determinants, have proved inadequate. By this means we can, at best, only speak in terms of a common denominator of needs. In doing so we not only ignore the most characteristic feature of human motives, but also the relation of needs to the self as culturally constituted. Referring to Cannon's theory of homeostasis, MacLeod writes:

> The studies of homeostasis show how, when a deficiency cannot be met readily by means of the resources of the body, a craving is generated which persists until, through behavior, the optimum condition is restored. Here we have the basis for an understanding of some of our most elementary forms of motivation. But we have also the basis for a redefinition of the concept of need. A need is generated when a self-regulating system is disrupted. Its strength and the character of its directedness are determined by the character of the system and by the nature of the disruption. A self-sufficient system will generate no needs. If we take this argument seriously, we may discard as artifacts the conventional lists of primary organismic needs, and possibly all other inventories of fundamental needs as well.

> Physiological homeostasis can account for the generation of some needs, but it does not follow that it will account for the generation of all needs. It would be pushing the physiological hypothesis to a ridiculous extreme if we were to insist that there must be a biochemical deficiency initiating every wish, ambition, hope, and inclination. Yet these are the stuff of which the motivation of real life is constituted. Under some circumstances I need friendship or need to catch a train just as truly as under other circumstances I may need water or calcium. Whence do these needs come, if not from the disruption of a physiological system? It has always been clear to everyone but the psychologist that there are needs of the self. And even the psychologist, goaded and shamed by the psychoanalyst, is beginning to concede reluctantly that whatever is denoted by the word 'self' may have some reality. Once we free ourselves of the compulsion to explain away the facts of direct experience by reducing them to atoms or tracing them back to non-observable origins we realize that the self is just as compelling, just as inescapable a datum, as is the

[1] T. M. Newcomb, *Social Psychology*, 1950, p. 131 seq.

135

perceptual object. When 'I need friendship' it is the 'I' that has the need. If we analyze away the 'I' we lose the meaning of the motivation, just as when we analyze away the perceptual object we lose the meaning of perception.[1]

If in approaching the problem of human needs we take into account the needs of the self, then it would seem necessary to investigate variant needs of the self in its behavioural environment. In this way we may be able to identify and discriminate motivational patterns in the psychological field of the individual that may escape us entirely if we rely exclusively upon any reductionistic approach.

It has been frequently pointed out that in the process of self-objectification, the self becomes an object of value for the human individual. Sherif and Cantril, for example, write, 'A characteristic fact that holds for any individual in *any culture* is that experience related to ego-attitudes, ego-experiences are felt by the individual with a peculiar warmth and familiarity.'[2] (italics mine) Accepting this generalization, I believe that a further point needs special emphasis. This positive evaluation of the self represents the keystone of the characteristic motivational structure that we find in man. This is due to the fact that cultures not only share a common function in mediating self-objectification, it is one of their concomitant functions to constitute the self as a primary object of value in a world of other objects. While self-love when considered in terms of the psychodynamics of the individual may have its own idiosyncratic patterns, and while there are undoubtedly cultural variables to be considered, it seems difficult to escape the conclusion that some *positive* rather than negative evaluation of self is one of the conditions necessary for a human level of normal psychological adjustment. Neither the principle of homeostasis nor an 'instinct of self preservation', account for the needs of the human individual at this level of adjustment. Motivations that are related to the needs of the self as an object of primary value are not in the same category as the needs of animals whose behaviour is motivated in a psychological field in which any form of self-reference is lacking.

With this fact in mind, concepts such as self-enhancement, self-defence,

[1] Robert B. MacLeod, 'Perceptual Constancy and the Problem of Motivation.' *Canadian Journal of Psychology*, 3, 1949, pp. 62-63.
[2] Sherif and Cantril, *op. cit.*, p. 119; Newcomb, *op. cit.*, p. 327, says: 'One's self is a value — a supreme value to most persons under most conditions'; Krech and Crutchfield, *op. cit.*, write: 'Among society's most pervasive effects on the individual is the development in him of self-regard. Self-regard, essentially, is the social in man. Self-regard is related to one's conception of himself; his proper role in life; his ideals, standards, and values. And in connection with self-regard some of the most potent demands and needs of the individual develop.' Ernest R. Hilgard, 'Human Motives and the Concept of the Self.' *American Psychologist*, 4, 1949, p. 378, likewise emphasizes the point that the 'self of awareness is an object of value.'

aspiration level,[1] become more meaningful in cross-cultural perspective. The same is true for a deeper psychological understanding of concepts such as selfishness, self-love, self-interest. That there are important cultural variables involved and that an examination of them is pertinent to motivation is implied by Fromm.[2] Of self-interest he observes, 'the deterioration of the meaning of the concept of self-interest is closely related to the change in the concept of self. In the Middle Ages man felt himself to be an intrinsic part of the social and religious community in reference to which he conceived his own self when he as an individual had not yet fully emerged from his group. Since the beginning of the modern era, when man as an individual was faced with the task of experiencing himself as an independent entity, his own identity became a problem. In the eighteenth and nineteenth centuries the concept of self was narrowed down increasingly; the self was felt to be constituted by the property one had. The formula for this concept of self was no longer "I am what I think", but "I am what I have", "what I possess".' From the standpoint of motivational orientation the phenomenon characterized as 'ego-involvement', the identification of the self with things, individuals and groups of individuals, is likewise of great importance. The range and character of ego-involvements[3] as constituted by variations in the structure of different behavioural environments needs detailed examination.

By way of illustration, a brief consideration of some of the foregoing concepts in relation to the interpretation of the motives of individuals in a non-literate culture with which I am personally familiar, may serve to highlight some of the essential problems.

Among the Ojibwa Indians, a hunting people, food-sharing beyond the immediate family circle might appear to suggest unselfishness, generosity, affection, kindness and love. Without denying altogether motives that such terms may suggest, I believe that any immediate interpretation of this sort is misleading. Nor can it be assumed that food-sharing is an indication that the individual has become so closely identified with other members of his group that there is an inseparable coalescence of interests. For it is demonstrable that one of the most potent motivations in food-sharing and hospitality is apprehension or fear of sorcery. Food-

---

[1] See Murphy, *op. cit.*, particularly ch. 22; Snygg and Combs, *op. cit.*, p. 58, define 'the basic human need as: the preservation and enhancement of the phenomenal self'.
[2] Fromm, *op. cit.*, pp. 119, 135-136.
[3] Sherif and Cantril, *op. cit.* Krech and Crutchfield, *op. cit.*, p. 20, write: 'The normal processes of growth and socialization of the individual is one of development and multiplication of various self-involvements with objects, people, groups, and social organization in the world about him. The involvements of the self in these more and more complex social relationships give birth to new needs, new demands and new goals as the horizons, interests and concerns of the individual continuously expand.' Cf. Sherif, *op. cit.*, chs. 11, 12.

sharing is an act of self-defence against possible aggression.[1] For sorcery is a potential danger that is always present; it is necessary to be continually on the alert. Consequently, food-sharing cannot be interpreted motivationally without further knowledge of relevant cultural facts.

Even from an economic point of view, food-sharing may be interpreted as a defence against a very realistic threat—starvation. In the aboriginal period and even in this century, there are vicissitudes inherent in Ojibwa economy and ecology that are potent with anxiety. While I may be very lucky in my hunting or fishing today, I am also likely to be periodically faced with starvation. For try as hard as I may, I cannot secure enough to feed my family. Thus a system of mutual sharing of food bridges lean periods for everyone. When considered in relation to sorcery it is not difficult to see how malevolent motives may be attributed to any individual who refuses to share food, or who fails to be hospitable. If I don't share what I have with you, when you need it, I must be hostile to you. At any rate, you may in turn become angry and attack me by means of sorcery. On the other hand, if I always share what I have no one will have reason to sorcerize me on that score, and I will suffer from much less anxiety. At the same time, by playing my expected role, any anxiety that I may have about what may happen to me in lean periods is allayed. The psychological reality of this motivational picture is supported by a case in which an Indian overlooked another man when he was passing around a bottle of whiskey. Later when this Indian became ill, he was certain that the man he overlooked got 'mad' and sorcerized him. His illness was a revengeful act in retaliation for not sharing the whiskey. This pattern of sharing is so deep-seated that I have seen very small children when given a stick of candy, immediately share it with their playmates.

If we consider motives to be intervening variables which, since they cannot be directly observed,[2] must always be inferred, it is even more apparent why the self must be given some motivational orientation. As observers of the behaviour of people in another cultural setting, it is almost inevitable that we go astray unless we have some understanding of this orientation. While the positive evaluation given the self implies the basic importance of self-defence in relation to motivation, the discrimination of the actual motives that have self-defence as their goal, requires some understanding of culturally constituted threats to the self. The fact that the Ojibwa live in a behavioural environment where the threat of sorcery exists, inevitably gives a characteristic colouring to

---

[1] See my discussion of aggression with illustrative case material: 'Aggression in Saulteaux Society.' *Psychiatry*, 3: 395–407, 1940.
[2] See Newcomb, *op. cit.*, p. 31, for a paradigm of motives conceived as intervening variables.

their motivational patterns related to self-defence. The need for some means of defence against sorcery becomes highly salient for them so that activities such as food-sharing, hospitality and lending which, in another culture might be placed in another motivational category, must here be considered in relation to self-defence.

There is another side to this picture, however, which requires parallel emphasis. A more ultimate goal than self-defence is what the Ojibwa phrase as *pimaduziwin*—Life in the most inclusive sense. One hears them utter this word in ceremonies over and over again. It means a long life and a life free from illness or other misfortune. To them it is far from a banal or commonplace ideal. Their daily existence is not an easy one and there are many things that threaten Life. Motivational orientation toward this central goal involves a consideration of culturally constituted means that assist the individual in reaching it. Among these, the help of other selves—entities that are willing to share their power with men are the most important. These are the *pawaganak*. They exist in the behavioural environment and they become primary goal-objects of the self in achieving *pimaduziwin*. Human beings are conceived as intrinsically weak and helpless, so far as what we would call 'natural' abilities are concerned. Consequently, it is essential that assistance be secured from other-than-human selves. This assistance is concretely conceived in the form of special blessings from the *pawaganak* that confer power upon human beings to do many things that would be otherwise impossible for them to do. The desire for such power thus constitutes the primary need of every Ojibwa man. For it is only by securing such power that he can be a successful hunter, practice curing, resist sorcery or retaliate in kind, and so on. It makes him feel that he can achieve Life.

The existence of such goal-objects as the *pawaganak* towards which they are so highly motivated, influence much of the conduct of the Ojibwa. The fact that from the standpoint of the outside observer, such objects are not in the geographical environment makes no psychological difference. Goal-objects, through symbolic representation can mediate the satisfaction of certain needs as well as material objects. If we wish to translate the need that is satisfied into psychological terminology we can say that the *pawaganak* are the major means of self-enhancement in the behavioural environment of the Ojibwa. They are the mainstay of a feeling of psychological security. This is why their native religion meant so much to the Ojibwa. Largely because of the way in which sorcery was conceived to operate, and for other reasons, the self could not achieve a basic sense of security through interpersonal relations with other human beings alone. Relations with and dependence upon the *pawaganak* were more vital. The crucial nature of this focus of Ojibwa needs, goals and motivations for an understanding of the dynamics of personal adjustment is heightened by knowledge of what has happened to them in the course of their contacts with white man and western culture. Under these conditions the structure of their behavioural environment has been radically modified and the primary needs of the self can no longer be met in the traditional way. Nor has any substitute been found. Acculturation in certain groups of Ojibwa has pushed their personality structure to the furtherest limits of its functional adequacy under these newer conditions, with dire results.[1]

I have tried to indicate that the motivational orientation that Ojibwa culture structures for the self includes dynamic relations with other-than-human beings. This must be the case in other cultures, too, although the psychological significance of the nature of these relationships requires examination. But once we assume the standpoint of the self rather than the viewpoint of an outside observer, the motivational orientation of the self throughout the entire range of its behavioural environment must be considered. This is why I have emphasized the importance of the *pawaganak* as goal-objects in relation to the satisfaction of needs of the self that cannot in *this* behavioural environment, be met through human contacts. Once this fact is recognized, we can deduce the 'isolation' of the Ojibwa self which, in turn, is consonant with the 'atomistic' character of their society. Especially among males, there is a latent suspicion based on the potential threat of magical attack, that operates as a barrier to genuine affective ties, even among blood relatives. This barrier does not exist in relations with the *pawaganak*. For even though superhuman in power, they are not the sources of hostility or punishment. The only real danger from them is when they are in the service of some human being who may invoke their aid against *me* because they have conferred power on *him*. On the other hand, I am in the same position in relation to him, through my own blessings. My *pawaganak* are my best and most loyal 'friends'. Who they are and how much power I have is my secret, as it is every other man's, until matters are put to a pragmatic test. Women do not customarily acquire power in the same way as men. But stories are told of what women have been able to do when the occasion has arisen.

5 Normative Orientation

A normative orientation is the *fifth* orientation with which a culture provides the self. Values, ideals, standards are intrinsic components of all

---

[1] Hallowell, 1950, *op. cit.*; 1951, *op. cit.*

cultures. Some of these may be implicit, other explicit. In any case, neither the psychological nor the sociological importance of this orientation of the self can be minimized.[1] On the one hand, motivational orientation in man cannot be fully understood without normative orientation, since values are an integral aspect of needs and goals. On the other hand, without normative orientation, self-awareness in man could not function in one of its most characteristic forms—self-appraisal of conduct. For the individual would have no standard by which to judge his own acts or those of others, nor any ideals to which he might aspire.

As has been pointed out earlier in this paper one of the most typical features of a human social order is that it is likewise a moral order. There is always the presumption that an individual is not only aware of his own personal identity and conduct in a spatio-temporal frame of reference, but that he is capable of judging his own conduct by the standards of his culture. Thus normative orientation is a necessary correlative of self-orientation. Among other things the individual must be motivated to consider whether his acts are right or wrong, good or bad. The outcome of this appraisal is, in turn, related to attitudes of self-esteem or self-respect and to the appraisal of others.

Implicit in moral appraisal is the concomitant assumption that the individual has volitional control over his own acts. This leads directly to the affective aspects of self-judgment—'In man', as Hilgard says, 'anxiety becomes intermingled with *guilt feelings*. The Mowrer and Miller experiments with animals carry the natural history of anxiety through the stages of fear and apprehension, but not to the stage of guilt-feelings. In many cases which come to the clinic, the apprehension includes the fear lest some past offense will be brought to light, or lest some act will be committed which deserves pain and punishment. It is such apprehensions which go by the name of guilt-feelings, because they imply the responsibility of the individual for his past or future misbehavior. To feel guilty is to conceive of the self as an agent capable of good or bad choices. It thus appears that at the point that anxiety becomes infused with guilt-feelings, self reference enters.'[2]

The fact that the human individual not only is motivated to become the moral judge of self-related acts, but reacts emotionally to this judgment is peculiarly human. At the conscious level, what the self feels guilty about or what particular acts arouse apprehension, is one of the con-

---

[1] E.g., Sherif, 1936, *op. cit.*, pp. 185-186, writes: 'Values are the chief constituents of the ego . . . these values are the social in man . . . the values set the standards for the ego . . . the violations of the standards of the ego and ego-misplacements are painful; they produce conflicts or feelings of guilt.' Cf. Krech and Crutchfield, *op. cit.*, p. 68.
[2] Hilgard, *op. cit.*

sequences of normative orientation. As for the unconscious aspects of this same orientation and the processes through which values incorporated in a superego become an integral part of the self, any discussion of this problem would divert us into the psychodynamics of human adjustment that is not our primary concern here.[1] But it is now clear that in relation to this adjustment process differential value systems are one important variable and that the orientation of the self with relation to these is of great importance. One broad conclusion seems inescapable: if the self were not motivated towards *conscious* self-appraisal, such unconscious mechanisms of self-defence as rationalization, repression, etc. would have no ostensible purpose. On the one hand, the individual is self-oriented through cultural means, in a manner which leads to the evaluation of the self as an object of primary value. Any kind of self-depreciation, loss of self-esteem, or threat to the self, impairs the complex motivational systems that focus upon the self and its needs. At the same time, self-evaluation through culturally recognized norms is inescapable. Awareness of these is necessary because the individual has to take account of explicitly formulated or institutionalized social sanctions. This imposes a characteristic psychological burden upon the human being, since it is not always possible to reconcile, at the level of self-awareness, idiosyncratic needs with the demands imposed by the normative orientation of the self. For animals without the capacity for self-awareness no such situation can arise. In man, therefore, unconscious mechanisms that operate at a psychological level that does not involve self-awareness may be viewed as an adaptive means that permits some measure of comprise between conflicting forces.[2] They may relieve the individual of part of the burden forced upon him by the requirements of the morally responsible existence that human society demands. Hilgard points out that in addition to the role which such mechanisms may play as defences against anxieties experienced by the

---

[1] See Hallowell, 1950, *op. cit.*, and Spiro, *op. cit.*, p. 34 seq.
[2] The nature of this conflict stated in terms of personality structure may be construed differently. With reference to normative orientation as discussed in the context of this paper, it is worth noting that O. W. Mowrer, 'Discipline and Mental Health.' *Harvard Educational Review*, 17, 1947, pp. 289-290, contends that 'anxiety, guilt, depression, feelings of inferiority, and the other forces of neurosis stem, not from an id-ego conflict, but from an ego-super ego conflict. The trouble, in other words, is between the individual's conscious self and the values implanted in him by his social training, rather than between the conscious self, or ego, and the biologically given impulses, or lust and hostility.' Also see O. W. Mowrer, *Learning Theory and Personality Dynamics: Selected Papers*, 1950, ch. 18, 'Learning Theory and the Neurotic Paradox.' On p. 445 he points out that 'Freud has repeatedly remarked that repression of an impulse or memory characteristically occurs when it arouses effects which are so strong that they threaten to overwhelm the "ego". To this extent repression is definitely a "defensive" mechanism, but the resulting advantages usually prove to be achieved at a great cost. Repression is effected by excluding the symbolic representative of certain impulses from consciousness, i.e., from the dominant integrative center of the personality. Although repression thus brings a temporary peace, the process is likely to be pathogenic for the reason that energies which formerly submitted themselves to the management of, and thereby strengthened, the "ego" are now withdrawn and left free to seek — through those habits called "symptoms" — their own irresponsible nonintegrative paths to gratification. This is why Freud has characterized repression as a reversion from the "reality principle" to the more primitive "pleasure principle", from the "ego" (consciousness) to the "id" (the unconscious).'

self, they likewise permit the 'bolstering [of] self-esteem through self-deception. . . . The need for self-deception arises because of a more fundamental need to maintain or to restore self-esteem. Anything belittling to the self is to be avoided. That is why the memories lost in amnesia are usually those with a self-reference, concealing episodes which are anxiety or guilt-producing. What is feared is loss of status, loss of security of the self. That is why aspects of the self which are disapproved are disguised.'[1] There seems to be little question that one of the crucial areas of human adjustment of necessity turns upon the tolerance with which the self views its own moral status and the sensitivity of the self to feelings of anxiety and guilt. It seems to me that a comprehensive understanding of this whole matter requires a better knowledge of the self-image viewed cross-culturally and of the manner in which the self is normatively oriented with reference to the values, ideals and standards of different cultures.

While concrete investigations in various directions come to mind I want to emphasize only a single point here. If, in cross-cultural perspective, we view normative orientation as one of the major orientations of the self in its behavioural environment, I believe it will become apparent that there are some novel areas of inquiry that suggest themselves. For, as previously emphasized in the discussion of the other basic orientations, the behavioural environment as constituted for the self must be considered in its entire phenomenal range. And just as in terms of a given self-image time and space, as viewed in naturalistic perspective, may be transcended in self-related experience and the self may interact socially with selves that are other than human, this fact must not be lost sight of in investigating differential patterns in the normative orientation of the self. It follows that the moral world of the self and the acts for which the self may feel morally responsible may not all be attributed to waking life, nor to a single mundane existence nor to interpersonal relations with human beings alone. For the selves of this latter category may be considered as only a single class of beings that exist in the total behavioural environment as constituted for the self. Consequently, one fundamental question that arises is the actual dimensions of the area within the behavioural environment to which the normative orientation of the self is directed and the consequences of this with reference to the observable behaviour of the individual. What does a consideration of the normative orientation of the self in his *total* behavioural environment contribute to our understanding of the role of values, ideals and recognized standards to the needs and motivations of the self?

---

[1] I.e., 'by denial of impulses, or of traits, or of memories . . . ' or 'through *disguise*, whereby the impulses, traits or memories are distorted, displaced or converted, so that we do not recognize them for what they are.' Higard, *op. cit.*

143

We have some reports in the literature, for example, where the moral responsibility of the self in dreams is viewed as continuous with waking life. Lincoln[1] refers to Ashanti dreams of adultery which subject the individual to fine and to the Kai where adultery dreams likewise are punishable. But much more detailed inquiry into these phenomena would be desirable.

A case of suttee that occurred in India at the beginning of the 19th century and which is reported by Sleeman[2] is of particular interest because it brings to a concrete focus all the orientations of the self that have been discussed here. The essential facts are these. A married man, a Brahman, died and his widow was persuaded not to join her husband on the funeral pyre. But on hearing of the death of this man a married woman of about sixty years of age, of lower caste, who lived with her husband in a village about two miles away, presented herself to members of the Brahman's family. She said she wished to burn on the pyre with the deceased man. This was because she had been his wife in three previous births and 'had already burnt herself with him three times, and had to burn with him four times more.' The Brahman's family were surprised to hear this and said there must be some mistake, particularly in view of the difference in caste. The old woman had no difficulty in explaining this. She said that in her last birth, at which time she resided in Benares with the Brahman, she had by mistake given a holy man who applied for charity salt, instead of sugar in his food. He told her that, in consequence, 'she should in the next birth, be separated from her husband, and be of inferior caste, but that, if she did her duty well in that state, she should be reunited to him in the following birth.' The Brahman's family would not, however, accede to her request. Among other things the widow insisted that 'if she were not allowed to burn herself, the other should not be allowed to take her place.' What happened was this. Despite the fact that the Brahman's family, at this time, was not convinced fully of the old woman's claims and denied her plea, she carried out her intentions nonetheless. She stole a handful of ashes from the pyre of her 'former' husband and prevailed upon her present husband and her mother to prepare the pyre upon which she immolated herself.

This had all happened twenty years before the youngest brother of the Brahman told the story to Sleeman. The latter requested his frank opinion. It turned out that, partly in view of a prophecy the old woman

[1] Lincoln, op. cit., p. 29.
[2] Sleeman was an Anglo-Indian administrator who had had thirty-five years experience in India when his book was first published in 1844. I am indebted to Dr. Dorothy Spencer for this reference.

made at the pyre and other circumstances, the family of her 'former' husband were, in the end, absolutely convinced that her claim was true. They defrayed all her funeral expense and the rites were carried out in relation to her 'real' social status. They also built her a tomb which Slee-man later visited. He found that everyone in her village and all the people in the town where her 'former' husband had lived were thoroughly convinced of her claims.

It is perfectly clear that the motivation of the old woman of lower caste cannot be separated from a culturally constituted self-image which involves the conviction of reincarnation. Consequently, she could appeal to experiences in a former existence, through 'recall', to make her plea intelligible. From the standpoint of normative orientation her motives were of the highest in terms of the values of her culture. Suttee was a noble and divinely sanctioned act on the part of a wife. Although suttee, if viewed from outside this behavioural environment, may be considered as suicide in the sense of self-destruction, from the standpoint of the self-related motivational structure of the old woman, any self-destruction was literally impossible. She had already lived with her 'former' husband during three births; she had only been separated from him during her present birth because of an error for which she had now paid the penalty; she had still other births ahead of her. The time had now come to rejoin her 'husband'. What suttee offered was an occasion for *self-enhancement* and self-continuity in thorough harmony with the continued maintenance of self-respect reinforced by the deeply rooted approval of her fellows.[1] Their behavioural environment was psychologically structured like hers so that her motivations and behaviour could be very easily coordinated with theirs in terms that were meaningful to them.

The role that normative orientation may play in giving moral unity to the relations of the self with *all* classes of animate beings throughout its behavioural environment, is illustrated by the Ojibwa. With reference to certain central values considered from the standpoint of the Ojibwa self,

---

[1] If suicide is *only* viewed in an 'objective' or 'naturalistic' frame of reference, it seems to contradict the 'instinct of self-preservation', and thus present a paradox. On the other hand, if it be assumed that the constitution of the self in its behavioural environment may pattern the motivational system of the human individual in various ways, it does not seem paradoxical to say that the individual may come to view himself in terms of a self-image that makes it possible to transcend *bodily* destruction. A culturally constituted self-image makes it possible to make use of a conceptual dichotomy that not only permits the individual to maintain a positive attitude towards the self as an object of value but, at the same time, to rule out self destruction as a consciously motivated act, since the self may be thought to be essentially indestructible. Consequently, it is possible to be highly motivated towards self-enhancement even if this involves bodily destruction. Where such an ideology prevails, any concept of 'self-destruction' must be completely reduced to an unconscious level of motivation. In order for bodily destruction to involve self-destruction at the level of self-awareness, there must be a self-image that conceives the body as a necessary substratum for the self. The so-called 'instinct of self-preservation' is really a misnomer, for the biological forces that operate to preserve the life of the individual organism are not equivalent to, nor do they explain, all of the acquired drives that may become self-regulated in man.

it is completely arbitrary to isolate conceptually the relations of human beings with each other from the relations of the self to other-than-human selves. And from the standpoint of psychological understanding it is likewise unrealistic to ignore the significance of the dimensions of the normative orientation of the self.

It has been said that the grammatical distinction between animate and inanimate gender in Ojibwa speech is arbitrary and hard to master. It only appears so to the outsider. Actually, it is precisely these distinctions which give the Ojibwa individual the necessary linguistic cues to the various classes of other selves that he must take account of in his behavioural environment. It is also significant that he is not an 'animist' in the classical sense. There are objects—an axe, a mountain, a canoe, a rainbow, that fall within the inanimate class. In addition to human beings and *pawaganak* all animals and most plants are classified as animate. So are Thunder, the Winds, Snow, Sun-Moon,[1] certain shells, stones, etc. I once asked an old man whether all stones were alive. His reply was 'Some are!' Another old man is said to have addressed a stone; another thought that a Thunder Bird spoke to him.

Many examples could be cited to show that on the assumption that animals have a body and a soul like man they are treated as if they had self-awareness and volition. Bears may be spoken to and expected to respond intelligently; the bones of animals that are killed have to be disposed of with care. Although the Ojibwa are hunters and depend upon the killing of wild game, nevertheless, cruelty is not only frowned upon but may be penalized by subsequent sickness.[2] Gigantic cannibal monsters exist in the behavioural environment of the Ojibwa. They have been seen and even fought with. To kill a *windigo* is a feat of the utmost heroism. It is a sure sign of greatness because it is impossible to accomplish without superhuman help. But cruelty to a *windigo* is not permitted and in one case I have recorded this was the reputed source of a man's illness.

Greed is not only disapproved in human relations. There is a story told of a boy who at his puberty fast wanted to dream of 'all the leaves on all the trees.' He was not satisfied with the blessing that had already been given him by the *pawaganak*. He insisted on more power. He did not live to enjoy the blessings he had been given.[3]

---

[1] *Gizis,* is the Ojibwa term; it might be translated 'luminary'.
[2] E.g., stretching a snake until it breaks in two; cutting off an animal's legs while it is alive and letting it go; pulling all the feathers from a live bird.
[3] Radin, *op. cit.,* p. 177, has called attention to the fact that 'throughout the area inhabited by the woodland tribes of Canada and the United States, over fasting entails death.' For the Winnebago he elaborates this point by analyzing three tales, showing in each case how one of the cardinal virtues of these Indians, a sense of proportion, is violated by over fasting. Other Ojibwa cases are found in the literature. In one of them the bones of a boy who had over fasted were found by his father.

The psychological significance of considering the normative orientation of the Ojibwa throughout its total range rests upon the fact that in relations with animals or 'spiritual' beings *departure* from traditional standards are subject to the same sanctions that apply to human relations. Any serious illness is believed to be a penalty for wrong-doing. The individual is encouraged to confess anything wrong he may have done in the past in order to facilitate recovery.[1] Consequently, it is possible to find out what the individual actually feels guilty about. It is demonstrable that in addition to guilt based upon interpersonal relations with human beings, self-related experiences that transcend these and involve relations with non-human selves, may likewise be the source of guilt.

In this paper I have advanced the hypothesis that by giving primary consideration to the self and its behavioural environment all cultures can be seen to share certain central functions. In order for self-awareness to emerge and function in human societies the individual must be given basic orientations that structure the psychological field in which the self is prepared to act. Thus, while the content of the behavioural environment of man may differ greatly and intermesh with the geographical environment in various ways, there are common functions that different cultural means must serve in order for a human level of psychodynamic adjustment to be maintained. At this level self-awareness is a major component of the personality structure of man. If we assume the point of view of the self in its behavioural environment it is likewise possible to gain a more direct insight into the psychological field of the individual as *he* experiences it than a purely objective cultural description affords.

THE OJIBWA SELF AND ITS BEHAVIOURAL ENVIRONMENT

Finally in order to illustrate the application of the orientational categories previously outlined by a concrete case I shall draw upon data collected in the course of my personal contacts with the Ojibwa Indians, particularly the Canadian Ojibwa (Saulteaux) of the Berens River. This branch of these people represented a relatively unacculturated group at the time I first began to visit them twenty years ago. A small proportion of them had not been Christianized. What kind of self-image do these people have? In what kind of behavioural environment is the Ojibwa self groomed to act?

---

[1] A. Irving Hallowell, 'Sin, Sex and Sickness in Saulteaux Belief.' *British Journal of Medical Psychology*, 8: 191-197, 1939; 'Psychosexual Adjustment, Personality and the Good Life in a Non-literate Society.' in P. H. Hoch and J. Zubin, eds., *Psychosexual Development in Health and Disease*, 1949; 'The Social Function of Anxiety in a Primitive Society.' *American Journal of Sociology*, 6: 869-881, 1941.

In the Ojibwa language there is no term for 'self'.[1] Linguistically, self-reference is dependent upon personal and possessive pronouns and personal names (usually nicknames). Every individual knows *who* he is, but he likewise knows what kind of a being he is. He entertains definite beliefs and concepts that relate to his own nature, and large areas of his most characteristic thinking, his affective experience, his needs, motivations, and goals are not thoroughly intelligible unless we take the content of his self-image into account.

I believe that the essential features of the self-image of the Ojibwa, in their full psychological reality, can best be communicated by indicating how they function as an integral part of the experience of an individual. To present the material in this form I have let a fictitious Indian, long deceased, speak in the first person, rather than attempt an abstract exposition. In order to cover as many aspects of the topic as possible and yet remain as close as possible to data collected in the field, I have attributed to my Indian speaker knowledge and experience derived from the statements of a number of different informants. Furthermore, the statements of my fictitious Indian speaker may be taken as a free translation of a possible Ojibwa text, since I have not used any English words that do not have a fairly good equivalent in Ojibwa. Beside this, Ojibwa terms for key concepts are cited. In parentheses I have added my comments on particular points in order to highlight significant concepts and have sometimes gone into further elaboration. In the footnotes are references to published articles or books where fuller data or case material highly abbreviated in the account given by my Indian speaker will be found.

When I was born I had a body, *miyo*, and I had a soul, *otcatcakwin*. My body came out of my mother's womb and when I was an old man it was buried in the earth [the body has a definite existence in time]. I was not one of these people who knew what was happening before he was born. But my father did. I remember hearing him say: 'Some people say that a child knows nothing when it is born. Four nights before I was born I knew that I would be born. My mind was as clear when I was born as it is now. I saw my father and mother, and I knew who they were. I knew the things an Indian uses, their names and what they were good for—an axe, a gun, a knife and even an ice-chisel. I used to tell this to my father and he replied: "Long ago the Indians used to be like that, but the ones that came after them were different." I have asked my own children about this, but there is only one of them

---

[1] Nor are there abstract terms equivalent to what we can note by colour, family, religion or beauty.

148

that remembers when he was in his mother's womb. People said to me: "You are one of those old people who died long ago and were born a second time.".'[1]

I have heard some other old people say that they had heard babies crying constantly until someone recognized the name they were trying to say. When they were given this name they stopped crying. This shows that someone who had once lived on the earth came back to live again. [Reincarnation is possible, even if occasional. There are special cues in such cases: the recall of prenatal memories; crying and babbling that only stops when the name of a deceased person is mentioned,[2] which indicates the importance of the personal name in self-identification. Another cue is the presence of a few gray hairs on the infant's head. In cases like this no personal identification may be made. Certain inferences are clear: the soul is independent of a particular body; it transcends the body in time; an implicit concept of self that is intimately connected with the idea of the soul. Self-objectification is clearly implied since self-awareness is even attributed to the foetus. The informant says that his father knew when he was going to be born. To the Ojibwa to know what is going to happen ahead of time is one of the signs of a 'great' man, i.e., a man with unusual powers.]

When I was living on the earth I had to be careful that nobody got hold of any part of my body. When my hair was cut I always burnt the part that was cut off. I was afraid that someone with power [magic] might get hold of it. If he wanted to, such a person could make me sick or even kill me. I didn't want to die before I had to. I wanted life, *pimaduziwin*. But someone did manage to kill me by sending something towards me that penetrated my body. That's when you need a *nibu-kiwinini* [an Indian doctor who tries to remove the object by sucking as part of his ritual]. Sometimes he will suck out a shell, a piece of metal, or a dog's tooth and show it to you. Then you can live. But he couldn't cure me. He didn't have enough power. The person who killed me had more. [The body is intimately connected with the self, so intimately that physical possession of even part of it is considered as endangering the self. The self can also be attacked by magically potent material substances projected into the body. In general, it may be said

---

[1] This is a translation of a statement made to me by Alec Keeper. Unfortunately, I did not follow up the reference made to the 'womb memories' of his son, Ketegas, whom I also knew. See Hallowell, 1940, *op. cit.*, pp. 49-50. Victor Barnouw, 'The Phantasy World of a Chippewa Woman." *Psychiatry*, 12: 67-76, 1949, cites verbatim the intra-uterine reminiscences of a Wisconsin Chippewa (Ojibwa) man and refers to specific examples of memories from early infancy on the part of other individuals.
[2] I discovered that the occurrences of identical personal names, sometimes more than a generation apart in my genealogies, could be explained in every case by reincarnation. None of these people were living at the time of my inquiries.

that bodily illness of any kind arouses great anxiety. The Ojibwa tend to be hypochondriacal. There are two points of interpretation that are relevant in this connection: Since serious illness, in many instances, is thought to be due to sorcery, it becomes a direct personal attack upon the self by an enemy. At the same time since illness, viewed from the standpoint of experience, involves the dysfunctioning of bodily processes, the bodily aspect of the self assumes great importance. The further implication is that an attack on the body destroys the balance that should exist between soul and body in order to realize the good Life, that is, life in terms of longevity, health and absence of misfortune. Since self-awareness is given content in terms of a self-image defined by this dichotomy, anxiety may be aroused if either soul or body is endangered. In a positive sense this is why *pimaduziwin* expresses a very central goal for the self—a level of aspiration towards which the self is motivated.][1]

When I died and my body was buried that was not the end of me. I still exist[2] in *djibaiaking*. Ghost land or the Land of the Dead. [Existence of self is not coordinate with bodily existence, in the ordinary human sense.] When I was dead people called me a *djibai*, ghost. Some Indians have seen *djibaiak* [plural] or heard them whistle. [In other words, a dead person has a form, a ghostly appearance that can be perceived by the living and without being visually perceived, may occasionally be heard by the living. Death involved metamorphosis because the body formerly associated with the soul has become detached from it and lies in the ground. On the other hand 'I' *know* when 'I' am a ghost; self-awareness, personal identity, personal memories persist; there is a continuity of the self maintained.]

It is a long hard journey to the Land of the Dead. To reach it you travel south.[3] [There are cases known in the past in which pagan Indians begged their Christianized relatives not to bury them in a coffin. They believed that they would have to carry it with them on the journey to the Land of the Dead, and they did not wish to be burdened with it. This journey is not conceived in 'spiritual' terms at all; the 'living' self can become emotionally disturbed by the anticipation of difficulties to be encountered by the 'dead' self. It is plain that, psychologically, the behavioural environment of the self is all of one piece.]

When I got there I found it to be a very fine place. The Indians who had died before me were glad to see me. Some of them had moss growing on their foreheads [like old rocks], they had died so long ago. I sang

---

[1] See Hallowell, 1950, *op. cit.*, where this goal is discussed with reference to what has happened to the Ojibwa as a consequence of acculturation.
[2] There is a term for existence that is applicable to any class of animate beings.
[3] See Hallowell, 1940, *op. cit.*, for details.

and danced with them. A few Indians have reached the Land of the Dead and then gone back to tell those who were alive what they saw there.[1] [The dead in appearance are thought of anthropomorphically, not as disembodied spirits. They live in wigwams. But there are differences. In one account a youth visiting the land of the dead was offered a food by his grandmother. It was decayed (i.e., phosphorescent) wood. When he refused she said: 'Naturally you are not truly dead. . . .' An essential point for emphasis is the continuation of a fundamental duality of essence. *Djibaiak* like *anicinabek* have souls, and some kind of *form*. As will become more apparent later, this duality holds for *all* orders of animate beings.]

If an Indian dies and a good medicine man starts after him quickly enough he may be brought back [i.e., his soul may be captured and returned to his body]. Then he can go on living as before. Once I saw Owl do this.[2] *Tcetcebu* was very ill. By the time Owl arrived where her father was encamped, she died. Owl tied a piece of red yarn around the girl's wrist at once [to enable him to identify her quickly in a crowd] and lay down beside her body. He lay in this position a long, long time. He was still; he did not move at all. Then I saw him move ever so little. The girl began to move a little also. Owl moved more. So did the girl. Owl raised himself up into a sitting posture. At the same moment the girl did the same. He had followed her to the Land of the Dead and caught her soul just in time. Everything has to have a soul in order to exist [as an animate being]. I'm in the Land of the Dead now but I have a soul just as I had one before I came here. [Death involves the departure of the soul from the body; the soul takes up its residence in a new locale. There is metamorphosis. The body becomes inanimate and 'selfless'. The persistence of the self in conjunction with the soul in its new form is implied in the self-awareness attributed to ghosts.]

If a conjurer, *djisakiwinini*, has power enough he can bring a soul back from the Land of the Dead into his 'shaking tent'.[3] I was called by a conjurer once because my son was ill and this man was trying to cure him. My grandchild went with me. When her mother, who was sitting with the other Indians outside the conjuring tent heard her speak, she cried.[4] I had to tell about something wrong I had done when I was living. This helped my son to get well.[5] [Under these circumstances the ghost has no perceptible form; only the soul is there. But functionally,

---

[1] *Ibid.*, for concrete instances.
[2] For this case see *ibid., and* p. 32 for a reputed case of resurrection.
[3] For details see A. Irving Hallowell, *The Role of Conjuring in Saulteaux Society*, 1942.
[4] *Ibid.*, pp. 57-59, for the full account.
[5] For the role of confession in relation to illness see Hallowell, 1939, *op. cit.*; 1941, *op. cit.*; 1949, *op. cit.*

a self continuous with a 'living' existence is implied because personal memories of an earlier period in life are recalled.]

When a person is sleeping anyone can see where his body is but you can't tell whether his soul is there or not. Some conjurer may have enough power to draw your soul into his shaking tent while you are asleep. If he has the power you can't resist. Perhaps he only wants to have you talk to the people in his camp and tell them the latest news. But he may want to kill you. If your soul doesn't get back to your body then you'll be a *djibai* by the next morning and have to start off to the Land of the Dead. I had a lucky escape once. I was only sixteen years old. A conjurer drew my soul into his conjuring lodge and I knew at once that he wanted to kill me, because I had made fun of his son who was a 'humpy' [hunchback.] I said 'I'm going out.' But the old man said, 'No! You can't go.' Then I saw my own head rolling about and the 'people' in the lodge were trying to catch it. [The 'people' were the guardian spirits, *pawaganak* of the conjurer—superhuman entities.] I thought to myself that if only I could catch my head everything would be all right. So I tried to grab it when it rolled near me and finally I caught it.[1] As soon as I got hold of it I could see my way out and I left. Then I woke up but I could not move my legs or arms. Only my fingers I could move. But finally I managed to speak. I called out to my mother. I told her I was sick. I was sick for a couple of days. No one saw my soul go to and fro but I knew where I had been. I told my father about it and he agreed with me. [It is quite clear from all this that the soul is detachable from the body and may occupy a different position in space. This is true both with respect to a dead person and a person asleep. It is also possible to infer with reasonable certainty that the soul cannot be conceptually dissociated from the self. Where a functioning self exists, there must be a soul. Where a soul exists there must be a self. In terms of an assumed dependent relationship the self-soul relation in Ojibwa thought logically parallels the self-body relation in our sophisticated thinking. We emphasize a certain kind of *physical* body or form as a necessary substratum for a functioning self. We are skeptics so far as any other kind of a structural substratum is concerned. On the other hand, the Ojibwa take it for granted that the soul is the only necessary substratum. Any particular form or appearance is incidental. Thus, various kinds of metamorphosis can be accepted so long as it is assumed that a soul continues to exist. What is particularly interesting to note, it seems to me, is that once we accept this assumption, it become more and more apparent that *functionally* the same generic attributes of the self as we understand it,

---

[1] Even in this 'dream' a *bodily* part of himself — his head — assumes vital importance. The dreamer gives himself 'form'.

and that we assume can only be manifested where a human bodily structure is present, are constant functions of the soul, as thought of by the Ojibwa. The soul of the living or the dead knows who it is, what it is, where it is, in space and time; it is conscious of past experiences, it has a capacity for volition, etc., irrespective of the form or appearance it may present to others at the moment. This interpretation is further illustrated by what follows.]

There was a *djibai* here who paid a visit to her grandfather. He was so very sad after she died. She visited him one day when he had put a mast up in his canoe and with a blanket for a sail was crossing a lake. She appeared to him as a little bird that alighted on the top of the mast. She didn't say anything but he knew who it was because he was a wise old man.[1] [The deceased—one of the very old people, *keteanicinabek*,— may be seen by a living person, not as a ghost but in the form of a bird. Metamorphosis is possible for a *djibai*; in this case from ghost to bird.]

The soul of a living person, too, after it leaves the body can look like an animal. A powerful medicine man can do a lot of harm because he can go about secretly at night. But you can see his body lying there in his wigwam all the time. A long time ago a friend of mine told me what he had seen.[2] He and his wife were living with an old man suspected of being a sorcerer. One night he thought the sorcerer was up to something. The latter lit his pipe and covered himself up completely with his blanket. My friend kept watch. After a long, long time had gone by, all of a sudden the sorcerer threw off the blanket and fell over towards the fire. Blood was running from his mouth; he was dead. My friend found out what killed him. At the very same time that the sorcerer was lying under his blanket so quietly, in another part of the camp Pindandakwan was waiting with a gun in the dark beside the body of his son who had been killed by sorcery. A kind of 'fire' had appeared around the camp several times before the boy died. This night Pindandakwan saw the 'fire' coming again. It[3] made a circle around the corpse, which was covered by birch bark. He heard a voice saying, 'This is finished.' Then he saw a bear trying to lift the bark near the head of his son. He

---

[1] Hallowell, 1940, *op. cit.*
[2] What I have given here is a highly abbreviated version of a longer, unpublished text.
[3] This reference to 'fire' illustrates the allusive manner of Indian narration. The listener is supposed to know what is meant. What is referred to here is made explicit in another anecdote: 'One night when I was asleep, I was suddenly awakened. My strength came to me and I managed to get on my feet and walk outside [the narrator had been very ill and thought he knew who had sorcerized him]. Right in front of me I saw something. It was a bear lying right outside the tent [wild animals do not ordinarily come so close to any human habitation]. I saw the flame when he breathed. I said to my wife very quietly, "Hand me the axe." She could not find it. The bear started to go. I tried to follow but I could not walk fast enough. I spoke to the bear. I said, "I know who you are and I want you to quit. I'm good natured but if you come back here again I won't spare you." He never came back and after that I gradually got better.'

153

was going to take what he wanted.[1] Pindandakwan shot the bear and he heard a man's voice crying out. Both the sorcerer and the boy were buried the next day. Everyone thought the old man was a bad one. No one blamed Pindandakwan.

This anecdote requires some lengthy comment, since it will enable us to penetrate further into Ojibwa thought and the basic premises involved. (a) It is obvious that there is not metamorphosis of the body of the sorcerer. The *miyo* remains in the wigwam in its usual form. (b) Unlike the previous case where the soul was drawn from the body by the power of another person, here the soul leaves the body behind through a volitional act of the conjurer himself. In fact, the Ojibwa would say that *he* left his body and point out that this was not the first time; his reputation for wickedness implies this kind of behaviour. And the 'fire' had been seen at Pindandakwan's camp before. (c) It is likewise obvious that, in this case, the conjurer was not understood to be prowling around *dressed up* in a bear skin. This was John Tanner's interpretation, over a century ago, of similar stories. He writes: '. . . by some composition of gunpowder, or other means [they] contrive to give the appearance of fire to the mouth and eyes of the bear skin, in which they go about the village late at night, bent on deeds of mischief, oftentimes of blood.'[2] This is simply Tanner's effort at an explanation intelligible to him. (d) I believe that all we need to say is that the self of the sorcerer was in Pindandakwan's camp. To say that *he* was there is the meaningful core of the whole situation; it was Pindandakwan's assumption that *he* would be there and he acted on this premise. In these terms the situation is as humanly intelligible to us as it is to the Ojibwa. What is always difficult for them is to explain that we would call the *mechanism* of events, exactly *how* they occur. To them, this line of thought seems 'pedantic'. Explanation is never pursued in much detail at this level (which is actually the level of science). But to say that *he* (the sorcerer) had visited Pindandawan's camp on several occasions, that *he* had killed Pindandakwan's son, that *he* was caught there on a particular night and killed by Pindandakwan in revenge is thoroughly meaningful to them. All they take for granted (as an implicit metaphysical principle) is that *multiform appearance* is an inherent potential of *all* animate beings. What is uniform, constant, visually imperceptible and

---

1 It is said that a sorcerer who kills a person in this way is bound to visit the grave. He cuts off the fingertips of the corpse, the tip of the tongue, and gouges out the eyes and stores them in a little box for magical use. This is why Pindándakwan made a pseudo-grave for his son outside the wigwam. It was a deliberate 'trap' for the sorcerer. Pindándakwan is an actual person who appears in my genealogies.
2 John Tanner, *Narrative of the Captivity and Adventures of John Tanner, etc.*, 1830, p. 343. Tanner was a white man captured by Indians as a boy. He lived with Ojibwa and Ottawa, learned their language and published his reminiscences in later life. For further information on bearwalking and the attitude of contemporary Indians towards it, see Richard M. Dorson, *Bloodstoppers and Bearwalkers. Folk Traditions of the Upper Peninsula*, 1952, pp. 26-29, 278.

vital is the soul. A sorcerer being a person of unusual power is able to leave his human body in one place and appear in another perceptible manifestation elsewhere. (e) There is an additional point to be noted. Inquiry revealed that Pindandakwan was known to have considerable power himself. Since he assumed it was a sorcerer prowling around and not an ordinary bear, he did not load his gun with an ordinary bullet. He mixed 'medicine', *muckiki* (having magical potency) with his gunpowder. Just as it is thought possible to attack a person's ordinary body with intent to kill by projecting a material object with magical properties into it, in the same way the sorcerer, in the bodily appearance of a bear, could be directly attacked through his body, although something more than an ordinary bullet was required. (Under the circumstances there was no way of focusing the attack on his soul.) In both instances the body is assumed to be a vulnerable point of attack. Since it is fairly clear that what death implies for the Ojibwa is the *separation* of the soul from its humanly formed body, I believe they would agree that the soul of the sorcerer did not succeed in getting back to his human body. This explains why his body was seen to collapse. It could not resume its normal functioning without a soul. This is why Owl was in such a hurry to capture the soul of *Tcetcebu.* Not being able to reach his body in time to resume living (which was, no doubt, part of the magic employed by Pindandakwan), the sorcerer's soul was compelled to assume the form of a ghost.

In a brief account of his puberty fast, to which our Indian speaker now refers, the reader will note another situation in which a *temporary* separation of the soul from the body occurs. To the Ojibwa there was nothing particularly unusual in such a personal experience. But we lack autobiographical anecdotes because there was a traditional tabu upon references to personal experiences during the puberty fast.

Long ago, when every boy used to go out alone in the woods to obtain his helpers his body remained in the *waisan*, nest, his father built for him.[1] If you had been there you could have seen his body for yourself. But his soul might have been elsewhere. One of his helpers might have taken him somewhere. This is what happened to me. When I was a boy

---

[1] The Ojibwa boy, at puberty or before, sought tutelaries or guardian spirits: without their help no man could be expected to get much out of life or amount to anything. The 'nest' referred to was a sort of stage constructed by laying poles across the branches of a tree about fifteen feet from the ground. The boy was expected to remain on this stage several days and nights without food or drink. He was only allowed to descend to the ground to urinate and defecate. This fast was the most crucial event in a man's life and to undertake it he had to be *pekize*, pure (without sexual experience). Failure to observe all preliminary conditions and the fasting regulations destroyed his chances of blessings from other than human entities — the pawáganak (literally, 'dream visitors') — who were more powerful than human beings. The situation is often described by the Ojibwa by saying that the pawáganak took 'pity' upon the kigúsämo, the faster. It was through dreams or visions, while the body lay inert, that direct experience of these entities occurred.

I went out to an island to fast. My father paddled me there. For several nights I dreamed of an *ogima* [Chief, superior person]. Finally he said to me 'Grandson, I think you are now ready to go with me.' Then *ogima* began dancing around me as I sat there on a rock and when I happened to glance down at my body I noticed that I had grown feathers. Soon I felt just like a bird, a golden eagle (*kiniu*). *Ogima* had turned into an eagle also and off he flew towards the south. I spread my wings and flew after him in the same direction. After a while we arrived at a place where there were lots of tents and lots of 'people'. It was the home of the Summer Birds . . . [After returning north again the boy was left at their starting point after his guardian spirit had promised help whenever he wanted it. The boy's father came for him and took him home again.[1] From this account it can be inferred that in addition to living Indians and deceased Indians, there are other classes of animate beings in the behavioural environment of the Ojibwa self with whom the individual comes into direct contact under certain circumstances. For it is apparent that the dreams of the puberty fast are interpreted as experiences of the self. The being that first appears as a human being and then is transformed into a bird is representative of a large class of other-than-human entities that maintain an existence independently of *anicinabek*, and are more powerful than man. The eagle-man is not the bird one ordinarily perceives but belongs to the class of 'owners' or 'bosses'. All animal species, such as the golden eagle, are thought of as having a *kadubenimikuwat*. These owners are *only* perceived, however, in dreams or visions.]

If we assume that dream experiences are interpreted by the Ojibwa as experiences of the self we then arrive at a very important deduction. The *pawaganak* are experienced as appearing in a specific form, that is, as having a bodily aspect, whether human or animal. Years ago I wrote in my notebook that Chief Berens, my most intelligent informant, said flatly that the *pawaganak* had 'bodies' and 'souls', but no 'ghosts'. Since my bias was to think of these *pawaganak* as 'spiritual beings', I did not at first see the implications of the general statement my informant had made. But, in our present discussion, its full import is clarifying. The soul is the essential and persisting attribute of *all* classes of animate beings, human or non-human. But the soul is never a direct object of *visual* perception under any conditions. What can be perceived visually is only the aspect of being that has some form of structure. Consequently, it is not surprising to find that when the *pawaganak* appear in dreams they are identifiable in a tangible visual form. This experiential fact

---

[1] This account was repeated to me by a man who said he had heard the dreamer narrate it when he was an old man.

taken at its face value indicates, of course, that they, too, have a body as well as a soul. Structurally, they are the counterpart of man. On the one hand, it is *not* assumed that they have a uniform or stable appearance. Metamorphosis is always possible, as in the dream reported. It may be inferred, therefore, that there are inherent attributes that remain constant for different classes of being. In the dream referred to, the being that appeared was a *pawagan* of a certain kind and not a human being, even though he first appeared in a human form. This is just the reverse of the bad old sorcerer who was essentially human even though he appeared as a bear on certain occasions. This means, of course, that in the behavioural world of the Ojibwa, no sharp line can be drawn between animals, *pawaganak*, man, or the spirits of the dead on the basis of outward bodily aspect or appearance alone. Myths illustrate this, too, and unless we are aware of the point I have just made it is utterly impossible to apprehend their veridical nature from the Ojibwa point of view. Myths are sacred stories because they rehearse actual events in which the super human *pawaganak* are the main characters. These *pawaganak* are specially adept at metamorphosis. This is part of the dramatic interest of the myths. Consequently, the Ojibwa are quite prepared to have the *pawaganak* manifest the same characteristic attribute in dreams. It is one of their essential attributes because metamorphosis, especially when volitionally induced, has the implication of 'power'. It is thought that the human being who is capable of metamorphosis has derived his power through the help of *pawaganak*. This is the source of it. When he possesses it he, therefore, becomes superior to his fellowmen in this regard. They have to respect him even though they fear him. The only metamorphosis of *all anicinabek* is brought about by death. The dead, however, have more power than the living; consequently they are more like *pawaganak*, including the power of metamorphosis. But the *pawaganak*, who are eternal, do not die; they never become *djibaiak*.

The only sensory mode under which it is possible for human beings to perceive directly the presence of souls of *any* category, and then under certain conditions only, is the auditory one. The chief context of this kind of experience is the conjuring tent where, as I have already pointed out, the souls of *djibaiak* may be present and *speak*.[1] It is only infrequently that ghosts may be heard to whistle, perhaps in the neighbourhood of a grave, where it is sometimes said they have been seen. It is

[1] The conjuring tent consists of a barrel-like structure, covered with bark or canvas, that conceals the conjurer who kneels within. Those who witness the performance are *outside* this structure. Since the pawáganak reputedly are *inside* they, like the conjurer himself, are invisible to the audience without. On the other hand, it is said that the *pawáganak* do have a visible aspect from inside the tent. They look like tiny stars or minute sparks. It is only under very exceptional circumstances, however, that any person except the conjurer ever has an opportunity to even peep inside the structure during the performance. Consequently, the sensory manifestation of the spirits is typically auditory, not visual. See Hallowell, 1942, *op. cit.*

from the conjuring tent, too, that the voices of *pawaganak* may be heard to issue. They cannot be seen. Thus from the standpoint of our central problem it is difficult not to draw the conclusion that, while according to Ojibwa dogma it is a soul that is present, even to them it is always an identifiable self—*pawaganak* or ghost—that speaks. For them *otcatcakwin* defines the conceptual substratum of beings with self-awareness and other related attributes (speech, memory, volition, etc.) that we associate only with a stabilized anthropomorphic structure. When Ojibwa speak of their own dream experiences or those of others, when they refer to what has been heard in conjuring performances, it is assumed that one's own soul or that of some other being was present and not the body. But this fact does not have to be explicitly stated any more than we have to be explicit about the presence of the body in referring to self-related experience or to social interaction with other selves. What is implied by the Ojibwa and by ourselves is an indication of the differences between their self-orientation and ours. What is held in common is a self-concept that assumes certain generic human attributes, despite conceptual differences in the nature of the substratum of a functioning self.

Returning once again to the puberty dream I should like to stress the fact that once dreams, on this occasion or any other, are construed as experiences of the self, we can only conclude that metamorphosis can be *personally* experienced. It follows from this, too, that to anyone who has had such a dream, episodes in myth, or anecdotes like those in which the sorcerer figured, cannot appear as strange or fantastic occurrences. In a dream, too, the self may experience the separation of the soul from the body and mobility over large distances. Accounts of such mobility also occur in myth and in anecdotes connected with conjuring. I was told by one informant that he once attended a conjuring performance to which another conjurer, from two hundred miles away, was called. He said, 'I was sleeping, but I heard you calling me.' People in the audience asked for news and received replies to questions. Then the soul of the visiting conjurer sang a song and departed for home.[1]

In addition to metamorphosis and spatial mobility, the self may likewise experience events in its dream phase that transcend the temporal schema of waking existence. Our autobiographer, for instance, not only made the long journey to the Land of the Summer Birds during his puberty fast; he stayed there all winter and flew north with the other birds under the guidance of his *ogima* in the spring. It is self-related experiences of this nature that coordinate the world as dramatized in myth with the world as

---

[1] *Ibid.*, p. 59, where other similar cases are given.

experienced by the self in certain phases of its existence. Myths are understood as past experiences of superhuman selves—the *pawaganak*. Dreams are among the past experiences of the self. Thus the world of the self is not essentially different from the world of the *pawaganak*. The cultural emphasis given to dream experiences helps to unify the world of the self through *experience*. For anthropomorphic entities such as *wisukedjak* may appear in both myth and dream as may the Winds, Snow, Thunder Birds, and so on, in personified form. No wonder that certain 'natural' objects belong to an animate rather than an inanimate gender in linguistic expression. Furthermore, all classes of *pawaganak* are linguistically integrated in the kinship terminology since, collectively, they are spoken of as 'our grandfathers'. And in the dream reported by our autobiographer the *pawagan* calls him *nozis*, 'grandson'.

The Ojibwa self is not oriented to a behavioural environment in which a distinction between human beings and supernatural beings is stressed. The fundamental differentiation of primary concern to the self is how other selves rank in order of *power*. 'Is he more powerful than I, or am I more powerful than he?' This is a crucial question applying to all human beings as well as to the *pawaganak*. But the fundamental distinction is that while other Indians may be more powerful than I, any *pawagan* is more powerful than any Indian. The power ranking of different classes of entities is so important because events only become intelligible in terms of their activities. All the effective agents of events throughout the entire behavioural environment of the Ojibwa are selves— my own self or other selves. *Impersonal* forces are never the causes of events. *Somebody* is always responsible. This is just as true for past events as the myths demonstrate. *Wiskedjak*, the 'culture hero' was responsible for certain events in the past that led, among other things, to the distinguishing characteristics of certain animals as known today.

A further assumption is this: While power may be used for good or evil ends, most of the *pawaganak*, but not all, are beneficent. Human beings, too, for the most part use their power for beneficial ends. This is exemplified by all those who specialize in curative functions. They have received their power to cure from the *pawaganak* and, in turn, they help their fellowmen. At the same time superhumanly acquired power may be used for malevolent ends.

Since 'magic' power, as we have seen, is the ultimate source of successful adaptation in every sphere of life—from hunting to defence against sorcery—and the ultimate source of this power rests in the hands of the *pawaganak*, the fundamental relationship of the Ojibwa self to the *pawaganak* is clearly defined. It is one of dependence and is the root of their deep motivational orientation toward these powerful beings. But there is a normative aspect of this relationship as well. I must fulfill certain obligations that my guardian spirits impose upon me. I may have to make certain sacrifices, perhaps material ones (*pagitcigun*). In the dream visit of W.B. to the *meneneweciwuk* these were mentioned. There is a story told about a man who, after he was married, went off hunting all winter. He never spoke to his wife or had sexual intercourse with her. She left him in the spring. It turned out that he had been observing taboos imposed upon him in his puberty fast as a condition of a long and healthy life. 'If she could only have held out three more moons', he said, 'it would have been all right.' He married again but did not follow the taboos. One of his children died, then his wife. A third wife died, too. This was all the result of his failure to live up to his side of the bargain with his *pawaganak*. Since all the relations between an individual and his *pawaganak* are based on dreams, their psychological reality is fundamental. It is what makes the puberty fast so important. The conceptual reality of all these beings the Ojibwa boy has been acquainted with from babyhood by listening to the myths recited on long winter nights becomes in the course of the fast a *personal* experience. If the puberty fast of the Ojibwa is crucial to them for living in their world, this same experience, viewed psychologically is equally crucial for making their world a reality for the self.

A. Irving Hallowell

MARSHALL McLUHAN, Professor of English, St. Michael's College, University of Toronto, is working on a book to be called *The End of the Gutenberg Era*.

DEREK SAVAGE, Tregoney Court, Mevagissey, Cornwall, is the author of *The Personal Principle* and *The Withered Branch*.

JACQUELINE TYRWHITT, Professor of Town and Regional Planning, University of Toronto, is now in India for the United Nations.

DOROTHY LEE, formerly Professor of Anthropology, Vassar College, is now with the Merrill-Palmer School.

EDMUND CARPENTER, Assistant Professor of Anthropology, University of Toronto, has done fieldwork in the Pacific and Canadian Arctic.

DONALD THEALL, Lecturer in English, St. Michael's College, University of Toronto, is interested in communication theory and contemporary poetry.

LORD RAGLAN, Cefntilla Court, Usk, Monmouthshire, has done fieldwork in the Sudan and Transjordan.

DAVID RIESMAN, Professor of Social Sciences, University of Chicago, is lecturing this spring at Johns Hopkins.

STANLEY EDGAR HYMAN, Professor of English, Bennington College, and associate editor of the *New Yorker*, is a literary folklorist.

A. IRVING HALLOWELL, Professor of Anthropology, University of Pennsylvania, and former President, American Anthropological Association, has lived among the Canadian tribes from Lake Winnipeg to the Labrador.

167

www.ingramcontent.com/pod-product-compliance
Lightning Source LLC
Chambersburg PA
CBHW071100280326
41928CB00050B/2575